WHISTLE FOR THE FLIES, JESUS - WHISTLE FOR THE BEES ON TERRY SHAFER

MITCH ARMAUGH

iUniverse, Inc.
Bloomington

iUniverse books may be ordered through booksellers or by contacting:

iUniverse
1663 Liberty Drive
Bloomington, IN 47403
www.iuniverse.com
1-800-Authors (1-800-288-4677)

ISBN: 978-1-4502-9602-1 (sc)
ISBN: 978-1-4502-9603-8 (ebook)

Printed in the United States of America

iUniverse rev. date: 03/30/2011

CONTENTS

Forward   xi

Preface   xiii

Chapter One – The troubled years   1

Chapter Two – The numbness sets in   84

Chapter Three – Why am I so stupid?   114

Chapter Four – Fasten your tray tables   176

Afterward   227

Appendix   229

To me, because I deserve better.

"This control will never get the best of me again – I will make it out without a sound."

Edison Glass. Songwriters: Morin, Joseph A Jr.; Morin, Joshua David; Silverberg, Joshua David; Usher, James Allen.

Isaiah 7:18 (See Afterword, page 227 – or just Google it)

"She runs into a wall of rank smell from Rocco's last greasy meal and detects his alcohol-saturated blood. It coagulates like pudding under his head, his eyes half open and dull, the chair overturned, the gun under his chest, every detail exactly as Rudy had left it. Blowflies buzz around his body, searching for the perfect piece of moist human real estate to appropriate for their eggs. Lucy stares, transfixed, at the frenzied insects." Patricia Cornwell, *Blow Fly*, 2003, G. Putnam's Sons, New York. Copyright Cornwell Enterprises, Inc.

PREFACE

9/8/2010 – A sad 9-year anniversary.

Do any of you know anybody who is happy with his or her Christian marriage? I don't. Not really.

Until recently, I have been a faithful Baptist churchgoer, Sunday-School class teacher and small group leader. I have been faithful at church for over 32 years. I have spoken at hundreds of Christian churches, schools, church conferences, education conferences – I have sold hundreds of books and videos to Christians and Christian educators. My articles have appeared in Christian publications dozens of times. Furthermore, I am internationally published in science journals from England, Germany and America. I have over 50 publications, including having my images published on the covers of 12 scientific journals. I own a U.S. Patent for a technical inspection device. Furthermore, a major university in Southern California, well known for its high quality research, currently employs me to assist in their research efforts. Please understand that I am not trying to glorify myself or to impress you with all this– I give all the glory to God for the opportunities I have had and for the accomplishments I have experienced. All of my accomplishments are just as filthy rags, as Isaiah 64 says. But I have been around the block a few times and I am not ignorant about love, marriage and the Biblical admonishments for married couples. Especially where the Bible specifically discusses it. I think I understand human relationships pretty well.

I don't need fame – I have enough fame, truth be told. If I were to give you my real name and you Googled it, at least eight pages of stuff would come up about my work and myself. I am not looking for attention!! I really just simply want to live a happy and quiet life and to be in love with someone who loves me in return.

But again I have to say-I just have never met a Christian couple that is crazy-mad in love with each other, who can't keep their hands off each other – who can't stand to be apart for even one night. Have you? Maybe you have, but I suspect that what you see in church on Sunday is far from the truth about so-called Christian marriages. I know that was the case in my marriage for over 400 Sundays.

I have been married to two different Christian women for a total of 31 years between both marriages. I did have a very happy marriage to my college sweetheart for a period of fabulous years, but neither of the "Christian" women I married ever seemed happy….with anything! I ended up empty handed and feeling worthless at the end of each relationship.

What follows is the story of my second marriage, which lasted a contentious nine years and ended by my leaving, moving away and Terry divorcing me. You might be wondering why a faithful Baptist would marry a second time-well my first marriage ended when colon cancer took down my college bride. I watched her become an angry, bitter and paranoid person as she dealt with her cancer without God and as she shipwrecked her life and the lives of those around her. I still had two of my three sons at home at the time she walked out on us and left us forever. I was needy and very lonely and I wanted a partner–a soul mate–someone who had the same Biblical ideals as I do–someone who had love to give and a need to receive it in kind.

Have you met and married your soul mate? I bet you $100 right here right now you have not. You never will.

You also might be wondering why a faithful Baptist would allow himself to be thrown out by his current wife and move over 200 miles away. Well… you are just going to have to read this one for yourself.

You need to know one important tidbit here as well. The names in this book have been changed (mine included) for obvious reasons–but there are a lot of folks out there who know my work and my reputation–so it won't be hard to figure out who I am and the same goes for the people I am describing here. After all, I am pretty well known in Christian circles. When folks figure it out, there will no doubt be some shock, but hopefully they will realize that I am just as human as anyone else. I have feet of clay too.

I really debated, however, whether or not I should change the names of a couple of so-called "Pastors" in this diary, because they acted like utter fools and not like decent and committed ministers of Jesus Christ. If you are going to earn your living on the hearts of others–on the donations to the church from the folks in the pews, then you had better live an exemplary life. You don't have to walk on water—none of us can claim that—but you had better not be a fool.

It is one thing to call yourself a Christian and blow it – I do that all the time and so do you, if you are a Christian. It is an entirely different matter, however to earn your living as a "set-apart" minister of Jesus and behave like an idiot. Men and women like that should be exposed to the whole world. I wish I could give the real names and locations of the two so-called pastors that played a large part in my saga, but maybe you can figure that out for yourself. In my humble opinion they should be exposed for who they are and maybe they would injure fewer people that they come in contact with.

You may also note that I switch from first person to third person in this book. Please know that I am not an accomplished writer of books and that this is essentially the diary that I penned during the traumatic years that I experienced with Terry. I was mostly concentrating on writing down what I was experiencing at the time, and that to try to determine whatever pattern there might have been in this so-called marriage. I only wanted to figure things out and fix them. Now I want you to experience my pain at the hands of a so-called Christian woman.

I also have one request of you as the reader of my saga. I have prepared a questionnaire at the end of this book that I hope you will take a few moments to reply to. I have an email address set up at the end of the questionnaire—would you take some moments after you read this book to email me your answers? I would greatly appreciate it.

All that being said, please allow me to set the tone for this book. The purpose of this book, besides describing my Twilight Zone adventure in this so-called marriage to Terry Loretta Armaugh (now Shafer once again), is to tell the world to avoid this skilled manipulator I was taken in by. I want you to know a little about the woman I tried to love and lay my life down for over the last eight years. There may well be other women like her on the hunt for some unsuspecting Baptist who would be susceptible to these kinds of manipulations, as I was. You have been warned.

Here is a copy of a note she wrote to herself early on in this marriage. If you cannot read her handwriting don't stress—I have typed the text of what she wrote just below the note.

11/6 What a relaxing, peaceful, stress-less evening I have had. Thank you, Jesus. My body is relaxed & I feel pretty & desirable. I cleaned up the kitchen, got things ready for tomorrow, did a load of laundry, did some crossword puzzles, watched the news, Jeopardy & a non-offensive movie

Here it is typed out: "11/6. What a relaxing, peaceful, stress-less evening I have had! Thank you Jesus. My body is relaxed & I feel pretty and desirable. I cleaned up the kitchen, got things ready for tomorrow, did a load of laundry, did some crossword puzzles, watched the news, Jeopardy, & a non-offensive movie."

Notice anything missing from this admission about what brings her happiness? People. People are always an impediment to Terry's happiness. She had a lot of folks fooled—both here in California and back home too. They all thought she was a giving and compassionate woman who cared about other people and wanted to give love and friendship away. Nothing could have been further from the truth.

Why did I want you to see this note at the front of this book? Because Terry is all about "I, I, I, I." She only feels relaxed, pretty, desirable, and stress free when she is alone with her crossword puzzle books, and the TV remote. Human interaction never relaxes her. I have asked several women what makes them feel pretty and desirable and their answers list none of the activities Terry mentioned in her note to Jesus. Most women I asked said that having a spa treatment, getting a new set of lingerie, getting nails, hair and toenails done go a long way towards feeling pretty and desirable towards the man they want to be with.

Having a devoted, loving, and attentive Christian man does not relax Terry or make her feel pretty or desirable. Relationships with other women don't make her feel pretty and desirable or the least bit relaxed. In the eight years that I knew her I never saw her share the Gospel with anyone. I never even saw her share her testimony with anyone in our small group or anyone at our wonderful, evangelistic and growing church over the eight years that she went there. In fact she has never had any relationship with another Christian woman at our church. She went to lunch with the wife of one of our Elders *one time*—and only because I begged her to. She is friendless and loves it that way. Terry is a lone wolf dressed in Christian trappings.

I didn't see that eight years ago when I asked her to marry me. I only saw it after writing 150 pages in my diary over eight years. She still doesn't see it.... She never will.

A little more background information is necessary here as well. While Terry and I were dating, and every time I drove over to Phoenix from LA to visit her (usually a Friday through Sunday noon), I would stay at her apartment (a crummy efficiency apartment near Bethany Home Road behind a hospital – not the best of areas). I would never sleep with her—so I would bring along my own air mattress and bunk out on her small kitchen floor with a fan blowing on me to keep me cool. She did not have a decent A/C system, so I sweated it out most of the time. Nevertheless after her kid Ronnie (a son she had out of wedlock with a drunk she had lived with 14 years before) went to bed, we would sit on the couch, watch TV and kiss a bit–then when she was ready for bed, I would sort of tuck her into bed for the night.

The reason I said "sort of" is because I actually gave her oral sex on her bed each time I was there. Yeah, I know–what a shocker, huh? Like I said–I am only human.

I never asked for anything in return from her, frankly because I was content to be patient and wait for marriage to have sex. I imagined that it was going to be a healthy physical relationship because she went nuts when I did oral on her–I figured that giving her oral sex was like putting money in the bank…

Terry would have the most intense orgasms I have ever seen a woman have, and it made her very happy, so I did it to please her. And boy did it please her. I expected great things to come…

Funny though–she never *offered* any reciprocation–not then (she would whisper, "Thank you" and roll over and go to sleep)–not even later in our so-called marriage, but like I say, I didn't really care at the time we were dating. I was making an investment in the future, right?

When we were married, just months later, however, she made me completely stop doing that regularly for her. I could never figure that one out. And she did not just say, "No, honey I don't need that," or something sweet like that. It was always a curt, "No, we aren't doing that." I figured out later that she was probably just too terrified to have to satisfy me sexually in return – so she became a Victorian prude and an ice princess. What a fun and one-sided love life we had. Had she done all that just to hook me for the greater prize of marriage and security? God alone knows.

On the Sundays I was there, we would go to her little backwater church called North City Baptist Church off Alice Avenue in Phoenix. Pastor Paul Keown was her Pastor and he was a nice enough guy, but typical of most (very small and almost dead) Baptist churches I have visited. He was remarkably shallow. Terry introduced me to every one she could there, and I got the shallow "So glad to meet you" routine. But I had been through this many times, since I speak so often at churches and church-related events that it didn't bother me.

On one Sunday after church, about the time we got engaged in the late fall of 2001, Pastor Keown pulled me aside and said, "In this woman [meaning Terry], there is no guile." That meant of course that in his opinion, Terry was incapable of lying (or performing any crafty or artful deception). I thought to myself at the time, "I'm not so sure I agree, buddy," but I just smiled and nodded.

I attended Sunday-school there, and some potluck dinners with the mostly bored, hen-pecked husbands and the predominantly fat, white women, and tried to be as nice and polite as possible. The sermons were placid soliloquies, the singing was very bad, and everyone scooted right after the last "Amen". I was often the loudest person during the singing and I was even holding my voice way back. That, however, did not prevent 2-3 people in front of us from turning around and staring at me…. What can I say? For years I sang with a Christian group in Florida and we even cut a live, double-album at the Grand Ole' Opry in Nashville. I was a trained tenor and I loved to sing praise music. I still do.

I even attended the wedding of one of the church couples with Terry there over one weekend-we held hands and smiled a lot at that event. People thought we were cute. Whatever...we were engaged, right?

Additionally, during the six months I commuted from LA to Phoenix to see Terry, Pastor Paul had us meet with him for "marital counseling" in order to pass his little compatibility test I suppose. I think we went in on about six Friday mornings to meet with him. On one particular day we went in and it was after my usual performance of oral sex on her the night before. So we were sitting there in front of his desk that Friday morning and he asked the question, "Have you two been intimate?" Within about 90 milliseconds of him enunciating the "t" on intimate, Terry blurted out, "NO!"

It was a pretty forceful and somewhat loud response and frankly it shocked me. Not because she lied, but because she sort of jumped all over his question—as if to drive the thought straight from Paul's mind. I remember formulating an answer that included the words, "Actually that is not true," and "I have been giving her oral sex," but I thought it might be prudent to keep my mouth shut and not ruin his perception that Terry had no guile in her. He did not pursue the matter further, but he should have.

I must have had a shocked look on my face, however because Paul studied me carefully for some moments before he continued.

Nothing else was noteworthy during our six sessions but in retrospect I sure wish I had opened up to him, and exposed her for the huge liar that she is. It might have saved me the 9 years of misery I have slogged through.

Recently, and over many months, I have emailed him and left him phone messages, but he has never returned my recent calls. I think he called me back once after I peppered his answering machine with about 20 messages over a 2-day period some years back, and then he returned one email, (and only to state that he wanted to "Hear Terry's side of the story"). I guess my side didn't count for much as I sought counseling from him.

Better to take the side of a high-school graduate, Paul–a woman who had a kid out of wedlock and who had never landed a guy in her 49 years, than to take the word of a man who had spoken to hundreds of churches, has two graduate degrees from Christian institutions of higher learning, who was internationally published in major scientific journals, and who had raised 3 fine sons after losing his wife and marriage to cancer. Obviously I didn't measure up to Paul's standards.

Just last month, I even sent him this entire recollection of my interactions with him and his sleepy church before this book went to press (with plenty of easy to spot typos), and asked him to make any edits he desired. No reply…so typical. No real Christian there.

Well here is a news flash Pastor Paul and all you shallow folks at North City Baptist Church…Terry is FULL of guile. Her guile is so crafty and accomplished that she can make you believe that she is pure and snow-white on the inside – when guile is really her game. She excels at it. Deception and trickery is her abode and she manipulates people very effectively with it. I have personally watched her use it in several situations, and once I was on to her little act it was easy for me to spot. She is a very highly skilled manipulator. Ever wonder why her son is such a loser, Pastor Paul? Why he moved back to Phoenix, covered himself in tattoos and body piercings and NEVER came back to the church that he won so many Awana awards at as a young kid? It is because he is a little mirror of Terry, Paul. Your spiritual progeny. Way to go minister of the Gospel.

Terry lied to me about so many things. Early on in our marriage, she lied to me about opening her own private checking and savings account and diverting her paycheck into it. She made up some story about how "It was the company's fault," and all. I knew she was just getting everything ready so she could easily bail out of the marriage. I found out about the clandestine checking account because she screwed up one time and had her whole paycheck diverted from automatically depositing into our jointly held account. In another instance she swore up and down that she was not emailing any other people about our marriage (and complaining about me behind my back). I figured out how to download letters and emails off her computer and she was doing just that, AND to multiple people at the same time—all the folks that she manipulated to believe her stupid stories about me. Terry is a skilled liar and it became full blown in her son as well.

During my many failed attempts to get our marriage working, I freely confessed to her that I was seeking advice from other women who were already in my life—the oncologist of my first wife, female professors at the university, female doctors that I associated with in my work, etc. They were all professionals and I knew that they could do a better job of diagnosing the sick marriage than I could. I did not hide any of that from Terry because I was openly *searching* for answers as to why *I could not* make our marriage work. I have been a problem solver all my life but this was one problem I could not solve. I searched for answers from anyone who would listen to me-she never searched for anything but freedom from personal responsibility. No guile indeed!

So when she comes back to North City, my dear shallow friends, (which I am sure she will do once she completes her mission to divorce me and sell off our home), take what she says with a grain of salt. Do yourself a favor—you will be happier in your interactions with her, and when you see the real Terry you won't feel played.

Some personal advice for you Paul—do a bit more checking on people before you place your seal of approval on them. You went straight to the bottom of my opinion poll on this one and you don't look so accomplished, or frankly even the least bit savvy when it comes to reading people that have been in your church for years and years.

I also remember one of the very first times I was over in Phoenix to visit with Terry; she needed some groceries, so I happily took her to the local Basha's grocery store and bought her what she needed. We stood in the checkout line with our cart of food and she directed my attention to a scantily clad blonde ahead of us who wore a pair of bright red stiletto heels and short jean shorts. I was trying not to notice her because frankly she was real eye candy, but I looked at Terry and said, "OK…". Terry pointed down to the girl's heels and whispered in my ear, "Do you know what those are called?" I told her I did not. She whispered, "FMP's." I did not know what that meant and told her so. She leaned in again, pressing up against me and whispered, "F*%k me pumps." I remember feeling hot all over and thinking, "Wow I cannot wait until my honeymoon with this girl!" But she was simply playing me – making sure I would commit and marry her. Like I said, she was highly skilled. All that went away after the "I do's" were said.

Terry knew how to manipulate my desire for a hot sexual relationship. She did things like that often during our engagement—and she had my full and rapt attention. Little did I know it was all a game to her—a method to hook me and reel me into her boat; a device to capture the man who would rescue her from her crappy and desperate life—a crappy and desperate neighborhood. I was such a willing subject. So enjoy my diary folks — watch me twist and turn on the end of her line and be forewarned—there are women like this out there. You could be next. I was played and nothing I tried worked. I ended up destitute as a result of this vicious little wanna-be "Christian."

Chapter One – The troubled years

1/1/03….My 50th birthday.

I started this diary today because of deep frustrations with my second so-called marriage to a Baptist girl who I met online (ChristianDate.com). I have been in this uneasy union with Terry Loretta Shafer (now Armaugh), since 4/6/02. Actually, I live in hell.

As all couples do, we have our differences, but we seem only marginally compatible. We sort of like the same things, although she constantly complains about being cold-outside, in the house, in the car, at church-even in the bed, (and even when I keep the house at 76 degrees). I think she is part lizard.

She and I do not have the same kind of humor (I admit I am kind of jaded after 26 years in Southern California). She is severely set in her ways, as I am sure that in some respects I am too, but she pretty much allows me to wait on her hand and foot. You heard right – I wait on this princess hand and foot.

Of course I believe that a man *should* wait hand and foot on his wife – *but* that he should be appreciated for it too. A little appreciation can go a long way for a man that is putting it all out there for his woman.

Do most Christian women deserve to be waited on hand and foot? Not in my experience. Most Christian women I have met are edgy, angry, independent, caustic and unforgiving. They act as if they deserve everything they can get their little fingers on and will quietly walk all over people to get it. I have very rarely met a Christian woman who had a 'quiet and gentle spirit,' such as described in 1 Peter 3:3-4.

Maybe you have met some that sure deserve to be waited on, but I have not. I have also never heard any Christian man tell me that his wife deserves to be waited on hand and foot. But I have always desired a relationship with a woman whom I could wait on hand and foot. I am a hopeful romantic.

In fairness, Terry does get up very early (4:30AM most mornings) and commutes about 100 miles per day to and from Irvine, California (a city in Orange County, CA). Her job is stressful, although she does sit at a very comfortable desk all day and does phone customer support. I mean; her company regularly buys them new workstations, new computers, new ergonometric chairs, new phones – the whole nine yards. But Terry does not, even after sleeping in late on Saturday morning, ever hold my hand, sit close or hold me or act like she desires any intimacy at all. She even seems annoyed that I want intimacy.

In actuality, she doesn't seem to go out of her way at all, really, to seek me out or engage me in any meaningful way whatsoever, except maybe to play cards (if I ask) or to facilitate *her* needs in some way. Whenever she sweetly says, "Hey honey?" it's because she is about to ask me to do something for her. So, mostly she seeks me out just to facilitate some need she has – then once I have satisfied her need (for some food or drink item, some object she requires to do a particular job, or maybe to supply some information she needs off the internet or the TV or whatever), she ignores me.

I get ignored a lot. Not that I need constant attention, but at 50, my desire for closeness hasn't been nailed into the coffin yet (much to her chagrin) – so yeah – I still love the intimacy stuff. But it never happens around here.

And so at the Armaugh home, I do pretty much all of the initiating physically, and those old feelings of desperation, loneliness and neediness, when it comes to needing sex with my wife (or just simple closeness and cuddling) are back in spades. I feel pretty much like a beggar. She doesn't care. I have even told her that I feel like she makes me beg. She just snorts and goes back to the TV or the crossword puzzle.

Terry never married before she met me. She was 48 when we met and although she had been shopping for a husband all her life (or so she said) she never sealed the deal with anybody. That should have been my first red flag. She once told me she had never had a good relationship with any man, including her father. There was so much that I ignored about her early on because I was so lonely. I was stupid.

But I do have a rich past of loving a woman with all my heart…I was married for 23 years to my college sweetheart – we had three wonderful sons together and then I lost it all when she got cancer. Life is not fair, huh? But at least I have those great memories and I still have my amazing three sons.

I am very grateful though, for the sacrifice Terry makes in her job, and naturally the nice health and retirement benefits that come with it – but I go way out of my way to show it to her every day. For eight months, she made that awful commute to work in her old beat up Toyota Tercel, which we towed from Phoenix after we married. However, I just plunked down $4200 cash in down payment money so she could have a nice new 2003 Honda Civic with all the extras. It is a classy little car, nice sound system and A/C, nice power windows, door locks, sunroof. I was happy to do it for her – and why? Well I want my wife safe and happy. Is that a bad thing?

I also do all the grocery shopping for the household (and its four members); I do all the cooking and 99% of the kitchen and house cleaning. I scrub the downstairs and upstairs tile floors and I also vacuum the carpets. I do all the laundry. She comes home to a nice, hot, delicious meal every night, which I make from scratch. I am actually becoming quite the cook, and I love to do it for her. Isn't that what a loving, Bible-believing husband should do?

Terry has all the carbonated water she can drink (which I also make for her with a carbonation machine that I bought because she likes it so much), all the fruit and chocolate she wants, and pretty much anything she really needs, including the many meds she takes, and the wine she likes to drink. I go out every week and get it all for her. All she has to do is put what she needs on the list that I hang on the fridge and presto-chango – she has it. I even anticipate her needs and write down the things I know she is getting low on. I have made it my business to find out exactly what she likes – what she doesn't like to eat, drink or use and then I make sure she always has it on hand. She says she loves me – she smiles and acts all friendly but things here are not normal. On paper we should be perfect together. Too bad life isn't on paper.

I handle all the cash flow and ensure that there is always money available to do what we need. I fill the cars with gas, although she sometimes fills hers-I pay all the bills and handle all the financial matters. To be fair, her paycheck gets deposited into the business account we have, but I always deposit more than she ever does from my own personal company business that I have run for 25 years. She also has full signatory rights to the business account because I took her straight to the bank after we married so she could get the money in case I die suddenly or something. I usually have a balance of over $5,000 at any given time in the account. She also has a bank debit card – so she could easily clean me out.

I have also taken her back to Arizona multiple times since we got married (about once per month), at no small cost in gas, hotel and food, so she could see her family and friends. So, let's face it – her life is pretty good, and I am a pretty nice guy. I am not perfect, but I am really trying.

Recently I was potentially exposed to HIV and Hepatitis from human blood specimens, (plus other workplace hazards that I won't discuss) at my old job at a small university in Los Angeles. Because I used my rights and complained to California OSHA about it (and they came in and did surprise inspections) I got fired. Not one to sit by for being fired as a whistleblower, I got an attorney and after 2 years of negotiations, I finally got a decent settlement (well into six figures) which will allow me to set up a modest lab and do the kind of teaching and research that I love to do, hopefully for years to come. But that money has to last! I can't just spend it on her – it is our new livelihood. And with people losing their jobs and income in these uncertain economic times, I love having a backup plan that will protect us.

When we got married, Ronnie, (Terry's son born out of wedlock to a man he has never met) stayed with friends in Phoenix until school was out at the end of 2002. Then when he finally moved to LA, I found him to be a spoiled brat. He was rude, insensitive and self-centered. All he wanted to do was play video games and just skate by in school with as little effort as possible. John Fredrick, with whom he stayed for 2 months in AZ to finish school, told me that he gave up on him in 2 weeks. Two weeks! Terry told me that he has ADHD and he has been taking *Ritalin* since he was 6 or 7 years old. How sad. It is strange, however because she interacts with him very little and his pills put him into a kind of a stupor. So she has this sort of chemical baby sitter that frees her up from him. Weird.

Ronnie's interpersonal skills were horrible. He interrupted most conversations, whined when he had to do any chores, and mostly talked about or asked questions about himself. He refused to eat most of what was put in front of him, and threw most of what he did not eat into the trash. I have never laid a hand on him, but I have worked very hard to discipline him and it has taken its toll. He does not like me at all (and shows me little respect), and now he is finally doing a little better (just ok, really) in school. He has harder classes and much more homework than he was accustomed to Arizona. He is also finally eating somewhat well; he does a few chores for the family, but he still just is a slacker at heart with no real ambitions.

Ronnie (I'll call him R) is basically responsible to ensure that his room and bathroom are clean since they are downstairs, right off the living room, and guests can see them when they come in the house. He has to be reminded frequently to air out the smell in his room, make his bed and work on his bathroom. He has poor hygiene and if not reminded, will rarely shower or do his laundry. He is a slob when he eats, chewing with his mouth open, spilling food all over – etc. From time to time I have him vacuum the stairs, which he does fairly well. He also is asked to take the trash bags from the kitchen and place them into the large garbage containers on the side of the house. That's it! That is all that is expected of my stepson, Ronnie. My youngest son, Patrick is here also in a nice upstairs room and he is a model citizen, but Ronnie does not want to emulate Patrick at all. It is always a battle to get him to do anything – even the most basic of things. He is sullen and disrespectful – he ignores me until it comes to a head and it always comes to a head. Then he runs to his mom to get the alternate opinion (the one that we all usually have to follow – the one that will let him slide). His mother never disciplines him.

Now something new is going on…..when I ask R to do other things his mom gets on my case! She actually starts an argument over it right in front of him and the two of them tag team me. Case in point – he wants to go to his youth group meeting on Sunday nights which means I or Terry have to drive him the 7 miles to church and pick him up again Sunday nights – a night that Terry is usually trying to relax before getting up very early for work the next day. And because she goes to bed by 8PM or so on Sunday nights, that means I now have to drive back and forth twice each Sunday – just so he can hang out with the other rebellious teens.

I am not at all opposed to him going, but now I am told that he wants to stay late every Sunday night and go out to eat even later with the group leaders – a cost of about $6-7 per week. He also has no self-control. He drinks lots of caffeine-filled drinks and he loves the sugar high, so he comes home and thrashes around all night in his room (which means a real possibility that he will mess up Monday morning and will miss school as well).

Seven dollars per week is not much money for his Sunday night jaunt, to be sure, but I said that he would have to do another chore to earn that money. (I believe that kids should earn the fun outings that they get to go on – it teaches then to appreciate the better things in life).

Well, Terry then gave me the silent treatment all day. Some New Year's Day celebration and birthday present for me, huh?

Here is one other thing I don't get. Terry complains to me when I have a little stubble on my face, or I have a little body odor, or my nails are a little long or dirty. So I have made it my mission to be as clean shaved, as good smelling and as presentable as possible. I mean the last thing I want to do is to repel my mate, right? But she simply ignores the stench that comes off of R's body and from his room. She has told me that my breath "smells like rotting meat." Real pretty, right? So I make sure my teeth are always brushed and that I have breath mints on hand (she prefers peppermint). But R can stink like Mozart's grave and she is oblivious to it. To top it off, this woman only bathes one day per week. Yup, and only on Sunday morning. All week I have to smell this daffodil of the valley, but she will not shower or bathe until Sunday morning. How lucky am I? Can someone say, "Double standard"?

Tuesday, January 2, 2003

I decided to call her at work today to try to reach out and to try to thaw things out between us, now that it is a new year and all. She has been harping on me because I just don't throw money at Ronnie every day. So, on the phone, I tried to explain that I was not playing favorites, that none of my boys ever got money for breathing, and that R should have to wash a car once a month, or do a little something extra for the privilege of going out to eat every Sunday night before a hard day of school on Monday morning. Dead silence on the phone. I told her I would call back, but I never did. Why do unmarried women ruin their kids by not allowing someone who has already successfully raised sons to help them? I don't get it. My three sons are all doing great. My two oldest are in the military (one of them is in Navy Nuclear Power School) and she considers me a dolt when it comes to kids.

I am basically really worn out over raising teenage boys, however. I am especially worn out over trying to educate mothers on what their spoiled brats really need, and I don't think I am going to do it anymore. I went through 23 years of that with Judy (who as I said, walked out after cancer) – not again. Terry can raise him. I will do the right thing by supplying him room and board, but I am tired of casting my pearls before swine. My son Patrick is going to do fine. He has a strong work ethic, is very disciplined and has admirable goals. Her kid is going to end up sniffing gasoline. I think I will concentrate on my career and future for once.

2/8/03

Last Saturday, Terry was kind enough to go with me (after early church service and Sunday school), down to Tustin, to help Mike Pontoy and I do the Microbiology Society mailing. It was a sacrifice because she did not get her normal 12-2PM Sunday nap that day (although after we got home she slept from 3 to about 4:30PM), but she did get a nice free lunch out at a great Orange County restaurant before we started the mailer. On the way home, she told me that she had not taken her *Neurontin* (for her severe back and muscle pain) and that she was about 2-3 hours late in taking it. She is very forgetful but she will just not write things down like I repeatedly ask her to. I have tried many approaches to help her deal with lack of memory. I myself have to write just about everything down because in this hectic life, I forget lots of things, so I keep my notebook with me and refer to it often. But not Terry – she does no advance-planning to speak of.

I had gone on the Internet a few months ago and bought her a very nice $120, 6-alarm watch to remind her of things she needed to do (like take pills on time). I even spent time and programmed it for her (because the instructions were too hard for her to understand), and made sure it worked properly for her. Look, I really try to look out for this girl and make sure she is taking her meds on time!

So I asked her why she had taken the alarm watch off and left it at home and she just came unglued. I could not believe the temper tantrum she started to throw and it was scary because she was driving about 75 on the freeway…I started to explain that even if the alarms were preset for the weekday times when she should be taking her pills, it would still give her a reminder on the weekends, and she could at least think about taking her much needed meds – she shouted at me that she could never do anything right and that she was tired of me making her feel that way. She started crying so I clammed up.

I had gently tried to explain to her that the whole point of her wearing that expensive watch was so that she would stay on her meds and not get the debilitating leg and back cramps that put her out of work for 6 months last year. But she just went off on me, so I stopped talking. We drove home in silence for 40 minutes. When we got home, she went straight to the bedroom and stayed there about 3 hours. I napped on the couch for a while, and then cooked a dinner of shrimp scampi because I know she loves it. I then asked Ronnie to get Patrick and Terry for dinner and then I went out in the office (I keep an office in the garage for my lab equipment service business.) She refused to eat (I guess this was part of the tantrum). Oh well. Silly me for trying to help her with logic.

Later, she came downstairs crying and said she wanted to talk and I said, "No – not now." About an hour later, she came out to the office where I was working and in tears apologized to me. I gently held her and explained to her that I was only always thinking about her, that I tried to serve her even by the things I said and that I wondered why she had taken her watch off earlier, but decided to let her take responsibility for it. We made up and had a nice rest of the evening, although her eyes and head were puffy from all the crying. But I am definitely feeling the pain – she just withholds herself from me in so many ways.

We were only intimate twice last weekend (which I guess is average but I sure am starved for intimacy) – once late on Friday night when I was just simply too hot and sweaty to continue and then on Saturday morning early, since I did not get to finish the night before. I did not give her the big O either time, as I wanted to see how interested she would become later in the week. Usually she is so satisfied that it is 2 weeks or more before she shows any interest in me.

All week this past week, she pretty much came home tired and went to bed early. I am losing interest in her, because she only responds by laughing and then pushing my hands away when I reach out and touch her. I am definitely not a groper, but I do rub her back and neck to see if she is at all interested in me. I try really hard to make sure I am well groomed, dressed well and act gently in the way I approach her, but I think she is trying to control me by laughing and pushing me away. It works. We go for days and days without sex.

Last night (Friday) she went to sleep at about 9PM. I purposely did not reach out to her to touch her in any way. This morning I cuddled with her in the bed a little, but I did not touch her romantically. We slept in until 8AM, when she got up, after 11 hours of sleep and left the bedroom. I lay in bed until 8:30 and then got up. I feigned a severe headache because I really wanted some space, especially from her and Ronnie. At about 9:30, as we sat together on the couch, she said we did not have to go to the free luncheon (at the Honda dealer, where I bought her new car) since I had a headache and all. I said hopefully I would feel OK. Later I suggested that she take Ronnie "because my headache is not getting any better", and she wholeheartedly agreed with a big smile. I feel like she would rather just be alone with Ronnie anyway – just like her old life in Phoenix. They were alone together for 14 years or so. I really believe that she wishes she was back in Phoenix and that this was all a bad dream she was having.

She never cuddled me on the couch to try to make me feel better; she only rubbed her hand across my forehead a couple of times and said she was sorry I felt bad. I never reached out to touch her. I am beginning to learn that it is basically a waste of time.

After a while, she got up off the couch, showered (a first for a Saturday), got dressed and did her hair. As she was finishing I went into the bathroom to tell her I was sorry I could not go with her. She turned around to hug me and I gave her a very tender hug. I ran my hands along her body and lightly touched the sides of her breasts, then I ran my hands back down her sides and rubbed her buns for a second. She seemed to like my hug and the bun rub and she kissed me. I will wait to see if she gets interested in me at all later. She has not had the big O in over 2 weeks (or more?) I just do not think she is interested in sex at all.

I am really glad she took Ronnie. Patrick (my 17 year old son now rooms with him upstairs) is not here to entertain him (his own words) and R wears us both out. Last night he would not eat his broccoli, so he is going to see it again on his plate tonight.

I have made Ronnie write about 30 lines this week (I know-horrible discipline, huh?) for not pouring his cereal into his bowl over the sink. In the morning he routinely pours Grape Nuts all over the floor and the table, so I now require him to do it over the sink. Hopefully, writing lines will help him to remember. We also decided that he has to tell me when he takes his *Ritalin* (because like his mom, he forgets all the time and then the house is in an upheaval because he is bouncing off the walls when he forgets to take it). So I told him he is going to have to write more lines if he keeps forgetting to do this.

2/18/03

Well, last week turned out pretty well, although the boys have been home two Mondays in a row. Terry and I were intimate a couple of times over the weekend (it was wonderful), she seemed very interested, so it seems to work to just not touch her for awhile. After my many requests, she agreed to give me oral on Monday, but then she cried for an hour and said she could not do it. It really bothered me that she was crying and crying over that. I am convinced she has some deep pathology there. She has no complaints when I do it for her, mind you – she always gyrates wildly and then has a deep, loud orgasm, so I don't know what the deal is here. More and more, however, she says she does not want me to do that for her. I think maybe she is feeling guilty that she does not pleasure me very much – and she sure goes out of her way to make me feel bad if I ask her for it or expect something new and different in the bedroom.

She also only wants just missionary style and it is boring to me. Is it wrong for a Christian man to desire his wife on top or side-by-side or some other position? You would think I was suggesting a major crime by her reaction to my request for other positions. I have never asked for anything kinky – I would not do that, but she loves to get oral, shouldn't I??

Ronnie and I continue to have our spats. He continues to do things like leave his part of the upstairs bathroom and bedroom messy and pour his cereal on the floor, etc. He refuses to wear a beautiful jean letter-jacket that was hanging in Patrick's closet on these cold winter days. It is probably a $150 jacket, but he would rather go to school in shirtsleeves and shiver all day. Go figure.

2/25

Well all caca hit the fan when R came home recently with a crappy report card. I was angry because his grades have been slipping for 2 months and he refuses to do the work. Terry just lets him play Nintendo, play the computer, watch TV, etc., for hours every night (in his room) with no restrictions or anything. Weekends he just runs free with his 'posse' of illiterate hoodlum friends. She only ever asks, "How was your day at school sweetie?" And of course, he always just says, "OK," and it goes no further. Doesn't she love him at all?

I have been gently warning her for months that this bad report card day would come and tried to steer things in the right direction but all I ever got was grief – from both of them.

So, I demanded that the TV be taken from his room and that he be grounded off everything until the next report card. That lasted about 3 days, because he whined and whined and so she relented. Now suddenly his TV is back in his room and he is playing computer and Nintendo again at all hours!! He even sucked Patrick into it and now his grades are suffering as well.

I hate to be the bad guy, but if R fails this grade he will be yanked back to Arcadia High (he is on an Inter-District transfer from Arcadia to a better school in Duarte). I have warned everybody about this. Nobody seems to be listening. This won't end well.

3/26/03

Well, things have really been about the same lately. Terry (she refers to me as M, so I guess I will call her T) still comes home exhausted and R still resists doing things around the house and staying on top of his homework, (he actually brought home a special progress report with 2 D's on it), but things have been somewhat peaceful, mostly because I say less and less about everything. If Dad shuts up and ignores the warning signs everyone is happy – regardless of the outcome (which is usually bad). I am concerned because R is really starting to drag Patrick down into his sewer.

4/3/03

Well all hell broke loose last night. Ronnie sassed me loudly and rebelliously in the car on the way home from school. It was all I could do to not drive off the road! None of my kids ever got away with that and he is going to be no exception. It shocked me how belligerent and ugly he was with me. I made him do a written assignment as a punishment and to try to teach him to show respect. Then Patrick got all up in my face about it. It got pretty hot and then Patrick would not back down when I told him to mind his own business – he got belligerent and I had to yell at him repeatedly to get him to be quiet and to back down. R is really rubbing off on Patrick.

Well you guessed it, Terry came unglued – crying hysterically. She and I went into the office to try to talk things out. I explained that I was going to be shown the proper respect that a Dad should be shown and that R was no exception. I was not being belligerent or loud, but she just could not take being told that her kid was a sassy brat. So she just stood there blaming me for the whole mess and refused to agree that R had to take responsibility for his actions – so I got madder.

I finally stormed out after throwing a small plastic cereal bowl on the garage cement floor. She took R and drove away in the car. They were gone three hours – I just could not believe it. They all provoke me to anger and then run away when I get upset over being ignored and sassed and provoked! I went out to the van (parked by our complex pool) and sat there for about two hours thinking. Later I came back home and I slept in the garage. Basically her kid has no respect for me because she has no respect for me and it is starting to rub off on my youngest, Patrick – what fun! This will definitely not end well.

Following is an email exchange today after she left me a phone message saying she wanted to talk to me:

>>-----Original Message-----
>> Thu, 3 Apr 2003 7:11:33 -0800 "Armaugh, Terry" <ArmT@Prudential.
com> writes:
>>Mitch, can we please talk about last night? I did not understand why
>>you slept in the garage.
>>
>>> Terry Armaugh
>>> Small Group Customer Service
>>
>>
>>From: mitch armaugh [mailto:micromitch@juno.com]
>>Sent: Thursday, April 03, 2003 8:08 AM
>>To: ArmT@Prudential.com
>>Subject: I don't really feel like talking
>>
>>
>>I have one son who repeatedly ignores my requests that he clean his
>>room and sasses me with complete disrespect.
>>I have another son who gets all up in my face when I try to
>discipline the first one.
>>I have a wife who gets in her car with her kid and drives away
>>in defiance of her husband's wishes.
>>
>>what is there to talk about?
>
>
>On Thu, 3 Apr 2003 08:35:59 -0800 "Armaugh, Terry"
><ArmT@Prudential.com> writes:
>>Mitch -- I did not drive away in defiance or disobedience of you. I
>>drove away because I was terrified of you. I am becoming more terrified
all
>>the time.
Please, may we PLEASE talk about this when I get home, in
>>private?
>>It is a hardship for me to carry on an email conversation email while
>>I am at work. -- T
>>
>>> Terry Armaugh
>>> Small Group Customer Service

>>

>>

>>

>From: mitch armaugh [mailto:micromitch@juno.com]

>Sent: Thursday, April 03, 2003 9:57 AM

>To: ArmT@Prudential.com

>Subject: Re: I don't really feel like talking

>

>here is your anniversary present

>http://www.candlelightpavilion.com/nowshowing.html

>you are reserved on the guest list for Saturday at 11am, table #807

>you may want to take your son since you are so afraid of me

>if not, tickets are non-refundable so you should call them to

>postpone by noon today

>

>

On Thu, 3 Apr 2003 10:13:36 -0800 "Armaugh, Terry" <ArmT@
Prudential.com> writes:

>Mitch -- Of course, I would want to go with you. I will go with you if

>you want to keep the reservation. I cannot visit this website due to our

>firewall. PLEASE , Mitch, this is so very difficult to do thru email >while
I am at work. -- T

>

>> Terry Armaugh

>> Small Group Customer Service

OK, so maybe my last email was a bit vindictive. I bought her a nice
dinner theatre outing as an anniversary present (three days away!), but
good Lord!!! This just gets worse and worse by the day. She ignores me
and treats me with little respect after all the ways I lay everything down
for them every day. I just cannot be treated like a butler. What do I do,
become a mouse?

Last night we ended up talking for about an hour. She says that
because I yelled at Patrick so loudly, I terrified her. Then she asked me not
to pick Ronnie up from school today. Apparently he refused to turn in a
homework assignment, so he had to stay at school until 5PM to get it all
done. Surprise, surprise. So I guess I have to be a mouse so as not to terrify
her and just not get involved in her son's growth and development.

4/4/03

Now I have Judy involved in how I discipline Ronnie!!! Geeze – why don't these women care more about his character???

She is all mad because Patrick is mad – she left me 2 phone messages today, sprinkled with swear words about how I am killing her – how I have "driven away three sons" (what does that mean?), now and I am on my fourth. She said she is going to fight now to get custody of my son Patrick– good luck woman. How messed up is that?

My sons are doing great – they are disciplined, self starters and are quite productive.

This may sound terrible, but I honestly wish she would leave us all the heck alone. Patrick does fine when she is not meddling. My boys have all turned out fine. They all did well in school and 2 of them are college bound after good military careers. I think I know how to raise boys.

But I guess I should follow my own advice and just ignore what the boys do. Whenever I try to discipline Ronnie, it always comes back on me. Terry gets upset and cries, or she cries because I "don't love him," or she pulls away from me (punishment?) because I am "too hard" on him – whatever. I hope she never asks me to adopt him! Man, that would be the day.

I must have asked him 10 times in the last two weeks why he won't take a lunch to school. The lunchmeat I buy (that he specifically requested) just sits there and rots in the fridge – I end up throwing good food away. I am simply not going to buy him lunch items anymore.

Patrick has earned a big fat dis from me – why should I do anything special for him when he gets all up in my face in defiance against me? So if I am going to be treated like a slave, a slave I shall be – I, like Ronnie's uncle in Mesa, AZ, have given up on Ronnie for the sake of peace with my wife (and what a fake peace it has become). Now with my luck she will start crying all the time if I don't fawn all over him.

4/5/03

Last night I gave Terry a nice flower arrangement for our anniversary, which is tomorrow. She seemed to like it very much and kissed me repeatedly, but she was not affectionate any more than that last night. I think she is still on her period, but we have not made love in over ten days. She has all but pulled away from me completely.

Later last night I wrote a note to her and placed it inside a large cup I found in Ronnie's room, filled with dried, crusty, hardened chocolate milk.

I explained that I had asked him several times not to leave stuff like that in his room, and now someone had to scrub it hard with a sponge just to get it clean. It also attracts ants into the bedrooms which we need like a hole in the head.

She never said a word to me, but she did end up washing the cup herself!! Why she will not teach that boy personal responsibility is beyond me. He just gets to sit in his room, with his own TV, Nintendo and heavy metal music and she never asks him to do any chores around the house. Never asks him about his homework.

I finally got at least 10 hours sleep last night, so I know she got about 11 or 12. I cuddled her this morning, and even slipped my hand under her T-shirt but she immediately pulled my hand out – I did not try again. I lay in bed about 20 minutes after she got up waiting to see if she would come back, but she just went down and made her coffee and cereal. She controls sex. Or should I say, she controls the lack of sex.

Today we are going to that dinner theatre I bought her as an anniversary present, but I am just going to wait and see how affectionate she is. I guess since I terrify her so much, she does not really want me anymore.

Pat came home at 11:30 last night to get some stuff to go stay at his friend's Neo's house. I guess he is having fun at his new job at the Pizza place. He did leave me a letter, though, telling me how sorry he was that he got all up in my face. He said he respected the fact that I was the head of the home and that he knew all the ways I was laying my life down for the three of them. I tucked that letter into my Bible.

Well she really enjoyed the dinner theater – we saw *Annie Get Your Gun*. It really was cool – the décor, the service the food and the performance – for about $170 I hope so. She thanked me multiple times during the show and on the way home. She sat close to me and held my hand, rubbed my arm and neck. Now we are at home – she went straight upstairs and got on her bed to take a nap. Lucky me.

4/6/03 2:20PM

So, it's my one-year wedding anniversary and I feel like running away. One year ago this moment, I thought I was madly in love – now I don't know how I feel. We cuddled last night mostly because it was cold – I should say, I cuddled, because all she seems to do is lay on her side facing away from me. Since we had to get up early for church, we were both awake at about 6:45AM. No cuddling then to be sure. But she got up and went straight down again and made her coffee and cereal. She did give me a nice new leather checkbook as a present. I do really like it and Lord knows I needed a new one. That was pretty much it, though – no "honey let's go back to bed" or anything. In fact she just came out to the office where I have been working, and told me that she was going up to take a nap. So here I am….wondering what it really means to be married to this woman. I am wondering if this is the way all Christian marriages are? Do all the guys I see at church have the same crappy unfulfilled life as I do?

After we got home from church today she sprung on me that she had written the 2 remaining blank checks I had given her from the business account – one to R's Hot Rod magazine (which he does not deserve in my humble opinion, I mean, coming home with a D in science and all last night)…the other check she wrote for $1700 – to a new savings account that she opened on her own last week. What?????

This is the first I have heard of this – and thanks for asking me in advance if any checks were going to be bounced with her writing a $1,700 check unannounced. No, "honey, as the head of our household, do you think I could do this?" or anything like that. Just the blunt announcement….wow. I am just in shock. I would *never* do that to my partner – *never*. I just looked at her in stunned silence.

So it begins, I guess; the dividing up of the income. I have heard how the prelude to separation and divorce is when one partner starts hoarding money. She has had full access to the business checking account since the day we were married. I deposit over $5,000 per month into that account and have always given her blank checks. Plus as I said she has a debit card with access to all the money. How stupid am I?

So this seems all too familiar and reminiscent of what other guys have told me, as I watch what Saint Terry is doing.

I mean, the $1,700 is her money from her bonus – she could have written the check to herself for $3200 or so, because that amount was her complete bonus amount, but what am I supposed to think? I'm just the slave here; I better not overstep my bounds. I just went ahead and meekly gave her 2 new blank checks. Don't couples discuss these things and work out the finances together? Is it normal for one spouse to decide that they want $1,700 and to just open up their own account that they alone have access to? Is this normal? I just want to run away.

She also just informed me that she is taking Ronnie to work with her tomorrow – I guess she is afraid to leave him home alone with me or something, (I might actually make him take a shower or something) so the poor kid has to get up at 5AM during his Spring Break and go sit at a library in Irvine all day.

Patrick is pretty much staying away as well. He spent Friday and Saturday night with his high school friend, Neo. I guess he will be at Neo's all week as well, plus he told me Neo's mom is going to take him to Pasadena on Tuesday to see his mom after some minor surgery she is having.

So-happy anniversary, Mitch – you screwed up by marrying this psycho "Christian". Maybe Judy was right last year when she said I was rushing into things and marrying Terry so quickly. I dated Terry for 9 months, I went to her church many times and got to know her Pastor and friends. We went to several "counseling" sessions with her Pastor. They all swooned and told me how lucky I was to be getting such a gem of a loving woman….

Where is this loving woman now? One year into this and I feel like she entrapped me with lies and deceit. She only seems to love herself and her brat. Her church friends don't know the real Terry like I do….

Can't cry over spilled milk though. I guess the plan is just to muddle through one day at a time – at least I have the appearance of being in a Christian marriage, until she decides to move out or something, then I can pretty much forget about being in any Christian ministry. I am beginning to understand (my brother) Mike's final action on Earth. He put a .357 Magnum in his mouth and squeezed the trigger.

Later…on my first wedding anniversary…

Well she slept a good 2+ hours for her nap – I worked the whole time in the office, then I went into the kitchen to make dinner for the 3 of us. She came in and hugged me while I was cooking. I set up tray tables in front of the TV and we watched "Jack" with Ronnie while we ate. She cried. Then we went for a walk, but not much was said during the walk. When she came home, I started the dishwasher and cleaned up the counters while she dressed for the hot tub – I walked her to the hot tub for awhile – helped her in and out – helped her dry off. I spent $7,500 on this nice hot tub on the back porch, with a nice covered lattice gazebo for her privacy, to help reduce her muscle stress from work and driving and all, thinking it would make her want me more….silly me.

She went and showered and washed her hair. She came down a couple of times after she showered, and told me she was going to be drying her hair, but after over an hour, at about 7:45 I went up to see what was going on. She was in bed, TV on, watching X-Men, playing solitaire. Story of my life. I am just an afterthought! She controls me. Just like that note you saw at the beginning of this sad tale – Terry only feels "pretty and desirable" when she is left completely alone – no human contact. Just crossword puzzles and the TV. Is this what Jesus meant when he said, "What God has brought together?"

I lay on the bed with my glass of wine – after about 15 minutes, she asked me if I wanted to play cards, I said sure OK. Then she put the cards away – I asked why, she said she changed her mind. She asked if we could make love (A FIRST!!) and turned to me and started caressing my beard. Long pregnant pause – finally I said I did not know how to act towards her anymore, since she had just told me I was "terrifying her more and more all the time." Well an hour and a half of tears later, she is finally drifted off to sleep. I told her it was hard for me to be intimate after what she had said and after the way she gave me the cold shoulder all the time. We talked about righteous anger. She said I was basically not being like Jesus to Ronnie – "let the little children come unto me" and all that.

I asked her how many teens had been stoned to death (in the Old Testament) by their parents for being disobedient and disrespectful to their parents, as Leviticus commanded parents to do (not that I am saying we should stone our kids – of course not! But it shows how much they should obey). She said she didn't want to know. I guess not. I told her Jesus wrote that passage of Scripture – the same Jesus who said, "Let the little children come unto me." I asked her if she would have been terrified about Jesus overturning tables, shouting and beating people with a whip in the Temple. She said she did not know. I said that she needed to get a complete picture of Jesus and not just have her little skewed picture of Jesus.

I told her I had to give up on Ronnie, because no one had the stomach for disciplining him and it was tearing my marriage apart and my relationship with my son Pat. I told her kids are like wet cement and you can mold them when they are young, but Ronnie's cement was too hard and had to be broken up – I told her that the price was too high and I was not going to pay it. She cried a lot. I tried to hold her.

She asked me how Ronnie was acting to show he did not want to be disciplined and to learn and grow up right. I told her that he never asked to help out with the trash, that he never asked to help out with the vacuuming, that he never asked to help out with the kitchen, that he never asked to help out with the laundry, that he never asked to help out with anything, just as one example. She asked if Pat did that and I said yes, all the time.

Just then, he came into the room and told her good night and that he was going to bed at 8:40. He ignored me of course. No "good night Dad" or anything. She sweetly gave him a goodnight kiss and slobbered him up pretty good. I watched him roll his eyes when she wasn't looking.

Funny, he just now turned off his TV and his light and it is 11PM. Not much common sense for a kid who has to get up at 5AM, huh?

So, I probably just wrecked the marriage single handedly by daring to try to have an adult conversation about her son and his desperate need for discipline, but whatever. She needs to know that I do not despise Ronnie, I just won't be his Dad. I'll be his guardian, his caretaker, his slave and provider, but he really doesn't want a Dad – he wants someone to keep him entertained at great expense with no strings attached. It sure will be fun to try to manufacture a fake love for a kid who detests me. God help me.

I printed this out and left it for her. She was not amused…

"Once upon a time a rather ordinary boy brought home a hungry girl puppy. He longed to love the puppy. He wanted nothing more than to grow old with it and love it forever. The puppy danced around his home with glee and searched every corner of its new life for interesting and fun things to do. Every time he went to feed the puppy however, it bit his hand. At first the bites were just nips – no flesh was broken; no blood was spilled, so the boy persisted beyond the mild pain.

The puppy grew and developed. She learned new tricks and explored new neighborhoods. Always when the puppy came home, she would drag herself through the door and fall fast asleep. The boy had no puppy to pet it seemed. As the puppy grew, her nips became stronger. Her sharp teeth began to cut into the boys flesh. At first, the boy would simply wash off the blood, tape up the wounds and press on. The puppy was now a dog and had many different interests, however. None of them involved the boy. One time, the doggy cleanly bit off one of the boy's fingers. The doggy never noticed, and strangely neither did the boy. It seems he had contracted a form of leprosy that had been transmitted by the dog's many bites. The nerves were deadened. He no longer felt the pain of his severed flesh.

Time went by. The boy longed for the doggy to play with him, but the doggy had pressing matters. The doggy would come home and occupy itself with what appeared to be important things – things that had to be done. But they were essentially trivial. The numbed boy continued to feed the doggy and the nipping went on – the flesh was slowly and systematically chewed away.

One day the boy prepared the doggie's meal. Everything was there. It was ready to be served but as the boy looked down, a shocking sight appeared to him – his hands were now stumps! He could no longer carry the doggie's dish to her.

The food sat on the counter, but the puppy was now being fed elsewhere, and he knew not where. He only knew that his dream of living with a loving puppy was forever dashed. He was paralyzed in his inability to even get the puppy's attention. The puppy forgot all about her feedings – not to worry though, plenty of other things met the doggie's needs.

I found someone new he said. WHO said she? Adventure and freedom said he. I am sleeping with ideas and fondling discovery. My bed is burning with concepts and conundrums. I fade away from you – I fade away. Wait, there she is calling me with some new theory – sorry, gotta go! Bye, bye puppy – bye."

I found the printed story crumpled up in her trashcan while I was doing chores. Boy that sure made an impact on my sweet wife, huh?

> "Perfect little dream the kind that hurts the most
> forgot how it feels well almost
> no one to blame always the same
> open my eyes wake up in flames
> it took you to make me realize
> it took you to make me realize
> it took you to make me realize
> it took you to make me see the light
> smashed up my sanity
> smashed up my integrity
> smashed up what i believed in
> smashed up what's left of me
> smashed up my everything
> smashed up all that was true

gonna smash myself to pieces – I don't know what else to do."
Word and Music, Trent Reznor, Nine Inch Nails.

5/8/03

Well it has been a busy week – with the typical no intimacy – par for the course.

T has not been sleeping well – she is waking up a lot, I wish I knew why. Maybe my words did have an impact, but you would not know it to watch the behavior around here.

Last Friday we left together for the Modern Laboratory meeting in San Diego.

Friday was a nice leisurely day and we did have sex that night in the hotel, but it was the only time over the whole long weekend of Friday-Monday.

I volunteered early Saturday morning to help at the meeting and went to some sessions after a nice lunch with T. She then napped. Sunday we went on Dan's (my oldest son) U.S. Navy submarine in San Diego, and she rested when we returned. I spent about $1,000 for the weekend – nice meals, expensive hotel and all, and she did thank me, but she seems to have no real deep passion. Ho hum. She controls me.

On the way home on Monday afternoon, we picked up the boys who both had a nice weekend away as well.

UPS had delivered two books on intimacy from Christian perspective that I bought for her. She thanked me a lot, but has not touched them all week. The little black book I gave her 15 months ago on "How to Satisfy a Man", she only opened because I dug it out of her boxes that we brought back from Phoenix and begged her again to read it. She simply ignored me the last time I asked her to read it when she was still in Phoenix. She did read about half of it about 10 days ago but hasn't touched it since.

Yesterday when we were on our evening walk, she said that "Ronnie is starving all the time" and that I needed to buy him some snacks. I pointed out that there are apples, peanuts, popcorn, carrots and *plenty* of his lunchmeat and bread (that he specifically requested) that has simply been ROTTING in the fridge since early March. I said it made me angry that he never makes a lunch for school so I have no sympathy for him. (Am I supposed to *make* his lunch as well? Is that one of the butler duties I have been falling behind on?) Of course, this was her cue to start crying uncontrollably which lasted for about 2 hours. After trying several times to reason with her and calm her down, I just finally walked home ahead of her and went into the office to work. When she came into the office, I explained to her that she was just shutting me down and that I was going to start filling up my time with other things than doting on her if it kept up (remember the puppy story?) I just cannot handle the pain of waiting on this woman hand and foot, anticipating her every need, planning special things for her, when she just a) ignores *all* my needs and b) stands defiantly in the way of me trying to instill character in her hooligan son.

She thinks I hate Ronnie, but I explained that I don't want to be the father any more since he does not really respect me. I am happy to be the provider, but I am no longer willing to be involved in disciplining him or trying to teach him manners, hygiene, etc. I made sure that she understood that she had short-circuited that.

I pick him up from school every day and he never says hi to me (or anything for that matter). He gets into the car in silence. I have purposefully driven home in silence just to see if he will initiate a conversation, but he never does – he is content to just treat me like his chauffer, cook, etc. He does usually thank me for dinner (over his shoulder as he throws most of it into the trash and walks away), but he never offers to do any chores (like loading the dishwasher, emptying the dishwasher, emptying the trash) and has to be repeatedly told to do his laundry, clean his toilet and bathroom, and SIMPLY BATHE. One weekend when he stayed with my ex-wife in Pasadena, she told me he did not bathe the entire weekend.

We went to Phoenix over Easter weekend to get all her stuff from storage and now the house is filled with boxes and extra (unneeded) furniture. I hope she will go through it all soon.

So, in short, the past month has been a cycle of me doing all the workload with little or no help, Ronnie sitting in his room with his TV, computer, X-box, and Nintendo (yes – he has them all again) every day after school except to come out for dinner (I can't wait to see his grades which come out next week). Of course, lets not forget T coming home after a hard day, every day, enjoying her dinner and after a 30 minute walk with me, basically going up to bed. Pat, my son has been working on weekends and spending a lot of time with Neo so he has not been around. My Christian life is so idyllic.

5/9/03

Well we slept in late for once – it felt really good. Then Terry actually asked me to make love to her (SECOND TIME IN A YEAR!!) I was so needy I didn't last long. But she still has not picked up the little black book I asked her to read nor has she cracked the 2 new books on intimacy I bought her.

5/10/03 Mother's Day

I had to get up at 5AM to go work cameras at church, but Judy came to church and Sunday School. She seemed to like SS class with Carol Burns (Pastor's wife). We all went out to lunch later and had a fairly good time. Especially since I paid $107 for it. Later I tried to nap with Terry, but the room was too hot for me, so I am going to do some research work on some rocks. She napped for about 2 hours after I left.

Well I worked the rest of the afternoon and then we spent some time together watching TV after eating a few leftovers that I warmed up for us. Then at about 8PM, she asked me to make love to her (wow!). I could definitely get used to this, but one thing really bugs me. Terry is simply unwilling to do anything but just lay there. She closes her eyes tightly and lays on her back and doesn't interact at all. I decided to ask her, "so you just want to lay there and make me do all the work?" and she said yes. She actually said that yes, she was just going to lay there!!! How exciting for me....So the evening wasn't a total loss, but she sure controls the sex. I wonder how long it will be before it is just too much effort? Is that her plan? Christian marriages are so awesome – everyone should have one...

5/14/03 Wednesday

I have been telling Terry that the floors are a filthy mess since we returned from our little getaway to Tucson last week. I just have not had the energy to power wash them, so this morning when I called her at work at 7AM, I told her I was going to do the floors. It took me 2 hours. The crap I pulled off it, especially in the kitchen, under the boys' chairs was ungodly. I should have saved that black water to show her. I purposely left the boys chairs out in the living room, so that they would have to go get them and bring them into the kitchen in hopes that they would notice how clean the floors were. I mentioned to each boy when they came in for dinner that the floors had been worked on and were now clean. I pointed out to Ronnie a messy spot under his chair that I had left for him so he could see the difference. Then I got down on my knees in front of him and cleaned it up with a rag and some Windex. I showed him the dirty rag – he snorted and walked away.

Ronnie was already sitting and eating when Patrick came in to make his plate at dinnertime. When Pat decided to make himself some chocolate milk, R jumped up and demanded to be part of the action, laughing loudly. Terry said nothing and just kept eating and ignoring the whole scene. I said they had better not spill any powdered chocolate – they all heard me. Ronnie was goofing around and laughing and sparring with Patrick. Sure enough, R spilled chocolate powder on the counter, the trashcan and the newly scrubbed floor. I was incensed and firmly said I better not find chocolate on my clean floor or there would be hell to pay. Ronnie thought that was funny and started laughing, making me even hotter. I warned them that I would go agro if I found chocolate on the floor. Terry said nothing and did nothing, except to just cover her face as if to say "here we go again". Why do I always have to be the bad guy?

No one made any attempt to even look and see if there was chocolate spilled on the floor – I was just simply ignored. After about 10 minutes, I got up to see, and there it was, all over the counter, the trashcan and the floor. I got upset and told Terry that a punishment was due and that I was very angry about it. She sat there and cried – saying nothing. I got on my knees and cleaned up the mess while complaining about it – she said Ronnie would clean it up. I thought, yeah right – he hasn't washed his bath towel for 16 weeks and he is going to clean up this floor?

Then I went and sat in the living room where it was cooler and watched TV. For the rest of the night, Terry ignored me. She spent all of her time in the bedroom. About an hour later, she pulled Ronnie out of the office (where I was allowing him to do homework) and after about 15 minutes he came out into the hallway – about 12 feet away and said to the floor from 12 feet away that he was sorry for spilling the powder. I said "Whatever." Terry went back upstairs. I went for a walk. When I came back, she was asleep. I went and got my pillow and slept in the garage. I think the one to be punished is Terry. She refuses to discipline her brat and she stands in the way when I ask for him to be disciplined. This is almost too painful for words.

Patrick gave me an ultimatum the other night. He said he just couldn't do his homework, get the rest he needs and stay disciplined sharing a room with R. So I discussed it with T and we decided to move R back into the den that is just off the living room. I work really hard to keep the den and living room neat and tidy in case any guests stop by. She actually agreed with me that we would work together to ensure that R would improve his personal hygiene habits and work to keep the den (his new bedroom) neat and tidy! Wow, progress at last! But it was short-lived, as usual. It became a pig-sty in less than a week, just like before.

I asked him several days ago to remove the dirt-encrusted cups and bowls from his room where he always leaves them. When people come over to visit, they see his room, as it is right next to the front door. I now even have to leave his room door and window open sometimes just to air it out because it smells so bad in there.

I wrote him a note on Monday telling him to get the cups out of there and into the kitchen sink. When he came home he threw the note in the trash and didn't touch the cups in his room. I took the note out of the trash and wrote to Terry on the back of it that Ronnie ignores my requests – I put it in her makeup box so she probably got it this morning.

I think I will sleep in the garage for the rest of the week – or maybe I will go to San Diego State (SDSU) where my lab is being built. Let them fend for themselves.

5/22/03

Well I dove away last Tuesday and went to San Diego for two days. I did not call her until I was an hour from home on my way back on Thursday. Apparently, she didn't sleep for 2 days and was weeping when I came home. We talked for about an hour and I made it clear that I was not going to be treated like crap by her and R, and ignored by her – I would just go find something else to do at SDSU or whatever. She begged me not to do that again – she thought I had just left her for good. I told her I would never leave her but I was trying to make a point. I begged her to work with me as a team to forge R's character. I begged her to finish reading the little black book -and she did!

After dinner she even asked me for sex (yippie!) and she got on top and apparently had the most intense orgasm she has ever had – I couldn't even finish she was so sensitive, so I went unsatisfied that night. Oh well, at least my partner was satisfied. I was really pleased about that. I thought, "Maybe she will see how selfless I am and she will appreciate me more."

But the crap goes on around here. Ronnie still ignores me – his room is messy – he does not clean up after himself. Last night he turned his nose up at the new crock-pot meatloaf I made because it had ketchup on it. Ketchup. Don't teenagers love ketchup? Never mind that he eats ketchup all over his fish sticks, hamburgers, fries – you name it – every meal you can think of. She just let him leave the table without eating. I made him put his food in a microwavable container and into the fridge. I bet myself a steak dinner that he will let it sit there and rot until it gets thrown away.

I asked Terry what she thought about the final chapter in the black book – where it talks about really paying attention to a man's needs and she said, "it was interesting." We had her style of sex (again) on Saturday and Sunday, but on Sunday I told her it was getting too boring for me – missionary all the time, her eyes closed, no kissing or closeness, no hugging afterwards. Plus, now there is a new twist to our wonderful love life. It now always has to be just before she falls asleep. So let me get this straight…. my wife is willing to have sex with me at night, missionary only, her eyes closed so she does not have to look at me, and then no afterglow, so she can go straight to sleep. Does that mean she has to get all sleepy and drowsy with her pills and wine so as to just tolerate me on her body before she passes out?

It is almost as if I am making love to a mannequin -just not worth the effort. I gave her pleasure until she moaned and then she fell asleep.

Today is Thursday again and she has not touched me since last Thursday. I rub myself regularly now so I won't go crazy. She has some serious pathology about sex – and oral sex – forget it. She just flat refuses to even discuss it. Of course, if I offer her oral sex, the bedroom door is quickly locked and she eagerly jumps on the bed.

She has barely read her first book on intimacy. I think she is on page 46. When did that come by UPS? Oh yeah, 17 days ago. Am I just being too selfish or something?

Sunday – Memorial Day weekend, 5/25/03

Yesterday Terry went through all her boxes that we brought back from Phoenix and thank God, she is donating most of it to charity. Now we can get back to having a normal living room. While she and Ronnie did that, I worked on the back porch. I dug up several plants (rose bushes –boy am I sore from that) and planted some palms and some prickly pears. I also lined up a lot of garbage bags to have hauled away. I then brought home a propane BBQ from Wallmart and assembled it so we can do some grilling.

While we were relaxing on the couch, my head was laying on her lap – I asked her for a favor this weekend – "would you please give me oral?" – she immediately (and loudly) said she didn't think she could do that. I said "Please?" several times and she said "No!" After a very long silence I told her I was getting depressed and felt like she did not really care about my needs at all. You guessed it – she started crying. I am not going to have intercourse again with this woman until she at least tries to give to me. She won't even try. She controls me – she controls sex. If it ain't missionary – it ain't happening. If it ain't just before she falls asleep at night I can forget it. We came home from church and I washed the van – she made some lunch, then after, she fell asleep on the couch.

Monday, May 26, 2003, Memorial Day

Yesterday Terry barely touched me and I did not reach out to her at all. At one point when we passed in the hallway, she gave me a hug, but I just patted her on the shoulder.

I grilled a delicious chicken dinner with corn on the cob and garlic potatoes – we went for our walk, but we did not hold hands. We sat together on the couch watching "Men of Honor", and then went upstairs to watch the rest of it on the bed – she only held my hand a little. It ended at 9:30 and she cried (funny how movies make her cry over how sweet they are but her sweet loving man just pisses her off), then she took her pills at 9:45 and fell asleep by 10PM. I got up at about 7:20 this morning and got into the shower – she was up having her coffee and watching the news when I came downstairs. I sat with her for a while until she finished her cereal and coffee – then she went to the bathroom and finally just came out and told me she was going up to shower (since she hasn't showered since last Sunday).

This is shaping up to be another sexless weekend in a string of sexless weeks. God, why did you do this to me? You stuck me with a woman who just has no desire whatsoever. I am bitter – I trusted You and now I face misery and sadness again – almost like when Judy walked out after her cancer. Is it me God? Am I ugly, smelly, detestable? What is wrong with me?

Ronnie just sat in his room all-day and stared at Nintendo, just like he did all day Saturday and Sunday. Can that be good for his *Ritalin* soaked brain? Pat came home Saturday evening at about 7PM then also sat on the computer until midnight. Yesterday he got on the computer at about 2 and was on it until 10PM. I do not like this series of computer binges – it never leads to anything good. Then he and Ronnie went to the hot tub. I must have been taking a nap when they came home.

3:30 same day. Well I have pretty much stayed away from Terry all day. She finished working on her boxes (her packed stuff from Phoenix) and I have been busy in the office, cleaning up, getting organized, making rock specimens. Earlier, at about 1:00 she took the boys to a friend's house – then she just went back to work on the boxes when she got home. The laundry is calling me – 3rd load – we'll see what happens later now that we are alone.

Saturday, May 31. Well, as you can imagine – Terry ignored me last Monday and pretty much all week. I guess it makes her feel "pretty and desirable."

I worked on the SCAS manuscript all day (a research journal that I am publishing in regularly) – Terry did whatever. I think she slept and watched TV. She has not read from the intimacy book at all lately. I did beg her for oral and she gave me about 1 minutes worth. Making progress, I guess. When we went for a walk we walked by the boys at the hot tub. They were with a neighbor girl named Kaitlyn, I think. I was trying to talk to Patrick about not spending too much time in the hot tub because of his art project, and Ronnie kept yelling "Whaaa" "Whaaa" over me very loudly, interrupting my conversation with Pat who was right next to him in the spa. I asked T after we walked away if she happened to notice the blatant disrespect her son was displaying towards me in front of others and she was oblivious to it – she said no!!! She did not even notice. I could not believe it! I asked her how much more evidence she needed that he is a disrespectful snot. I could tell she was going to cry so I dropped it.

Sunday, June 1

Getting ready for church I asked T what she found out from Ronnie last night about his disrespectful display towards me at the pool. She said he had claimed that he has water in his ear and was trying to say "What?" I told her that was a crock, that I recognized blatant disrespect and that was clearly it – and she went ballistic. She threw a temper tantrum the likes of which I have never seen….she refused to get ready for church and said she and Ronnie were staying home. I told her repeatedly and gently that the boys were going to Sunday-School and that I would come back for her to go church. She screamed and cried and threw a real tantrum. I took the boys and came back home to get ready for church. She was still crying and typing on her computer. I went to church without her.

Later, I found the letter she typed and printed out for me. She just goes on and on about how she feels like a prisoner and has no rights, that I just tell her to obey – whew! Since when have I said, "Obey"??? She went on and on about how I am barely civil to the boy, but he essentially ignores me, my requests, etc., and shows me disdain and disrespect. It's really hard for me to be lovey-dovey with him if he will not do as I ask. I am a doormat around here, and I simply have to be that, just to keep the peace!

Later she hand wrote me an apology note and taped it to my office door. She says wants to be a good wife, and it is hard for her to give up all the independence she once had. Yeah right. Terry gives up nothing. This will not end well.

Thursday, June 6

Well we had sex tonight for the first time since May 22. It has been a pretty typical week – She gets up at 4, I get up at 5 to sit and pray with her and walk her to her car. I get the boys to school and do housework, rock work, (and this week a lot of school work in preparation for the trip to VA for my second graduate degree). Last weekend was a nightmare and even though she apologized in writing to me, she has not been very close. Granted, she started her period this week, but she knows how much I need affection. She is still on page 46 of her intimacy book. What a great investment that book was.

June 13, Thursday

Well the crap has hit the fan again. Ronnie is disobedient and a liar and I proved it to her. I know he has been sneaking into my office now that it is summer break, when I am not here (and against my express wishes and will). He knows he is not allowed out there without my express permission. I guess this is what I get for sending him out to my quiet, spacious office to do his homework when he gets distracted. I have thousands of dollars worth of equipment and other things including loaded guns in my office. Course, they are locked up in a locked cabinet but he could break into it if he wanted to….every other week we hear about stuff like that on the news. I have begged Terry to support me in this but she simply gets teary-eyed or ignores me.

R just finished mandated summer school for the summer on Tuesday and was home all day Wednesday. This was his second straight summer in summer school. What joy.

I set up a video recorder with a camera in my office on Tuesday (because I knew he was going to go in there right after I drove away) and asked Terry to please tell him to stay out of the office while I was going to be gone. Again, I just *knew* he was going to go out there and snoop around. He was going to be home alone all day and he has no self-control. He is flagrantly disobedient. Before I left to go to SDSU, I asked her again if she told him to stay out of the office – she said yes – so I left and she went to work.

When I came home late that day, I asked her if R had been in the office. She said R told her no – he had not gone out there. I thought, "yeah right," so I went down and rewound the tape. Surprise, surprise, guess who appeared on candid camera?

Well tonight we got into a discussion about him just before bed and I was trying to make the point to her that he does not obey – either her or me. If looks could have killed she would have macerated me with a chainsaw. She was pretty sharp with me because I feel he needs more discipline and she thinks I am too hard on him – so I said, "If I can prove to you beyond a shadow of a doubt that he blatantly disobeys you and lies to your face would you believe me?" She defiantly said, "Yes!" – knowing me to be a bastard and her angel of a son to be a true saint. So I produced the videotape shot earlier that very day of him going into my office not once but 2 separate times to snoop around in my things. He was on tape for several minutes rummaging around.

He also went upstairs several times from his downstairs bedroom, as the camera clearly showed. She cried and cried, and said she was utterly shocked. I was silent, thinking, "Finally my dear wife will listen to me and will work with me as a team for the betterment of her son." But then she asked me in tears if I was videotaping her!!! What??? I thought this was about exposing her kid as a lying jerk. Now she makes this about me and not her idiot son? What man would put up with a woman like this like I do? I simply left the bedroom and slept in the garage.

I did prove it to her though-maybe now she believes me that her little angel is not so perfect, but I am not holding my breath. I fear that it is just making her hate me even more, because I am right and she cannot stand me being right about R.

I told her that this summer if I have to go anywhere – guess who is coming with me? I am *not* leaving him home alone to mess with my office things, my chemicals, my loaded guns, etc. How much fun would it be if he started playing with my guns?

June 20, Friday.

Last night I asked her for oral and she just started crying. She just cannot do it – she cannot stand it for whatever reason. Course, if I offer it to her, the doors get locked pretty fast and she is all naked, spread eagle and moaning… am I just an idiot? I just can't ask her for oral again I guess – of course, I can't ask her about anything sexual. She just huffs and puffs and walks away.

I am praying that I won't get depressed. I am trying to encourage her a lot because tomorrow we get on a plane to VA for a whole week. I have been taking Ronnie with me every time I get in the car and have to go somewhere. Nobody is overtly complaining and at least I don't have to worry about him messing around in the office while I am gone. But I could get frostbite from all the icy feelings towards me.

July 21, Monday.

Terry is at work – it is about 7:30AM and Ronnie is asleep after being up until about 1AM. Pat is with Jay (my middle son) in Calabasas. Well the VA trip went pretty well. It was exhausting for me to be in class all day – five days straight, and Terry was a big help to me, I have to say. She would bring me lunch every day (after I showed her how to go to the cafeteria and gave her enough money for the whole week). I thanked her repeatedly. We did have a good time sitting together just having lunch and talking. I never asked her to do oral on me during the trip, and I think we had the usual "eyes-closed and wincing" missionary style once and that was it – what fun. But it was pretty stressful. I had papers to write just about every night. I just have to get a laptop before I go next time. Since we returned home I have left her pretty much alone. I rub myself just about every day now. Once last week, she did get on top and did me until she had her big O. She has a pretty hard come when she does that and I like to do it for her because it relaxes her so much afterwards, but for me to get on her and get busy again after that is impossible – she is just too sensitive. So I get left in the cold after she gets her rocks off.

I guess she loves me; she comes home every night, right? Isn't that love? She rarely shows any affection. I think she is just heartbroken about having to leave Phoenix. She won't admit it but I know she hates California. She now has become a total control freak about driving. She HAS to drive everywhere we go – even when we go to AZ. She can come home on a Friday – exhausted after working her horrible schedule all week, after being completely sleep-deprived and she INSISTS on driving the car (or my big van) when we go to AZ – a seven-hour trip! I had better stay alert and awake on the trips in case I have to grab the wheel when she passes out, but I also had better comply and not say a word.

I took her back to her pitiful friends and church over the weekend, since I was speaking at the AZ science meetings. I nearly died in the heat, but she loved it. She was sullen and silent all the way home back to CA; she even cried silently to herself. Usually we hold hands while we drive around together, but I did not initiate – neither did she. So, I guess this marriage is just one of companionship and convenience. Two sexless, platonic fools are better at facing the world than one. Aren't they? Aren't I better off with this frigid woman than if I was utterly alone? There is no fire or passion in this relationship. I guess I will have to read books and watch movies to have any romance in my life. She is on page 106 of her intimacy book. That is about 1 page per day. I guess I can't ask for much more. How lucky am I?

I know she must hate living here but she is so dishonest about it. She just refuses to tell me the truth but her actions speak much more loudly than her feeble attempt to hide her disdain for me and for Southern California.

On a whim today, I decided to watch our wedding ceremony video – mainly to watch and listen closely to the vows portion of our wedding ceremony. I found it interesting that her pastor – Pastor Paul in Phoenix, had her recite different vows than me. My vows were, "To love, honor and cherish" her. Which I would say again in a heartbeat because I am convinced that God wants me to really love and serve this woman. BUT…. her vows were different…Pastor Paul had her repeat, "Love, honor and *obey*." I wondered why he would ask here to repeat those vows? I certainly have never demanded that she obey me or simply expected her to just blindly do everything I ever asked. I have always given her the opportunity to express her feelings and opinions about any decision that had to be made that affected both of us or us and the boys. So I decided that the next time I get over to his little sleepy church, I would ask Pastor Paul why he used those words with her during our ceremony.

One shocker, however, on the video tape…..I had not realized that Terry's bridal shower was on the beginning of the tape that was used to record our ceremony. I had never watched the shower portion -(being a guy and all), so I decided to take some time to watch and listen to it. It was basically Terry and a bunch of very talkative (and highly opinionated) overweight women from her church in one of the very plain and sterile white church rooms.

Of course they were all chowing down on cake and carbs – but what else is new? Those women were all married. They had already entrapped some poor sap of a man and they had no need to look lovely or desirable for their now entrapped Baptist husbands – why shouldn't they scarf down mass quantities of fattening foods? Women like that disgust me. I mean I tried during my marriage to Terry to stay as fit as I could – to walk every night, to eat few carbs, to be aware of my personal grooming….no wonder the men of North Village Baptist church never hung around their fat and ugly wives.

Nevertheless, the topic of Terry moving to Southern California came up during the shower. Several of the women wanted to know how she was going to "handle" living in Southern California. Terry responded by tearfully saying, "Oh I really don't want to live there, so *please, please* pray that God will move me back to my beloved Phoenix!!" So there you have it folks…..from the very beginning this girl did not want to move away from her sick little church in her hellish neighborhood. Why in God's name did she pursue me? I always made it plain I was not ever going to live in Phoenix! The heat is oppressive to me and I never hid that from her. What was she thinking?

"Yes I am alone but then again I always was as far back as I can tell.

I think maybe it's because, because you were never really real to begin with. I just made you up to hurt myself. And it worked."

Words and music Trent Reznor, Nine Inch Nails.

Tuesday

We haven't had sex in over 9 days. Last night I told Terry that I didn't even feel married anymore. She said her boobs were hurting. I told her I was trying to leave her alone, and she thanked me. Huh. Would I feel better if she held me and said, "Baby, I know you need me and I want to satisfy you – I am just uncomfortable right now? Would you give me a day or two to recover?" I know that's what I would say if I were a married woman and had a needy man...

She came home early at 3:45 and we were alone. We ate dinner and she showered and washed her hair. I bet she smelled nice, but I will never know since she didn't touch me all evening and went up to bed at 8PM. Ronnie came home at 7:30. That means we were alone for 4 hours and she never even kissed me. My life sucks.

Wednesday July 23.

I asked Terry not to wake me up today, but she woke me at 4:50AM. I never went back to sleep. I have been in a daze all day long and cannot even think. In frustration, I told her when she came home that I think she is torturing me with sex deprivation and sleep deprivation. I asked her not to cry but she did a little – I told her I was sorry but that I was feeling that she did not care about me. She seemed sorry and she did make love to me right after dinner. Three guesses what position? Whose eyes were closed tightly? It feels like I am raping her. Is that her intended effect?

Thursday. I drove to Ventura today but I bought us movie tickets to see Hulk and took R and T to the movie and dinner at PF Changs. We all had a good time. She then told me she had started her period today, but she did make love to me that night. She had a good big O. World first campers – 2 nights of sex in a row. Now I guess I have to wait a year again to have her.

Friday 7/23. It is 4:45PM and Terry is in bed. I fed her at 3:45 and she went straight up to bed. Her period is pretty heavy and her boobs are sore, so I can't go near her.

Sunday 7/27/03

Yesterday I went to SDSU at 7AM and returned at 6:30PM. Terry had the whole day to herself with Ronnie. She got new eyeglasses – did her hair, did her nails and cooked a roast. Wow. She was still on her period, so I did not bother her. Today the boys left at 1PM for camp. We came home after dropping them at church and she went to bed for about 2 hours. Then she got up and sat on the couch with me. We had leftovers for dinner. She showed me no affection whatsoever. At about 6PM, after we had been alone in a quiet house for 5 hours I asked her if we could mess around tonight. She said her period was still heavy. I asked her if she could oral me and she got upset, saying, "Probably not." We went for a walk and I did not say a word. When we got home she went in the spa. So her period is too heavy for me but not for soaking in the spa?? We sat on the couch together for about 45 minutes – then she went to bed at about 7:50.

She is still on page 106 of her book. What a life. Are all Christian marriages this wonderful?

Tuesday 7/29/03

I begged her last night to come home tonight and attack me before I go crazy. It has been seven days. It took some significant begging when she got home, but she did take me by the hand upstairs and she threw me on the bed and kissed me and caressed me until I took over. I sure love to beg – it really pumps my self-esteem. I did make her get on top, but she did not come. I printed off a copy of some of the text of "How to satisfy your man every time," the book I asked her to read months and months ago, and stuck it in her "new" Christian intimacy book. I underlined the parts about really paying attention to your man and what happens when sex gets boring. She never mentioned getting it. It is now missing from her book. I bet she threw it away.

Thursday 7/31

I have been up since 3:52AM when Terry left the hall light blazing into the bedroom with the door standing wide open. Am I in a Chinese torture chamber? I was pretty upset about that but did not say a word. I seriously think she is trying to disorient me. She left the bathroom door open again last night while I was trying to cool the upstairs so I could sleep. I try to keep "unnecessary" rooms closed because the AC just cannot handle these wide-open spaces and vaulted ceilings. She and I have discussed this over and over and over again but it goes into one ear and out the other.

I simply cannot sleep when it is 76 degrees or above up there. I yelled at her and she started crying. Silly me for thinking that yelling would work. Only humble servitude works – and even that not so much. I purposely waited until it was 83 degrees up there last night to not have to run the air and spend a wad of cash. It takes all evening of cooling with the AC just to get down to 75, where I won't stick to the sheets. So I had to wait until 11PM to go to bed. Then she wakes me up at 3:52. What a miracle woman this is.

The electric bill came yesterday and it was over $350. I told her I was canceling the $100/month life insurance bill to pay for the electric and asked her to find a policy for me at work. She never did. She only works at a Fortune 500 life insurance company. I bet a $15,000 policy on me would be free. I guess I am not worth even that much to her.

This morning I got up to help her out the door at 4:43AM and she kicked me in the head while I was sitting groggy on the stairs waiting for her. She said she was sorry, but that she could not see me sitting there. Hello??? All the lights in the house were on and I am not some midget.

I think she thinks I have a lover. Last night the phone rang and she answered "Hello," and got a click. She hung up the phone saying, "Oh, when a female voice answers, hang up, right?" I asked her if she thought that was my lover or something -she said no. I guess that is all she got from the text copy from the Christian intimacy book I stuck in her crossword puzzle book – that men go looking for sex if they don't get it at home. She has not said a word to me about that and she has not budged a page in her intimacy book. We are probably going to have missionary until I die of boredom. Plus, it is always such an effort to get her butt off the couch every night to go for a walk. From the time I feed her at about 3:40 until about 8PM, she is glued to the TV and the couch – and her butt looks like – well you can guess. Last night she was asleep by 7:30PM. Must be nice. I'm still doing the kitchen at that hour….

Friday August 1

    T got home and ate dinner. She went to bed at about 4:50 and slept until about 8:15 and then got up. We did have sex but she did not want to come. Wonder why? I must not be her knight in shining armor any more. I beg her to open her eyes during sex but nope. It ain't gonna happen. I feel so special staring at her eyelids during our special time together.

Saturday – our last morning alone without the boys before their return from camp – she did not want to be close at all – not even holding hands on the couch. So I basically stayed away from her. Sunday the boys spent the whole day at Neo's after church – did she want to get intimate? Nope.

Tuesday August 5

    Yesterday I drove 275 miles to SDSU and back and ran the equipment there for a few hours. I even beat T home at 3PM and cooked dinner. She took the boys shopping after dinner and drank a chocolate mocha. It kept her up until 9:45. I tried to touch her but she pushed me away. She just pushes me away! She controls sex (and that means no sex…)

    Today I busted my butt getting the house ready for the appraiser who came at noon to appraise the place for the refinance loan. Before that I had to meet with a supervisor from the trash truck company, since their truck decided to dig an 18-inch gash in my front lawn last week when the picked up the trash.

    I cooked an awesome grilled dinner, which she scarfed down and then she fell asleep on the couch for almost 3 hours. She woke up and went to make coffee, as she does every night, only her jumbo-sized coffee can was empty. All she could say was "There's no more coffee???? WHY is there NO MORE COFFEEE????"

    Naturally she was upset when I asked her why she could not write *Coffee* on the grocery list, seeing as though she is the one that does her coffee pot every night. That sealed the evening. We went for a walk, but she mostly walked about 3 feet behind me-she never said two words. After about 20 minutes of that I tried to hold her hand and show her some compassion – she pretty much ignored me, but to her credit, she did not pull her hand away and sock me in the face.

When we got home I ignored her for the rest of the night. She went up to bed at 8:20 after soaking alone in the spa without even saying good night. Some marriage. Jesus has really made her special. I bet He loves her something fierce.

Wednesday August 6, 2003

I got up at 4:41 to help her get out the door. She didn't say much other than "Love you" before I closed her car door. I tried to go back to sleep but could not, so I got up around 5:00. I noticed that she must have read about 4 pages in her book last night. Maybe I should have more fights with her. If I did, by Christmas she could be done with the book. She has still NOT, however, said anything about the page I photocopied and put in her crossword puzzle book days and days ago. Silence is golden, huh?

She called at 8:30AM and asked me if I was still upset about the coffee. I said "No, I am upset because you treat me like s**t." She started to cry and said, "I have failed you again." She asked me "Why – what have I done?" I told her that I didn't want to talk about it and to just forget it because she would just cry and go back into that "I am a failure" mode. I told her I did not want to upset her at work. She said she could not forget about it. I told her I am a human being with feelings. Then I changed the subject.

She will never become a giving person. Her idea of giving is being in the same room with you and smiling at you when she is not already preoccupied with something that is more interesting than you are. I don't think she will ever learn to initiate tenderness and closeness – I think she really feels threatened by that, so she would rather be passive and wait until somebody reaches out to her. She truly has a detachment disorder.

Well we went to the movies tonight with Aya, our Japanese exchange student friend and then to eat Chinese. Everybody seemed to have a good time – I spent $99. T did ask to go for a walk tonight and then she said she was sorry she had shut me out yesterday. But it was 8:30 when we got back so she pretty much went straight to bed. Oh well. I think her apology was supposed to make me feel better. Too bad I don't.

Monday, August 11, 2003

Well Patrick and I worked at UCLA all day Friday and again all day Saturday servicing laboratory equipment. It was a long, hard weekend. Terry pretty much rested up all weekend. Saturday night we tried to make love but my back was hurting. I gave her an oral orgasm and she went wild. Funny how she loves it when I do it for her, huh? She would never cry and push me away on that offer….In fact she spreads wide open so I miss nothing in my attempt to give her the wildest time of her life….

But should I ask for a little of the same, the waterworks comes on. After that, she took a 2-hour nap on Sunday and I left her alone. Tonight I tried to get intimate with her and she kept pushing me away. Surprise, surprise. Momma is satisfied – and you want what???

Tuesday, 8/12

Tonight she came home tired because she has been staying up late watching TV every night. After a delicious dinner for which she did not thank me she said, "I want to lay down" and went straight to bed – about 4:30. She slept until 6:30. I did the kitchen, as I always do. What else is new?

Afterwards, she came down to the couch where I was relaxing and sat next to me. I tried to touch her – she pushed my hands away. She did not want to but I made her go for a walk after much cajoling. When we came home, I made some cold fizzy water. Before I could get the bottle to my thirsty lips, she had a cup on the counter and was begging me to fill it. I filled her glass and she gulped it down. I think I heard her grunt a "Thank you," but maybe it was just a burp.

She made her coffee and came out to the couch – I was watching a game show because there was literally nothing on. She took the remote and started flipping through the channel guide. I tried to touch her again and was met with the same push off. She said "Oh, 'A Walk in the clouds!'" and stood up. "I'm going upstairs to watch this," blurted out of her mouth she and went up without so much as a "Honey, come with me?" nothing. I stayed downstairs for about 45 minutes and then feeling guilty – (silly me) went up to sit with her on the bed. She was all tucked in watching, but an advertisement was on. I told her the Beach Boys final concert from 1960 in England was on- she ignored me. I asked her how many times she had watched 'A Walk in the Clouds' – she said, "two or three". I bet myself it was two or three dozen.

I asked her if she had ever watched the final Beach Boys concert – she said "No" and she said she only wanted to watch her movie. I said, "what

Terry wants, Terry gets", and she started to cry, with "Mitch are you saying I am selfish or something?" (What gave it away???)

I stayed up there another 15 minutes or so, while she cried and watched her show and then I walked out. This is no marriage. Marriage is when 2 people try to out give each other. This is a sick relationship, where one person holds intimacy over the other and only gives out just enough to keep the other person (who gives all the time) from giving up and leaving.

Monday, 8/25/03

Well it is 8:30PM and Terry is already asleep. Oh well. She gets really tired sitting at her desk at her job I guess. Tomorrow I am going to service lab equipment at Palmdale College and I am staying over to get the job done without having to drive a lot. She just said, "OK."

We did make love twice over the weekend – after about 4 weeks with no sex, though and she read about 38 pages in her book, so what am I complaining about? I get wincing missionary from her once a month and she pretends to be interested in the books I buy her. Stop complaining dude! You could be alone (and happy?)

Friday, September 26, 2003.

Well, we are down to sex one time every 10-12 days now, if I am a model citizen and don't rock the boat. She doesn't really touch me much anymore even when sitting together on the couch, and I haven't reached out to her that much. She controls me and she controls the sex. I did rearrange the couches in the living room and put the loveseat facing the TV inside of the larger long couch. Silly me, I thought she would love to be closer to me but she hates it.

Of course we have had a rough couple of weeks lately with Ronnie's ear infection, but he is well over that now and he's been well for about three days. I have been keeping a diary in my day timer of the dates that we actually are intimate. And as I said, so far were running about one time every ten days. Terry was off all last week, and we went to Moorpark College to service lab equipment on Wednesday and Thursday, but even during the times and we were alone together, she didn't really reach out to me that much. I have been telling her that I think she doesn't really want me anymore because I am too small or ineffective or a bad lover or something. But all she says is "Oh stop it", but then she never reaches out to me.

Every night at the same story -she either goes to bed for a nap right after dinner or she is so tired between dinner and bedtime, that she just doesn't reach out to me and then she goes to sleep in about 8:00 or 8:30. Or she just flat refuses and pushes me away. She really freaked out during Ronnie's ear sickness and I guess that took a lot out of her because she has just really been tired since then. Oh well.

Sunday September 29, 2003.

I really don't know what to say anymore. I am just burying myself in my work and my studies. Terry seems content to just do her thing. She sits on the couch and watches TV, she does her crossword puzzle book. Lately she has been reading a diet book that has all kinds of new foods that I guess I am going to have to buy for her. If she would just get up and walk, she would lose a lot of her weight. And if she would eat salads at night and take the dinner I make for lunch the next day, I think she would lose weight. I am not that attracted to her anymore either which compounds the problem. I don't know. I tried to get her to walk Friday night and she whined because it was too dark. I went alone. When I got home, after an hour, I went out to the office – she went to bed, so we never spoke from about 7:30PM on that night.

I pretty much avoided her all day Saturday; I just worked out in the office for as long as I could, doing different things. Then she asked me in the afternoon if I wanted to go upstairs and lay down together-and I said no. I think that hurt her, but I guess I just wanted to hurt her back. Sorry, God, but I am just worn out by this sick marriage.

Last night we walked together, but mostly in silence. I am so hurt that she just doesn't reach out to me that I don't know what to say to her anymore. After we walked, she went in the spa and then sat on the couch next to me. The boys were at a school luau, so we were alone. She did reach over for me then on the couch and I couldn't stand it anymore – I begged like a street urchin. A man shouldn't have to wait to have release just once every ten days. We went upstairs and made love, she had a very intense orgasm. Mine hurt it had been so long. Then today I started feeling isolated from her again. I don't know what it is and I don't know what to do. This is so screwed up.

We walked again tonight, mostly in silence. I made a mean remark to her on our walk when we saw a bug covered in ants on the sidewalk. She said ever since she was a little girl and got covered in ants one time, she hates that. I said I would remember that for her birthday. When we got home, I went back to my studies and she went upstairs. Later I went up and apologized for saying what I did to her. She cried a little. I don't understand why she doesn't see that I need intimacy from her. Can she live without a man's touch for years? Obviously she can because she lived that way for 14 years – alone with Ronnie.

What am I to do? I feel the same way I used to do when I lived with Judy. I want to say mean and vindictive things to her to get back at her for being so cold. I want to ignore her and not give to her, not touch her. I want to stay really busy so she does not see my hurt, my need. I hate women. I hate what they do to me. I guess I am merely a roommate that takes care of all her chores. Like Paul McCartney sang in "Maybe, I'm amazed" – I feel like a lonely man who's in the middle of something that he doesn't really understand…

Monday 9/29/03

I decided to send her an email today at work. I told her that today was the 2nd anniversary of us buying her ring together. I told her I hope it still shines for her. I said that no matter how she feels about herself, that she is still the most desirable woman to me. I went for a walk and prayed to understand her more. I think she just has really bad self-esteem. I think she feels fat and unlovely. I called her after lunch and she told me she got my email and that it made her smile a lot. I told her I wanted her to feel loved today – that I loved her and I wanted to make her happy. She said she loved me and that she wants to make me happy too. I hope I can just keep giving to her to make her feel "pretty and desirable". Then maybe she will want to give herself to me more.

Monday night

I worked hard to really give to her tonight. Patrick was in San Diego, and Ronnie just stayed in his room, so I gave T a nice back rub and we went upstairs. I made slow love to her and she exploded with pleasure. She said it was the greatest ever. But she refused to go for a walk later on. She said her legs were too shaky. I can see that. I walked alone.

Wednesday 10/1

Last night T only would walk part way with me. Now she is taking part of dinner to eat at work every day and she is eating a full dinner when she gets home. She quit eating just fruit for lunch, and she quit just eating a salad for dinner. Now she is just plain eating. She is just getting fatter.

Tonight I tried to tell Ronnie (again – after countless times) to sit up at the table. He sits slouched over like some homeless dude with his forearms (not elbows but forearms) glued to the table. He just got up and walked away and went into his room. She interrupted and made me angry because she was essentially arguing with me about how to discipline him. I got up from the table very upset and told her I wanted to talk with her about it afterwards. Then I was trying to put away the leftovers she said she wanted them for lunch tomorrow. Off to the fat farm we go. I got really mad and went out to the office to blow off some steam.

About 10 minutes later, she came out crying and asked me what I wanted to talk about. I tried to explain to her that when she argues with me in front of her son about my discipline of him, it completely undermines my authority in the home. Then she started crying worse and got all weepy saying she didn't understand how she was doing that. She said she didn't understand how she is actually defying me. It is maddening. I told her that she has succeeded in making me not care at all about how Ronnie looks or comes across because she just gets on my case when I try to correct him. Finally I told her to go away, that I did not want to talk to her any more. Her answer? She got Ronnie and got in the car and drove away for three hours. Crap. What a nice signal that is for the kid. When Dad says something we don't like, we just drive away. I wonder what they talk about?

I went for a walk at 6:30 and came home about an hour later. Her car was parked out front, and Ronnie's bedroom door is closed, so I assume she came back home.

I do not know what she wants from me. She obviously does not want a husband, because she will not submit to me like her Pastor told her to when he married us. Not that I demand submission, but dang it – I serve this woman daily! Couldn't she at least hear me out? Couldn't she give me the benefit of the doubt and try it my way for once?

She obviously does not want a father for her kid because she will not let me discipline him. His room is an absolute sty. I will tell you one thing. The time will come when he will get physical with me. I will try to get him to do something and he will assault me, maybe even batter me. On that day I will call the cops and have him sent to Youth Hall.

Thursday 10/2/03

She wrote me a 7 page letter apologizing to me for defying me, although she says she still does not understand how she defies my wishes. I went up and gave her a long backrub and held her until she went to sleep. I got up with her at 4:45 this morning and prayed with her. I have already called her two times at work to tell her I love her, and it is barely nine o'clock in the morning. I guess I just need to learn to completely walk away when she does stuff like that. I need some place to go, I guess. A comfortable hideaway that I can run off to when she does stuff like that. She does not respond at all to my criticism. Does anyone criticize Terry? To be sure, no one changes her – not even God.

Wednesday 10/8/03

Well last week T was complaining about her hair, and how it "makes her look like an old lady". I have told her since we started dating 3 years ago that I cannot stand short hair on a woman, but she just cried and cried. She knows how strongly I feel about her wearing long hair – it has been one of my intense desires since we started dating years ago. She has always worn her hair long – even for years before we met and I think she looks really good with it – especially in a pony-tail. She told me she would just trim it a bit, because she knows how much I want her to wear her hair long. The last time she went to get her hair cut she about cut it all off. Well today she went and got it cut even shorter. She looks like crap. I almost can't even stand to look at her. I said nothing, but I am so incredibly freaking depressed I just want to run away. It makes her look even older – like some Midwest biddy from the blue hair and cribbage club. When we went for a walk, she started crying and I did too. I told her I loved her and not to worry, but I am so depressed about it. She looks like my grandmother or something.

Thursday 10/16

Well it took me 2 days to even talk to her again. She just looks like crap with her cut hair. Everyone at church loved it…I nearly threw up in disgust. It has been about 10 days since we had any intimacy. Tonight she went to the parent teacher conference. She brought home Pat's grades – all A's and B's. R's grades? F in French, D in Biology, F in English, D in Algebra, and a B in Art. She was trying to tell me that he is just about failing in everything because *he is not encouraged enough at home* and she took the blame! My God woman, have you never heard of tough love???

So she is now taking the blame for the kid not turning in assignments, not participating in class, and not doing his work (yet he sits in his room and watches Nintendo and TV all night, etc). It is after 11PM and he is still up doing who knows what in his room. Today I asked him (since he was off school) to wash his sheets and make his bed, since he has been sleeping on a bare mattress for 2 weeks. A bare mattress. I had left him a note two weeks ago to do it, but he just ignored me and threw the note away. I told her again in an email yesterday that he ignores me.

I tried to talk to her on our walk tonight about how it is time for Ronnie to reach down inside himself and suck it up and do the work. I explained that independence, self-reliance and personal responsibility are what she needs to cultivate in him. She mostly cried. I got silence followed by tears. I told her that she is enabling this behavior and that it will not improve as long as she lets the child dictate what the conditions for his success are. Children do not tell adults what the conditions are. Adults set the bar and children must try their best to rise over it. No one is perfect to be sure – and you have to reward them, but they have to at least try!!

I told her that if Ronnie was getting up early to hit the books and studying at night and if he failed after doing all that, I would buy him a month of tickets to Disneyland, because I would know he failed in spite of really trying. But the kid has no goals, no aspirations – he just wants to slide and be a lazy bum.

Later that night she let him eat food in his room, over my objections. When I said I would prefer that he eat at the table, she faced me and sternly said, "I told him he could eat in there," as if it was a done deal and I should just shut up.

I got pretty upset and told her I am sick of being treated like a second-class citizen. She stormed off to the bedroom crying while saying she is a failure in everything. So once again, when I act like a Dad and a husband and I say anything critical, I end up paying for it. Everyone gets upset at me. Remember, Mitch, you are the Butler…. that is all. Tomorrow is grocery day and the floor needs to be scrubbed. Face it. Ronnie does not want your input, and neither does his mother. Just do your job and shut up.

Friday 10/17

I didn't call her at all at work today, but I did go out and get her a thank you card. I told her how much I appreciated her working so hard. She did thank me and kissed me when she came home and opened it. But that was about it. She went to bed at about 9PM. I spent the evening getting ready to go to the lab on Saturday.

10/19 Sunday night.

Well it is 8:30 and she is in bed already. We were intimate yesterday, but only because I begged and begged. Boy does that help my self-esteem. I had gone to San Diego at 6AM and came back at around 12:30, so she had some space. But she really did not act interested in me in any way. It was almost painful when I reached orgasm (after about 30 seconds….). I told her it hurt and she said "Oh, honey I'm sorry," and rolled over and went to sleep. I wonder if she is rubbing herself in the morning before she goes to work or something, because I have not given her an orgasm in about 3 weeks. Maybe she has a man on the side. Tonight we sat in the couch together but she just yawned a lot and complained because I had the A/C on. It is still about 86 degrees outside at 9PM – of course I have the air on. Any normal person would.

Wednesday 10/22

Well the week has been pretty much the same. She leaves early for work; I work around the house and do rock research and I study. It gets blistering hot, she comes home and eats and doesn't want to go for a walk because it is too hot, she is too tired, etc. I walk alone. We sit on the couch and she goes to bed at 8:30.

On Monday night, I asked her to go tell Ronnie to get up 15 minutes early on Tuesday, so that I would not be late to my photography class. I had a lot of darkroom work to do for the research photos I need.

Well he was sitting at the Nintendo drooling when she told him, and he had been sitting there several hours. So it probably went in one ear and out the other. So Tuesday morning, he gets up at the regular time because he never set his alarm. I had woken Pat up 15 minutes early because I wake him up every day. Ronnie has an alarm that he was supposed to set but didn't because he was too stupefied by Nintendo. I asked him if he was told to get up early that day. He said he forgot, I asked him the same question again, He said yes. So I told him right away that he had 20 minutes to be ready to go out the door, and if he were not, he would lose cable TV to his room. So I give him the 20 minutes and guess what? He was sitting and watching TV in his room. At 7:20, I asked him, why he didn't brush his teeth and is therefore not ready? He had no answer. I said, "Because you are not ready, you lose the cable TV hookup to your room."

Well tonight he tells his mom at dinner that he couldn't eat a decent dinner because he had cake at school. I asked her after dinner if she thought it was OK for him to not eat any lunch, eat cake at school, and then come home and not eat dinner. She decides to go talk to him. She finds out that he had a top ramen and a granola bar for lunch. Some protein! Meanwhile he tells her that I cut off his cable because he got up late. In other words, he basically lied to her about why he was being punished. So all hell breaks loose – she is crying for over an hour, and finally when she calls him up to the bedroom – he confesses that I had given him 20 minutes to get ready and he was watching the TV. He said he can't get ready if the TV is not on! Oh my GOSH!

I told her that one of us has to give, and if that it had to be me, I would just move out and disappear. That made her cry worse. I told her again that I do not feel that she ever disciplines him much, and that he manipulates her to the max. I also told her that this was the reason I told her I was getting cold feet before we got married. I knew then that we were not compatible and we are not. She just lets anything he does (or does not do) slide completely.

Needless to say, I walked alone tonight for exercise.

Sunday 10/26/03

Well Friday night Patrick had 3 friends over for a sleepover. They did OK, although it got rowdy at about 10:30 when we were trying to go to sleep. T and I were intimate at about 8PM when the boys were at the spa. I told her that she just does not have a libido anymore and she said, "No way!" No way? What planet is she living on? I asked her when the last time was that she had a big O. She could not remember. I told her it was 3 weeks ago (I wrote it in my Daytimer). She was pretty quiet about it. Otherwise it was an uneventful weekend. She slept a lot on Saturday and Sunday but we were not intimate again all weekend. I took everyone out to Sizzler after church on Sunday.

Wednesday 10/29/03

T has come home tired every night, and since the fires have been burning in the local hills, we have not gone for a walk (the smoke is really bad). Nevertheless, she has just gone to bed early and has not really reached out to me. Last night she fell asleep on the couch at about 5:30, and went up to bed at 7:50. So I made it an early night too. How lonely am I?

Sunday, 11/02/03

Terry is not curtailing her eating. Two days in a row this week she went out to lunch at work and ate a big meal, then she came home and ate again. She has gained a lot of weight and it turns me off. Last night she wanted to make love, but I was so turned off I could not even get aroused. So we rolled over and went to sleep. Tonight we made love for the first time in 9 days. I gave her the big O and she passed out asleep.

Sunday 11/15/03

In the last 13 days we have been intimate twice. We are still only averaging once every ten to twelve days, and it is "missionary with eyes closed" or nothing. T is finally eating mostly only a salad at night, but tonight when I told her I thought all women were pretty selfish and weren't interested in meeting their men's needs she just huffed off and went to bed. She didn't even say good night. My theory is probably right. She only wanted a man to care for her, to protect her and keep her company. As long as I am doing that and doing the cooking, cleaning, shopping, etc., I guess I am useful, but she *never* has come to me in almost 2 years of marriage and exposed her body to me and said, "Take me honey, I'm yours." She has *never* really initiated with me, or pulled me into the laundry room or anything except to ask me to make love to her on what, three occasions?" She has absolutely no passion whatsoever. She has not read in the books I gave her since August 25th. That is almost 3 months…...

11/20/03

T has lost all affection for me. She gives me a peck when she comes home, but does not hold me, reach out for my hand – nothing. I quit calling her at work in the morning to encourage her. What's the point? It only reminds me of what a cold fish she is and what a tomb of a marriage we have. Tonight I left the doors and windows open. It got cold inside. We sat on the couch together and all she did was cover herself in a blanket. She sat by herself, 15 inches from me, shivering….She knows how warm I am. She never once reached out to me or asked me to cuddle her…nothing. She never ever does. She has a warm, cuddly man sitting near her, dying for tenderness and affection, but she ignores me, even though I always put out heat like a furnace.

When we went for a walk, she said nothing. We walked in silence for pretty much an hour. I held her hand for a while, but stopped and she never reached out for my hand again. At dinner, I talked about how I want the boys' bathrooms painted a dark red, and she went nuts. She said, "Absolutely not." I reminded her that the whole freaking house was painted exactly the way she wanted it, and that now it was my turn and their bathrooms were going to be dark. I think she was pouting the rest of the night.

11/29/03 Saturday night

I cooked for Thanksgiving – turkey, honey-ham all the trimmings. The last 2 nights she has had really bad stomach pains. I think it was from the ham. Ronnie came home Wednesday with another stellar report card. He went from two F's and two D's to one F and two D's, mostly because he was dropped from French. But T has just let him gorge himself on Nintendo and Playstation and X-box all weekend long (yes, he does have all three in his room and is unrestricted). I finally kicked him off of it last night at 10PM after a 2-day marathon.

Today I got the phone bill and lo and behold he has been making long distance calls to a girl in Canoga Park!!!! I asked him if he made the calls and he said, "That was a long time ago," as if that answered my question (and as if that made it OK). I said, "10 days is a long time ago?" I showed her the bill and asked her if she knew he was talking for 49 minutes at a clip to some strange girl in Canoga Park and racking up a huge bill. She did her usual clam up routine and started to cry. She said she would talk to him. Later when I asked her about it, she said there were going to be more calls on the next bill too! Wow – I am so glad to be part of this family. Good thing I don't just walk away so their bills can be paid on time. So, according to him it was so long ago, it just happened and I haven't even been billed for it. Wow, I got some learning to do....

On our walk tonight, I asked her if she had decided how to punish him. She said she had not. I said that it seemed like she was just rewarding him by letting him sit in front of the computer in spite of his behavior and his horrible grades. I told her that whenever I try to tell her that he is not the angel she thinks he is, she just clams up and starts to cry. She started to cry and said nothing to me for the rest of our one-hour walk. When we got home, she went straight up to the bedroom and closed the door. What a nice arranged companionship we have. This is madness – dear God help me!

11/30/03 Well today she said she has a yeast infection. I wonder whom she got it from – she hasn't touched me in 7 days. Maybe her dried up vagina is showing its lack of use.

12/3/03 Wednesday. Today she went to see the doctor because her infection is even worse than before. Apparently it is raging pretty badly. She is now on a stronger antibiotic. I have not reached out to her for days. I do not hug her or kiss her....I am basically just as much of a cold fish to her that she is to me. We have not been intimate for 10 days and with her new prescription, it will be another week at least. I have pretty much lost interest in her anyway. We didn't walk tonight because she was too tired and I didn't feel like walking alone. She went to Wallmart on the way home last night and punctured her tire in the parking lot there somehow, so she spent a couple of hours waiting for the tow truck and having her tire fixed. I didn't feel like rescuing her. What's wrong with me? This must all be my fault.

12/4/03 We walked in silence again tonight. She held my hand once for a few minutes, but she was asleep by 8:29. How blessed am I?

12/5/03 Friday. She has a business luncheon today at a fancy restaurant. I have not called her at work in weeks. I should probably call her today and encourage her to have a good time. She has made a small effort to read in her book, and has actually underlined some things and written some comments, but I cannot understand why she just does not reach out to me. WHAT IS WRONG WITH ME THAT MAKES ME SO UNDESIRABLE?

She thinks I do not value her opinion. I always listen to her, but I usually argue my case pretty well. That's the way I grew up – you argue your case and if somebody else's logic kicks your butt you acknowledge that and move on....I guess I need to ask her if she minds if I argue my case.

She wrote in her book that she wonders if she is miserable because she has wrinkles and does not look pretty. Wow. Is she a narcissist?

12/6/03 Saturday. Well I did call her at work yesterday and told her to have a real nice time, and I guess she did. She ate a lot from what I can tell and then came home and had more to eat. We sat on the couch for awhile but we were not close. She fell asleep at about 9:30PM. Today we slept in but I did not reach out for her. She pretty much sat around all day. I fixed a large lunch for everyone and then we went to a dessert play at church. She ate her own cheesecake and then said she wanted to eat mine, so I let her have it after I took a bite. We came home and went for a walk – pretty much in silence. Then we watched the Disney movie "Holes". She never touched me as we sat on the couch. Never even acted like she wanted to be near me. DEAR GOD I AM IN HELL.

Then she went up to get in the bed. I went up at about nine. She pretty much ignored me and went to sleep at 9:30. So this is what being married to a real Christian woman is like. Holy heck, I'm so glad she is close to Jesus. If I got a lobotomy would I be better?

Monday 12/8/03

Well yesterday, T started getting close to me during church – holding my hand, touching my leg and sitting close and all – it was bizarre and something entirely new. Pat's girlfriend, Jackie came to church so we all went out to lunch afterwards. During lunch, T kept touching my back and leg. Meanwhile I am wondering – what does this mean?" When we got home I got busy doing some things and then we sat on the couch for awhile. We watched 'Meet Joe Black' and she kept cuddling me. I asked her why she was all lovey-dovey all of a sudden. She said her boobs didn't hurt and her yeast infection was gone. I told her that she had really hurt me by being so cold to me over the last three weeks and reminded her that it had been four weeks since she let me ascend into the heavenly temple between her legs. She said my bitterness hurt her. Crap – this woman has a retort for every hurt that I have! Nothing works!

I told her that I didn't need sex all the time, but that I needed *closeness*, and that when she draws away from me it tears me up. She acted cold and indifferent. It seems like every time I try to be vulnerable and express my hurts, she gets ice cold. I just cannot understand this woman.

I told her it was too painful for me and that it was making me bitter. I said I did not want to be bitter, but rather I wanted to be close and in love.

We both said we were sorry and we kissed and held each other. She asked me to go upstairs with her and we cuddled in the bed. She got on me and had a raging O. I hope she understands how much I need her to be close to me. I don't know how else to say it to her.

Sunday December 28

Well, let's see. I think I am beginning to understand why T has such trouble with intimacy. She has opened up to me in the last couple of weeks about some of the abuse she suffered with Ronnie's father. About 10 days ago, she sobbed to me that he used to choke her by the neck during sex, spitting on her and calling her "c*nt". She had told me before why she hates that word and now I know why. Last week, she said he used to beat on Ronnie also. I guess he also shook him violently when he was very little which completely freaked her out. Yeah, I get that.

She is doing a little better at trying to be close to me, but not that much. We have been intimate a total of 13 times in 50 days since the last entry. I keep a little symbol in my Daytimer to note the times we have been intimate. That is a little over one time per week.

The other night, she snapped at me and walked away from me during a walk, and stayed ahead of me for the rest of the walk. I left her alone the rest of the night – she didn't seem to mind. She just watched TV alone and then went off to bed. I slept in the garage. The next morning (yesterday) she apologized to me. Later on she asked me to go upstairs and make love to her, which she really enjoyed. Every time she has a big O, I can't touch her for a week. I tried touching her again today, and she just laughs and pushes my hands away.

I don't think she has been reading in the books I gave her (how long ago now? Almost 7 months). She has, however, been reading a book she just got for Christmas from one of her friends about being a praying wife. Swell. Maybe she can pray herself a new figure. Maybe she can pray herself to be "pretty and desirable," as she eats her way into fat history.

She told me she had just finished reading a chapter about "praying about his sexuality". Maybe she should pray to BE sexual. She told me she does not want to hear anything about my past life with Judy my college sweetheart. She said it demeans her. (What??)

I was trying to share with her about my past so she could understand me more, and maybe try to meet my needs. I guess ignorance is bliss for her. If she doesn't have to hear about what pleases me and what I need, then she won't have to worry about it, I guess.

I often wonder what my life would be like if I had not married her. I would probably be living in a 2-bedroom apartment with Patrick, trying to survive. I most certainly would not have my lab at SDSU, but who knows? I might have been more reckless and aggressive with my former employer if it was just Pat and me. Maybe I would have gone to the media and made a big national stink and gotten more money, but then uncle Sam would have taken it all, right?

January 13, 2004

Welcome to the New Year. Life goes on. We average intimacy once per 7-10 days, and only when I beg. She never initiates any closeness. I usually start trying to touch her on the couch as we sit together. She always laughs and pushes my hands away. Finally after an hour of this she says, "We can go upstairs". That makes it so special for me.

She NEVER cuddles up to me and says "Come and make love to me", although she has done that two or three times in our so-called marriage.

She still basically goes to work and then comes home moaning in pain and falls asleep at 8:30 after an hour of TV.

She is now mad at me because I cut off Ronnie's TV cable to his room. I told him if I keep seeing dirty dishes in his room, there will be no cable, and it has been off for about 3 weeks now. Still there are dirty dishes and cups in his room.

He has less than 10 days to bring his grades up to a 2.30 GPA or he is booted out of Arcadia High according to the Vice Principal. Every night he just sits and plays Nintendo and she lets him, no matter what I say. He started getting sick again and she wants me to leave him home alone while I am gone. I said no way, so she is mad about that too. I can't trust him – how can I leave him home alone? He won't go to bed at a decent hour (or even early-last night it was after 10:30), he won't take vitamins or drink orange juice, so-whatever. I don't really care if he gets sick and I will rearrange my schedule to stay home and make his life uncomfortable if and when he does. At least I won't have to drive him to and from school like I do every day.

Friday 1/16/04

Well Ronnie is now sicker and she just won't stay on him to take his vitamins, meds, etc. Last night I made him go to bed at 9PM. She went to bed at 5PM, got up for an hour at 8 and then went back to bed at 9. I have done the best I could to not touch her all week and she seems very content. Last night I slept in the garage again, and she called today to thank me for doing so!! What does that tell you? My wife is now happy that I sleep in the garage – holy CRAP!!!

She only touched me three times this week. And I literally mean touch. Even if we pass in the hall, she avoids touching me. Once on Tuesday when we were walking she took my hand for a little while and then 2 nights in a row she laid her arm on me when she went to sleep. Sure is nice to be married. Do I have the plague or something?

Saturday

The boys left at 8AM to go to an all day beach trip with their youth group. She drove them to church and then came home and sat on the couch until 11. I sat with her for a while, drinking my coffee and having my cereal. Then at 11 AM she announced she was going up to bed. So she has been in bed for 2.5 hours, so I am just resigned to getting things done in the office. No matter, I have plenty to keep me busy.

Tonight we went out to dinner with Don Phips an old friend from science circles and his new squeeze Cindy. The time together was strained because when T and I were dressing earlier, before we had to leave, she stripped and stood in front of me with a big smile on her face showing off her naked body that she has held back from me for weeks.

Boy did that piss me off. I told her that I could not believe that she flashed me like that when she has left me hanging for weeks and now we had to run out the door to a meeting.

Well she went off on me – telling me that she could not believe that she was doing something wrong again that did not please me! She said she thought I liked seeing her nude. I told her you don't starve a man and then just before he has to go out for the evening, show him a nice juicy steak that he obviously cannot have due to other commitments! Well we rode in silence for an hour until we got to the meeting place. Once there I tried to engage her again but she was still pretty upset, so once again I did not touch her the entire evening. I barely talked to her. We rode home pretty much in silence too and she just went off to bed. How bizarre and screwed up is this?

Sunday 1/18/04

Once again I have not really reached out to T in any way physically – especially since the flashing incident yesterday. I sat next to her in church and Sunday school, but I would not touch her and when she tried to touch me, I pulled away. By the time we were singing in church, she was weeping. I really did not know why, but I guess she has started to figure it out. When we got home, she cried and cried and told me she was sorry that she tortured me. I told her I needed to have her closeness, that she could not continue to reject me and then show off her naked body and have me be all happy with her. I told her it just hurt too much to be rejected and not feel close to her, and it just shuts me down. I said, "If all you want is a roommate, fine I would be that for you and nothing more." She was really intimate with me the rest of the day, but it never seems to last. She will be over it in about 12 hours – trust me.

Thursday 1/22/04

Well, like I said, nothing lasts forever, and she just really seems to have trouble being close. Now she has another yeast infection, so I am probably out of luck until sometime next week. Tonight was another nightmare. Ronnie took some finals today and has more to do tomorrow, but all he does is play X-box, which is in his room along with the endless stream of electronic gadgetry. When I say "Ronnie, this is your last chance to not get thrown out of Duarte High School- you will be at Arcadia High School if you don't stop screwing around," his mother screams at me to leave him alone. Whatever. Why in God's holy name do I even care anymore? When will I learn to just shut up and ignore all this sickness?

Tonight when we were walking, she kept interrupting me and just blowing off what I was talking about. I made the mistake of commenting on it – that she always interrupts and can't she pay a little attention to me and hear me out?

We'll you guessed it...she went off crying with the "I do everything wrong" routine. She cried for 20 minutes and "got a severe headache". We made up when we got home, but I really think I just can never criticize her, the kid, or anything either of them do or are involved in. It always turns into a nightmare, and we end up not talking, not being close – the whole 9 yards.

My role is to be the mouse, pay the bills, manage the house and money and try to squeeze in my doctorate and, oh yes, bring in some cash every now and then with my lab equipment business. If she pays attention to me, I am just plain lucky. If I get affection or intimacy, it is because she got bored with everything else and woke up horny or something. It has been a year and 10 days since I started this diary. I imagine I will add to it every now and then, but I finally figured it out. I am the surrogate big brother here. This is no "love, honor and cherish" thing. This is no "forsake all others" thing. This is "Take care of us and don't complain or we will get all up in your face."

"Take care of me, give me space to do my thing, but don't ever try to change me. Don't ever ask too much of me and don't you dare criticize my child or me." Is this what Jesus had in mind? God teach me to be the best mouse in the whole world.

Wed 1/28/04 – one week later.

Well last night we were sitting on the couch together. She wanted to watch "Friends", a show that features lots of scantily clad women and plenty of sexual situations. After an hour and a half of this eye candy, I commented that Jennifer Anniston had hard nipples in one scene (what... I should NOT notice?) So T starts crying and moaning that she is tired of me talking about other women's breasts, that I am obsessed with women's breasts, and she doesn't want to hear anymore about other women's breasts. Wow.

So not only can I not have sex, I can't talk about sex, and I have to keep quiet when she watches TV shows displaying sexy women. Needless to say we were not close the rest of that night! She went upstairs and read her Bible. Never mind that she still hasn't finished the book on intimacy I gave her *almost eight months ago*. I am so glad she is close to Jesus. Maybe the Bible will teach her about being holy and pure when she gets to heaven. I'm not holding my breath but I am sure all the Saints are cheering her on.

Thursday

Well yesterday I did not call her at work, which I used to do every day – what….months ago? After I got all the groceries home and put away, she called to thank me for the lunch she had just enjoyed (from leftovers the night before). She said she really enjoyed it and that she loved me. I said 'uh huh'. I have no words any more.

Last night she wanted to watch some Shakespearean play on TV featuring Peter O'Toole. It bored me for at least an hour. Finally she went upstairs and watched it until she went to bed. I never went upstairs, except to turn off her TV after she had fallen asleep, and to get my pillow. I slept in the garage.

I still have not called her today. It is 9:30 and I am leaving to see a client in Thousand Oaks.

Saturday 1/31/04

Last night I was actually glad to see her when she came home. What is wrong with me?

She took Ronnie to a shrink on the way home last night. He has to go several more times, I guess. We had dinner (I made steak stroganoff), which she piled high on her plate – especially the noodles. The six-pack of Slim Fast cans that I bought her (because she asked me to) has sat on the counter for nine days. I finally put them under the sink to get them out of the way. She hasn't noticed.

So at dinner, Ronnie asks her why she is eating such a big portion, "Didn't you eat lunch?" I was shocked and tried not to stare at the two of them. Was something seminal about to happen? She said nothing. Finally after a very long time of R sitting there and looking at her with a quizzical look on his face I blurted out, "Because she wants to be obese." She started crying.

OK so I am stupid, but oh my gosh – this is the Twilight Zone!

Then we went for a walk. I started a conversation, which she promptly interrupted. I let it go. Then I tried to draw attention to the really cool fog bank that was rolling in like a large front from the west, and I said, "Doesn't that look cool?" She retorted with a strong "No."

So I said she was retarded and that she really pisses me off. (I know, I am STUPID!!) She got upset because I called her retarded. So I clammed up for the rest of the walk. She asked me a few questions, which I answered curtly. She tried to hold my hand a couple of times, but I did not squeeze back. She is just so self-centered and I am supposed to grin and bear it – act all lovey-dovey. We walked in silence. I admit that I am just wanting to cut her down with my words. I hate myself for that.

When we got home she immediately sat in front of the TV, but now she had her Bible on her lap. I guess she was waiting for some "Word from the Lord" or something. I went to work for a while in the office. When I came back out, I sat with her while I ate my bowl of fruit. She said she was sorry, and I told her when you beat someone down enough don't be surprised when they don't come back up. She kept saying she was sorry, but she did not touch me or try to be close to me. I went back out to the office. When I came back into the living room about an hour later, she was asleep on the couch. It was 8PM. She had gotten up at 3:15AM Friday morning, so I knew she was tired.

I watched a scary movie in the bedroom until she came up at nine. Then I turned off the TV and went downstairs to finish the movie. She went to bed. I slept in the garage again until 8:45 AM this morning. She was up and in front of the TV but had her Bible again. Maybe she should tie it around her neck. I took a shower, thanked her for making my coffee and sat with her while she read her Bible with the TV on. I wonder if all that reading will make her a more loving person? I still do not understand why she will not read the books on intimacy that I bought her. Probably because I bought them. I wondered if I could bribe R to give her some books to read. I believe she would read them without stopping if he did that. She wants to be spiritual, but she won't love her husband. I am sure God just loves her deeply due to the way she treats me. How lucky am I?

After awhile, she asked if we were still going to take her car for detailing and then her to a nice lunch? I said, "Why don't you take Ronnie?" You didn't have to ask her twice. She ran upstairs and got ready to go. He was playing video games in his room (which is a pig sty as always).

After she was ready, she sat next to me on the couch and asked if we were going to Phoenix over the Valentines weekend, I said "I don't know." I know she wants to take Ronnie out of school on that Friday and take him with us. How romantic. Maybe when his report card comes back again with F's and D's and they throw him out of the Duarte District, she will figure it out. This will end badly.

Well I went and got the mail....Ronnie's report card sported 2 F's – grade point 1.50

I am sure he is now kicked out of Duarte High. Can't wait for the fun way the wife will treat me later on.....

Monday 2/2/04

Well Saturday night was fun...I gave her the report card and she went in to talk to Ronnie. I don't know what was discussed, but he still has a TV and Nintendo in his room. She told me that he is off the Nintendo, but I saw him playing it last night after she went to bed and he probably was this morning too. Instead of the Nintendo being on top of his VCR, it is now nicely tucked into the entertainment center, (harder to remove that way, huh?)

When we went for a walk Sunday night, I was distant again. She begged me to talk to her, she said I had to tell her what was wrong. So I told her that she was a cold fish, she was self-absorbed, self-centered, and unable to express intimacy. I told her she cries to control the situation (and me), and that whenever I try to correct her or give her direction as her husband, she cries and throws a temper tantrum.

I told her I foresaw all of this when I told her before we got married that I was having doubts and getting cold feet way back before our marriage. Then she said, "When did you tell me that?" I could not believe it! I reminded her of the big cry fest we had at Rainbow Lake where I used to live when I told her I was having doubts about marrying her in 2001, and so she just cried and cried. She said she could not remember. She kept asking "Then why did you marry me?" Good question, huh? I wonder why she married me. She sure doesn't love me.

She told me (while crying bitterly) that she could never forgive herself for having sex just one time before we got married. This I cannot understand. We dated for about 6 months. We were engaged for about 4 months. During that time, when I would go over to Phoenix, I would always give her an orgasm (orally of course), and I would ask for nothing in return. Probably a dozen or more times, I performed oral sex on her. She loudly enjoyed it and never told me to stop or protested in any way. When we met with her Pastor, he asked if we had been intimate, and she quickly told him "No!" I am sure I had a very puzzled look on my face because he looked at me a long time.

Then about a month or so before we got married I told her I had to know that we could be compatible sexually. I did not force myself on her, but asked her to have intercourse. I did not beg, I simply asked. She said OK and we did. So she is really upset about us having sex ONE TIME before marriage, but she is not upset about her getting to have oral sex dozens of times before the "I do's"! I don't get it.

I told her that she needs professional help. I said that her baggage with her violent father and her violent boyfriend (who fathered Ronnie) had ruined her ability to express affection and intimacy. I told her I just could not go on without us getting some kind of Christian professional help.

I then told her that I had been keeping a diary for 13 months and she cried even more, saying, "Oh you are keeping track of every little thing I do wrong."

She wanted to go to a secular marriage counselor, but I said no, my experience with them was that they could not deal with these kinds of issues. I told her that I was pretty much convinced that she was like every other woman I had ever met, they just want someone to take care of them and leave them alone. Let the man pay for every thing, but don't expect her to be close to him. I told her I would never leave her physically, that I would always be there for her, but that I was really close to leaving her emotionally. I felt like I would be her roommate, her butler, etc., but not to expect much more….

Later that night, on the couch she said she really didn't want to lose me and she was going to try really hard to be a wife and to be more intimate with me. Yeah, when pigs fly.

On Sunday, I went to SDSU at 4AM, and on my return, I met her and the boys at noon for lunch after they left church. Later that afternoon, she asked me to come take a nap with her and we were intimate. She said she is going to call Ronnie's new shrink to try to find someone we can all go to together. We'll see.

Monday 2/9/04

Well, a week has gone by and not much has really changed. I went to my photography processing class on Tuesday, and did the grocery and the laundry thing last week, but she came home tired every night and pretty much acted like a lump. I taught several classes of school kids about the scientific method, a "must do" for my doctoral program- on Friday, I had 2nd, 3rd and 4th graders.

Friday night we watched "Finding Nemo" and she passed out on the couch early. I tried to caress her several times, but she pushed my hands away. She can even do it in her sleep! Saturday morning I would not let her get out of bed until she was intimate with me, but that was it for the weekend. I spent all my capital on that and I knew it was going to cost me. She did not want to be touched in any way and showed no interest the rest of the weekend. Saturday at lunchtime I took everyone out for an expensive lunch at Spaghetti Eddies – they all stuffed themselves. She came home and went to bed. After a nice long nap, she did not want to go for a walk, so I pretty much forced her. She would not let me touch her while we sat on the couch together and she went to be early. I went to the office and worked until 11:15PM.

That night she woke me up about 3 times with her kicking and sleep talking. I got very little sleep and was cross on Sunday morning – I was so tired. I took everyone out for lunch again on Sunday after church. She took her usual nap without me on Sunday afternoon, and that night she kept pushing my hands and advances away. At 8:10 she went up to bed and was asleep by 8:50.

I went and slept in the garage Sunday night. She is just a cold fish.

Tuesday 2/10/04

Last night I tried to caress her while we sat on the couch. She pushed my hands away again. When we got upstairs I tried again and she said OK, and to close the door. We started to make love but she was dry and it was uncomfortable for me. She always rushes foreplay, which completely mystifies me-so she is usually not ready for intercourse. It is almost as if she just wants to get it over and done with.

While we were making love I moved her hand to her pelvis so she could stimulate herself. It had the intended effect of making her more lubricated. She started to get close to having an orgasm, so I moved her hand away. She started crying and weeping and saying I never let her finish (WHAT A BIG LIE! – I always satisfy her and often do at my own expense). She went on crying, even when I said I was sorry and asked her to continue, but she refused saying it was "too late"-so needless to say the mood was ruined and the intimacy abruptly ended for the evening.

Tonight at dinner, Ronnie was yakking on with a mouth full of food about all manner of things. When Patrick came in to dish up his food, I noticed that his portions were small. I asked him if he had had a big lunch and he said yes, Neo (his friend) had treated him to Burger King. Ronnie then had to pipe up bragging about how he had mooched a whole lunch from several people at school. I have had this conversation with him and his mother countless times. I have a refrigerator full of the bread and lunch meats he likes but he REFUSES to make himself a lunch and his mother ignores this. So I said I was totally embarrassed that he acted in such a way at school. Immediately Terry launched into me, defending Ronnie and saying that Patrick used to do it all the time last year, and I never said a thing about it, (which is not true – I always supplied their lunch preparations and asked them both to make lunches). I could not believe that she was using some trumped behavior on Pat's part to now justify what her own son was doing. I said "So, are you saying that,,,?" Then I stopped myself and said, "OK, I understand, I understand what you are saying.... save it for the marriage counselor," and I walked out of the kitchen.

The rest of the night went downhill from there. We walked in utter silence for an hour. She went in the spa to soak and then went up to the bed to watch TV when I started to read a book downstairs. Having a moody roommate (in no way is she a wife) certainly is a blast. Why should her brat obey me when she publicly humiliates me and denigrates my advice and wisdom in front of him? I am not going to touch her for a year. I swear.

Thursday February 12.

Yesterday, I got up at 3:30 a.m., and drove to San Diego to do a hands-on science workshop with Patrick. When I got into the bathroom, I found a handwritten note from T. Basically, she says she was sorry for the way she reacted the other night, in trying to defend Ronnie's behavior at school. What struck me was at the end of the note; she said she does not want to "displease me so much all of the time." It's not at all that I'm displeased, but that I'm **disgraced** by Ronnie's behavior at school. I'm actually thankful that he does not bear my last name. It has nothing to do about being displeased – it has everything to do with character, but she just cannot grasp that. She thinks that I have to be made happy all the time or something. IT IS ABOUT CHARACTER.

So yesterday was a long day and I did not call her all-day. After the workshop, when Pat and I were grabbing a quick bite to eat, she called me on my cell phone from her car. We talked a little and said goodbye. Later, we sat together and watched TV when I got home, but we really didn't discuss what happened the day before.

Monday 2/16/04

So, this past weekend I wanted to be intimate several times. After all it is a 4-day weekend including today, and Valentines Day weekend as well. I took her to a nice lunch on Friday and gave her a big card, and then took her shopping at IKEA for about 2 hours, but we were only intimate on Friday AM (and *only* because I *made* her come back to bed in the morning after I got up early and took the boys to school and had come back home). Then on Saturday after she made me wait all day, and just before she was about to pass out at 9:00PM for the night, she says, "It's OK now," (i.e. hurry up). I have to say that is SUCH a major turn on for me to be able to make love to my sleeping wife. Well, actually it is *sick*. Why can't she see that?

She always keeps pushing my hands away, like she has done countless times. The boys were gone after church on Sunday from 3PM to 10PM, but she just kept putting me off, pushing me away or getting up and walking away from me. Then after we went upstairs she just got into the bed and went to sleep at 9:30. How am I supposed to feel? I am so pleased Jesus has made such an impact in her life. It sure has enriched mine. Isn't Christianity wonderful?

Today I got up early and went out early to do some lab equipment business. When I got back she was up and putting her makeup on. I sat with her awhile while I did some paperwork and then I took her to an expensive lunch at Acapulco with Annie from PSU. She had a great time. When we got home, she announced that she wanted to watch 'Alice in Wonderland' (the video). So she went upstairs to lay on the bed and watch TV. She just does not seem to want to be around me. I went up after about 20 minutes and lay down next to her. I tried to cuddle and she resisted. I fell asleep for a while. After an hour we got up but she had not rested, I guess because of my snoring. I tried to cuddle her on the couch later that night, but she was not interested. We went upstairs at 8 to watch a movie – she was falling asleep at 8:30. I slept in the garage.

I have discovered once again that if I satisfy her physically she pushes me away for days and days.

Tuesday 2/17/04

Terry forgot to wear her alarm watch that I bought her, so she woke up almost 2 hours late for work. She rushed out without eating her breakfast. Now I will have to reset her alarms so she can get up even earlier tomorrow to have to make up the time at work (she still doesn't know how to do it and she whines and asks me to do it because it is "too hard.")

When I walked outside this morning to take the boys to school, I noticed the hose running at the front of the house – water just running everywhere. I asked Patrick if he had used the hose last night. He said no. I asked Ronnie – he said he had to give water to the neighborhood dog that he walks. I told him the hose was running and to turn it off. He immediately blurted out "No, it's not!" I told him again to turn it off and to not argue with me. I am so sick of him arguing with me when he gets defensive over something he has done and refuses to accept responsibility for. I told him he needs my permission from now on to use that hose.

Tonight we went to the secular psychologist together for marriage counseling. Basically she sat there and accused me of being angry and hostile all the time. I was stunned and when I asked her for specifics and she could name none. She had a major cry fest in his office. Wow – what an event that was. I tried to explain to him that she had real problems with intimacy and closeness – she was a cold fish and could not express any intimacy. I told him I was going to email him my diary, and I did, the very next morning. Never heard back. Surprise, surprise. Another professional who is not interested in actually helping someone, yet wants to earn his living that way.

Sat 3/6/04 – almost a month later

I purposely have not written in my diary recently because not much has changed. I told T that I was probably not going to go back to the psychologist for a while, as I had already sent him my diary and she and he could work on things together.

I slept in the garage all last week, because she really just does not seem to want me sleeping in the same bed with her, nor does she seem to want to be with me – not at all.

I cannot open the window, or she "will die" of the cold, consequently, the bedroom is too hot for me to be comfortable. My snoring apparently wakes her up, and she wakes me up several times a night in turn, with her violent twitching, thus I get no rest. All in all, I got great sleep every night last week in the garage, and she seemed to do OK. Until it gets too hot, I think I will continue to sleep down in the garage.

Her brat Ronnie went into my office today again without permission. He decided he wanted to plug in my DSL modem, which I had left unplugged overnight. He was in Patrick's room doing who knows what on the computer until after 11:30PM which is when I unplugged the DSL modem downstairs and finally went to bed. She never checks to see what he is doing online, but hey, he is not my kid…..how bad can it be anyway, right?

So this morning, after he got up, I guess he needed more of a fix and when he found that Pat's computer was offline, he decided to walk unannounced into my office and mess with the modem. I got really pissed about it and told her so, but I was very controlled about it. It didn't help – she only talked to him and then he came to me and said he was sorry. I was very mad and told him he was grounded, to call his friends and tell them that he was not going to the arcade with them today to waste money on even more video games. We have been through this before, so many times!!! I cannot trust him to stay out of my things in my office and he knows the rule. He told her he had forgotten about the rule. He just forgot – poor little brat. Is that supposed to make me sad like it makes her?

She actually told me that he probably has a brain defect (what???). I told her he has an anti-authority defect and he was like a drug addict – willing to do whatever to get his fix. All I need is for him to break something or get injured out in my office.

But she turned it into a cry fest again. She cried and cried and said I was overreacting and her head hurt, etc., etc. She begged me to take her computer out of my office (where all the physical connections are for the computers) and put it into his room. HIS ROOM!?? I told her that was like putting the fox in charge of the chickens.

She did pretty much nothing to him for going unannounced into my office, and it made me even more upset. He needs to be grounded. She let him run out the door with his friends for a day at the arcade (more junkie computer game fixes) and all she made him do later was to write some lines. Lesson learned? Do what he wants -even invading my personal space and wait for mom to throw a temper tantrum. Then he gets off scot-free.

Now I have to start locking my office to keep him out. I am going to buy a locking handle for the door and I am going to have the only key.

Sunday. Well yesterday after he left for the arcade, she wanted to take me out to lunch. So we went to get Mexican. When we came home, she wanted to nap, so I said "OK, but can I come up into the bed with you?" She acted like she didn't want me to so I didn't press my luck. She put me off until later. Well, later came and went and so I went to bed needy again. This morning I tried to caress her in the bed before we got up, but no dice. She just complained that her leg was hurting. Now it is 2PM and she has been back in bed for an hour. So, my sick "marriage" goes on. I found out that she had cancelled her appointment with the Psychologist after I asked her to go and talk to him alone. Hopefully she will go back and talk to him….he received a copy of my diary, so maybe he can piece it together, who knows. I am just the ignorant butler.

Friday, March 12, 2004

Well I just cannot resist talking about two things. The other night while T and I were watching TV (America's Funniest Home Videos – various marriage proposals on film), she commented that she wished *she* had been really surprised when I proposed to her! The truth comes out – it seems I even botched the proposal. No matter that I did it publicly, in a nice restaurant in front of a bunch of strangers. No matter that I did it when she least expected it. Apparently I was a jerk in the way I did it and she let me know it.

Later, she said she was sorry but the damage was done. The truth comes out. I couldn't even do the proposal right, so this thing was nixed from the start as far as she was concerned. Oh well.

Later, I read in her papers that she wishes she had stayed single and that I should have married someone else. How lucky am I? Why the heck did she marry me? If I was so stupid from the start – if she was so bent on staying single why on God's earth did she marry me? She could have saved us both the trouble by saying no. The only thing that keeps me here is the vow I made to God, "Till death us do part." That's it.

Last night R came home with failing grades again. She stopped at the parent teacher conference on the way home. She would not let me see his grades, nor would she talk to me about it. She started crying when I asked her about it. Today she plans to stop and see the Vice Principal at the school, to beg for mercy – but the same-old-same-old is in place. He is about to be thrown out, but he never studies or does any homework – he plays video games constantly and she lets him have free reign. Why?? Does she secretly hate him???

Today she is taking him to the movies and tomorrow he gets to go to the video game arcade. He won't change-mark my words. This will end badly.

Saturday. Well she told me that she grounded him off TV/video/computer, everything. We will see how long this lasts. I personally don't believe it. She still has not talked to me about his grades or her talk with the vice-principal. I peeked a look, because the grade sheet was on top of her purse...2 F's and a D. At least 2 teachers said he does not turn in homework. Same old story.

We were intimate today but only because I relentlessly groped her. She finally gave in and dutifully walked me upstairs, but she did not want me to satisfy her. I am so fulfilled by my Christian wife.

Monday, 3/15/04

Well I went to SDSU early yesterday and worked until noon. I was home when they came home from church and she did sit and watch TV with me but at 3PM she went up for a nap. I tried groping her again, but she just put me off. On our walk I finally asked her what the Vice Principal said. Apparently they were about to send Ronnie off packing immediately to Arcadia High (!), but she begged and cried and Mr. Martinez gave in to her. Join the club buddy – the crying thing really works! You got played.

So now, apparently if he fails to turn in one thing, he goes packing, or so Mr. Martinez says. She said R is having problems because he has such low self-esteem. I said what does that have to do with not turning in homework? She cried, so I quit asking stupid questions like that. The main complaint from his teachers is that he does not do the work. She said everyone in his life is so negative. I said he goes to a great Church, a great Youth Group, a great school – he has a safe, quiet home environment, an older step-brother who actually loves to be with him and wants to involve him in his life-and yet he has low self-esteem? She said people are negative around him all the time. I asked her if she was blaming me. She said "He thinks you don't like him", I said, "I don't like his behavior. I predict that he will be in Arcadia before June. They will throw him out of school because he is a slacker."

She got her bonus from work again this year. It was about $3200 and she deposited into the shared checking account. I was shocked she did not just keep it. She asked how much of it I wanted to pay bills. I told her none, so I wrote her a check for all of it except for the cost of a Chinese dinner, which she agreed to pay for. Who knows what she will do with the money? I bet she runs away to AZ for some time away alone. Must be nice to have $3200 in your checking account to just play around with…

Friday March 19

Last night she came home late but she had slept in late and left late in the morning. Things were the way they usually are around here. I fed her, put her in the spa, rubbed her back and shoulders, tried to cuddle her on the couch and got nowhere. I asked her if it was doing anything for her. She said, "You know it always does," (Really? That's news to me!!) Then she said "We can do something when we get upstairs". Nothing happened – she just pushed me away as always. Promises, promises. Doesn't the Bible have something to say about that?

She is off today, no work, and was going to drive R to school at 7:30AM. I asked her to please come back and get back in bed with me after, but she didn't want to. Actually I begged (that sure helps my self esteem). She said she had a 9AM appointment with the chiropractor and she didn't want to drive all the way back over here just for 10 minutes (what a giving wife!). So she just sat across town for over an hour until her appointment. See what I am talking about, God? You gave me a frigid woman. We have not been intimate for many days, and she has not had a big O for at least fourteen days……what do I do? I guess I just suffer as Jesus would…in silence. Will she be more attracted to me if I do that?

After she came home, I took her to meet Annie from PSU for lunch. Naturally, I had to pay for everybody. We had a pretty good lunch and came home. She sat on the couch and watched TV. I sat next to her and worked on my rock specimens. She never asked me to go upstairs with her. She did touch my hand once and my leg once. I swear I will never touch her again. If she wants sex, she can initiate…I am done. She can go pound sand.

The boys are going to an all-nighter at church against my best wishes. They are going out to get Starbucks and then they are going over to church. I cannot wait until tomorrow.

Saturday

Well the boys came home and brought Jackie (Pat's girlfriend) with them. They slept for about 3 hours in the upstairs room and then Pat and Jackie got up and went to do something. Ronnie finally got up and was sick (his bowels). Turns out he gorged himself on sodas, pizza, junk food and other stuff last night. He also said he was dizzy.

Terry sat on the couch most of the day – all she wanted to do was watch TV, so I sat and kept myself busy next to her with the rocks. Later on I went out to the office and worked for about 2 hours on some other things.

Later that afternoon we sat together and I relentlessly kept touching her arms and legs. Finally she said she would like to go upstairs. So we did and she had such a deep big O that she nearly ripped my pecs off with her fingernails. I was sore for the rest of the day where she clawed me. I worked really hard to give to her all day and to show her my appreciation. The boys were in and out most of the afternoon and evening but finally they went to bed at a decent hour.

Monday 3/22/04

Well this was supposed to be a romantic weekend. Now she is avoiding me – I guess I screwed up again, mostly because of Ronnie. Actually I was supposed to take her to Phoenix, but since her friend Eddie could not get off work, she scrapped the plans. I guess if she can't be with Eddie, she just blows off her beloved Arizona. Who knows?

Yesterday the boys had a bit of trouble getting up, but they did and we went to church. Afterwards we ran some errands then we came home and I fixed everybody lunch. We had to be at church again at 2:40 to participate in the new building dedication, but the boys wanted to go by themselves, in Patrick's car. At the dedication they were serving sandwiches, fruit, drinks and cake. Guess what Ronnie went straight for? The cake. He claims he only ate one piece, but I doubt it. His mother did nothing when she saw him eating cake for dinner. Then they went to get tacos and drove themselves back to church for youth group. They must have had more junk food and sodas because Ronnie came home and was up until after 11:30PM, which is when I went to bed. Well lo and behold, I slept in this AM (because Pat can drive himself and Ronnie to school now), and at 8AM the boys were still in bed!! Pat managed to get up and eat and leave for school, only missing one class, but Ronnie refused to get up. Terry had breakfast and got in the spa (holiday for her), then she got ready for her appointment with the counselor. I asked her if she wanted me to go with her. She said only if I wanted to. I said I wanted to and can you talk with me there without crying? She said no, and that I should maybe wait a few sessions before going. So I said OK. She said she would like to take me out to lunch and to take her ($1400) engagement ring to get serviced. I said great. I asked her if she wanted to go upstairs and she said, "No I don't have time." I hugged her and asked her to please not leave me hanging, and she said she would not. Now she is napping and I am not holding my breath. I hope you enjoyed your romantic weekend, Mitch; it was between 4PM Saturday and 10PM Sunday night. Too bad you didn't get lucky.

After she left, Ronnie got up (about 10) and showered. He asked me what he could eat and I said cereal. He never took his medication (*Ritalin*). She got home at 11 and I asked her if I should get ready. She said yes, so I got ready, thinking we would take Ronnie to school and then go out to lunch and such. Well, surprise, surprise-she wanted to leave R home alone! I said no way; he could not stay home alone. She started to cry and I went out and started to sweep the back porch because I knew what was coming. She came out and begged me and said he knew he was not allowed in my office. I reminded her that just 2 weeks ago, he knew that and went into my office anyway. I told her it was a matter of trust and that he had broken it too many times. So guess what? It turned into another cry fest. So now she hates me again because I do not trust her son. He has no will power, and to boot, he is not on his *Ritalin* today, so anything can happen. He gorged himself on crap on Friday night. He went straight to the cake on Sunday night – today he is nauseous and dizzy (go figure) and she wants me to leave him home alone? No freakin' way. I said let's take him to school and she refused.

So once again, my marriage sucks because I am such a mean, negative person. She would not let me cook his soup for lunch or make a lunch for her. So I ate alone and later she came and ate with Ronnie. Now it is 8PM; I am alone again and she is up in the bed sleeping.

Sunday April 4, 2004. 2 days before my 2nd wedding anniversary.

Terry says she loves me. She gets upset when I say she does not love me. Maybe she loves me as one would love a neighbor or something, but she is not *in love* with me. She never touches me, or if she does, it is only to proffer a quick peck on the lips. Maybe she touches my arm or hand from time to time. But she is not crazy about me – not even remotely. She does not reach out to me for affection, she has rarely initiated sex in our married life – on our honeymoon up in the mountains over Santa Cruz, she came to me naked and said make love to me. Maybe three or four times since then she has asked me for intimacy, but that was the only time she ever took off all her clothes and approached me. She has never finished reading the books I gave her over 1 year ago – in fact she has never even cracked open one of them.

Today we took R to the airport after church. She is flying him to Phoenix for spring break. She paid for it out of the $3200 she kept from her bonus. She also had me take her to Costco to load up on things we really don't need (OK, the Gatorade and snacks for the boy's lunches, I can see that, but not the other stuff we bought). I already have 2 freezers full of food at home. But she is doing what she wants with "her money".

I would love to have held back $3200 from the $22,000 I have already deposited into the general account this year from my own work. But that would be "cheating" on my part. I have to cough up everything I make but not her. She is special. She doesn't have to share like I do. It is so swell to live with a Christian woman.

Anyway, when we got home, I went into R's room to close the blinds and noticed that he had been sticking posters up on the wall with double sided tape. I had told everyone when I spent $4000 of my own cash to paint this place 2 years ago that if they wanted things on the walls, they had to be hung, like regular pictures. So I took the posters down. Then I said (very gently to her), "Sweetie, can you please ask Ronnie not to tape posters to his wall?" Well she whipped around and said "Mitch, I have never had any paint come off the wall when I used double sided tape," as if she was defending herself against a direct and personal attack. I asked her how her behavior matched up with the submission series of sermons we were having at church just then? No answer.....

I told her that she and the boys could do whatever the heck they wanted to because I was "just the fffing butler." She has since apologized, but this is the same old pattern. No matter how docile, how accommodating, how emasculated I am, she is going to have her way no matter what. It matters little that Ephesians 5:22-23 says that women are to be submissive to their husbands in everything – she is submissive in little. I am the submissive one around here.

I find one thing particularly odd – speaking of pictures on walls. She brought this big box of family pictures and stuff with her from Phoenix-all kinds of family pictures that she had on her walls in her old place before we married. When we moved in to our new place, I pointed out that the nice high and empty walls all along the stairwell would be perfect for her to hang all her family photos. She agreed but she has never hung even one picture from her past on any of our walls. Not one. The only photo from her past is our wedding ceremony photo on her dresser upstairs (frequently hiding behind her washed and folded old lady panties.)

Thursday, May 6, 2004.

Terry just does not want to be with me anymore. We went to Dr. Condant (psychologist) together on Tuesday, and it basically was an accusation match. I'm not going back to see him with her anymore. It's not productive at all. In fact it is counter productive. I made the point during the session that I don't feel like she is a partner with me in this marriage. I talked about how she reacted when I told her that we had not been intimate in the last 12 days. She had said, "No way!" but it's true because I have it recorded on my desk calendar. I talked about how I don't feel she is committed to the marriage, because it is like pulling hen's teeth to get her to be intimate with me. I think it fell on 2 sets of deaf ears, one of which we were paying for. Condant just sits there and scribbles – he does not explore anything I say…what a waste.

We were on a weeklong vacation in La Jolla last week (where I spent about $1800), and she was only intimate with me once (the whole week). Once again, it's been about 15 or 16 days, and we've only had sex one time. When I came back from La Jolla, I moved out of the master bedroom into the downstairs den and bath. She is now alone in the master bedroom, and I am squeezed into a den with hardly any room to walk around my bed. I bet she is thrilled. Last night, she went up to bed at 8:45 p.m., saying how tired she was then she proceeded to read for about 20 minutes (her book on praying for her husband). She just doesn't want to be with me – she would rather be with a book about praying to Jesus in her sanctuary of a master bedroom than to be with a husband who serves her and wants to be in love with her.

Something else about the recent counseling session; I made the point that she's not financially committed to the marriage. I asked her how much she thought each of us had deposited into the general account since the beginning of the year. She started crying and said, "Mitch, I have deposited ALL my paychecks into the general account," which is not true because of the $3200 bonus she recently kept for herself. I asked her again how much she thought it was, and she said she didn't know. I had written down the figures, so I brought them out. She has deposited a little over $8,000, and I have deposited almost $28,000 over the same period. I made a point that she withdrew her $3200 bonus, because it was "her money." She then complained bitterly that I had told her it was OK. I said, "I only told you it was OK because from the minute you started telling me that you were about to get a bonus, you called it 'your money' and 'your bonus'."

I told Dr. Condant that these were all just symptoms of the real problem. The real problem is that she's not committed to the marriage, or to me and that is why we don't have sex, or any intimacy or even a decent conversation. He grunted and scribbled. I wish I was getting $150 an hour to grunt and scribble. I asked him if he had ever read my diary and he grunted and scribbled.

She never reaches out for me. She doesn't share her bonus with the family because she is selfish. Later that day, she wrote a check to me for $1,000 saying she was feeling selfish for taking her bonus money. Wow, I should talk about her in front of other people more often.

Friday 5/7/04

Last night she had to take Ronnie to his shrink appointment. I never know what goes on there because they never talk about it and I never ask. She sat with me from about 8:10 to 8:18 while I watched "Survivor," then she announced she had to go upstairs. She got up and kissed me three times on the face. She went up and her light was on for another 30 minutes until about 8:50, as she was probably reading. She now has a stack of spiritual books on her bedside table, (of course on top of the books on intimacy I gave her, that she has ignored and/or never finished), that she has been reading. All that spirituality and no love for her husband. What a city on a hill she is – she's a truly sanctified believer!!!! Lucky me.

Saturday, May 8, 2004

Today had been uneventful until this evening. Terry slept in late today – she must have been tired last night because she got over 11 hours sleep. Or maybe she is christening her new large bedroom by masturbating and going back to sleep for several hours – who knows? I definitely am no object of affection or love for her that is for sure. She sat on her butt and watched TV all day. She even ate all three meals on the couch. Whatever. I don't really care. I just ignored her and stayed busy balancing the checkbook, paying bills, planning cash flow to cover the mortgage, auto insurance, home insurance, electric bill, gas bill, water bill, sewer bill, phone bill, cable bill, car payment – the list is endless. I would love to sit on my fat butt watching TV all day and not have to worry about all the bills.

After she chowed down on her dinner she left the couch and went up to her sanctuary and closed the door from 4PM until about 5:35. Maybe she masturbated again because she sure doesn't need me. I was finally sitting on the couch, after working all day enjoying some mindless TV. I figured that she had left the downstairs for the night – as she had done wordlessly so many times before, so I did not expect her to come down. I also had some paperwork with me, that I was working on during commercials, and I had the TV muted with the remote on the couch next to me.

Well came down and she plopped herself on the couch without so much as a burp – let alone a hello, or how are you? I don't think she had spoken even one word to me all day…

She immediately grabbed the remote and started flipping channels. I quietly mentioned that there was a show I was interested in watching at 7PM and she grunted. After 10 minutes of her flipping channels (and basically ignoring me and the show I had been watching), I went into my bedroom and pulled the door ½-way closed. My light was on and I was working but I was ignored for the rest of the night. She settled on a movie at 6:00 and watched it straight through until 9PM. She then turned off the TV, turned of the lights and went upstairs – I assumed to go to bed. My show (and my expressed desire to watch my show) was left in the dust.

The next morning the following note was folded and leaned up against my coffee cup on the kitchen counter:

M—

I am sorry for my selfishness last night. I had expected that you would have come out of your room at 7pm to remind me that it was time for you to watch want you wanted. But, I took advantage of it when you didnt and I should have come & told you it was time to watch want you wanted. I am sorry. It kept me awake & I had an awful night. I hope that you have a good day and that you feel even better from the meds you have to take.

I love you,

J

Some love she has for me, huh? So sorry you lost sleep and had "an awful night" Terry. I have had an awful 2 years…

Sunday, May 16, 2004

Ronnie had his appendix out, so last week was not much fun. Nobody slept a whole lot. We were intimate yesterday – finally-mostly because I kept begging. I am so tired of begging. That was the first time in 17 days. I will never touch her again. She is so freakin' selfish. But I always get so needy I end up begging like a loser. I am such a loser.

She always goes up to her room an hour before bed now and just watches TV alone before falling asleep. Tonight she went up at 8:40 and watched TV until about 9:30. She never asks me to come upstairs, she just goes up alone, unannounced. Last Sunday on the way home from church she was crying her eyes out because of the sermon we heard on wives. She said she was such a bad wife. No kidding. She wrote me a note that said she knew she was a bad wife and that she wanted to learn. But she never will. The conviction will wear off quickly, trust me. It takes her about 12 hours to forget what a narcissist she is and then her old pattern is back in spades.

Monday May 17

The cold war goes on. Tonight she went upstairs at 8:15. It is 9PM and her TV is still on, but she doesn't want to be with me.

Wednesday.

Last night she sat with me for all of about 5 minutes on the couch. At 8PM, I was switching channels and saw Alanis Morriset live on the Oxygen channel. Alanis was explaining that there was a 7 second delay on the live transmission, so any 4-letter words she might let slip (and then she said a few) were bleeped out, and they were actually bleeped out with a big bleep. It was really funny and she was so cute doing it. They also blackened over her torso as she lifted her blouse to expose her breasts –you could not see anything – it was all covered over! I laughed out loud because it was so funny, and Terry got up in a huff and went upstairs. That was it for the night. She never said goodnight – she never came back down.

I wrote her a letter and put it on the seat of her car. I told her I was fed up at the way she treated me, that it was clear that she did not love me, that she was committing sexual blackmail against me, as Pastor said in the sermon on wives last Sunday. I also told her I would never touch her again.

She left me 2 sobbing voice mails at 5AM. I have not spoken to her all day and I do not intend to see her until as late tomorrow as I absolutely have to. I am fed up. She is just completely messed up. I am going to San Diego overnight.

Ronnie now has to go to summer school (again) and he also has to go to Arcadia High because they kicked him out of Duarte High- *just like I predicted months ago*, remember fans? This should be a real lesson for him. He has to take 2 math courses or he will fail the grade. T wanted me to drive him to school all summer, but I said, "Why should I be punished because he would not do the work?" I refused to drive him to and from school every day, so he is going to have to ride his bike. Tough luck, Charlie.

June 28, 2004

We had a fight the night before Father's Day (last weekend). I told her to not have Ronnie call me "Father" or "Dad", since he pretty much ignores me. We sort of made up the next day, but nothing much has changed. She never touches me. She gives me a peck here and there, but we have no intimacy.

Last night we had another fight. She has been talking about divorce and separation for weeks now – she mentions it at every turn on this twisted path. She keeps asking me if she should leave. I don't want a divorce and I have made that plain but she keeps bringing it up. I am so confused – God what do I do? You say you hate divorce but this screwed up woman who says she loves you so much won't shut up about it.

I gave her space all weekend. I let her sleep in on Saturday and did not bother her all morning. I took her to see "Shrek 2" and then after we got home I let her take a nap by herself. She pretty much just did her thing all day. Amazingly she is blissfully happy when I do not interact with her, except to reply to her when I am spoken to and to supply the food, wine, chocolate and carbonated water she needs.

It was too hot to walk that night and my back was hurting, so we came home after 15 minutes of trying it. As usual, she never reached out to me or tried to be intimate in any way. We did not sleep together over the weekend – in fact, we have not slept in the same bed for weeks. During our argument, she admitted to me that **she masturbates when she wakes up in the morning**. I knew it!!! She finally admitted to me what I have known all along! She said that is what she often does right when she wakes up!!! Why then does she need me? No wonder she is always pushing me away!! What the heck?

Sunday – same thing – I left her alone. She napped after church but pretty much didn't touch me at all. She cooked dinner, and I helped – she burned the burgers, just like I said she would because she was not watching the grill, which she was running at full flame. You would think a 50 year-old woman would know this by now… Afterwards, we played cards on the couch for about an hour while we watched TV. Then at about 8:40PM – right at her bedtime, she asks me if I wanted to go upstairs. I said no thanks. She said "No…to fool around". I said no thanks, that I had already serviced myself earlier. It has been 7 days, and I am sorry but I am not waiting and waiting for her anymore – if she can masturbate, so can I. I told her. "I don't need your 'pity sex' (like Pastor mentioned weeks ago), and besides since you are servicing yourself, why can't I?"

Well you guessed it-it started. She cried that she was afraid about my back last night and that I might not have been up to it, and that is why she did not offer sex. (Ever hear of TALKING ABOUT THINGS WITH YOUR HUSBAND?)

I said what about Friday and all day Saturday? She never offered then either. I told her that she was not acting like a wife, but it was like she was only just a roommate. I explained that if that was all she wanted, fine, I would be her roommate, but that this was not a marriage. So it went for about 30 minutes, back and forth between us. She tried to hold back tears while she went on an on about how she needed to be loved like Jesus loved her. (And how is that?) Meanwhile, it was getting later and she was really crying and needing to go to bed so she could get up on time the next morning.

She actually told me that she could not be an Ephesians 5 wife if she had to work and drive 100 miles a day! She said it was tearing her apart to try to be both. (Course I am bringing in more money than she is AND running the household AND going to school in a doctoral program – what does that make me? A canonized Saint?)

I told her, "Fine, I will get a 'real job', complete with benefits and you can be an at-home wife – no problem." I told her she was more important than my doctorate, and that I would give it up for her. She said no, that was not what she wanted. What does she want?

We went up to her bedroom to continue talking. She said that she was not secure in my love and that is why she could not touch me or try to be intimate with me. She said her lack of security was holding her back. She did not feel secure. What the heck? What more do I have to do to make this nut-job feel secure?

I said, "I don't know how much more I can do to make you feel secure!" I do all the laundry, dishes, grocery shopping, cooking, bill paying, garbage emptying, floor washing, etc., etc. I give her BLANK checks that she can spend on anything she wants – I don't even ask her about her expenditures any more or the phone bills that her brat rings up, etc., etc. I am ALWAYS here for her EVERY NIGHT when she comes home, except for the occasional night when I have to go away and I ALWAYS tell her about a week in advance when I have to leave.

I have tried to call her at work at least once per day to encourage her (and which she takes as an intrusion on her privacy.) I am a mouse around here – an eviscerated male-I always tell her in advance when I have to travel or I have to go call on customers – I always talk to her several times on her cell phone that I bought her for her commute home. I meet her at her car and help her bring in her things, so she won't have to carry them. I always have a hot meal ready for her.

Many nights I let her take a nap right away and don't bother her in any way. I let her have her space and don't burden her with household chores, bills, etc., etc. How was that not making her feel secure?

I told her after 28 years of marriage to 2 different women, I still did not know what women wanted.

She retorted by saying I always just find fault with her, telling her to turn off lights all the time, telling her things about what Ronnie does, etc…. I asked, "Am I just supposed to shut up about everything I see? Just keep cleaning up for everyone and not try to help people to change and be responsible? Just let all the lights blaze and pay $397.00 electric bills?" (As was our last bill).

I told her that I was practical and logical in everything I did, that I was not finding fault, I was just pointing out the expedient and practical things to do. She then said I did not love her like Jesus loved Mary, that I was like Martha, always concerned about everything….She also told me she could not touch me because she did not feel worthy of me, (what the hell does that mean?)

She said she really loved me, and I said, "I don't believe you." She said "Oh, I know, because you don't see it..." I said, "Yes, you are right!" On and on this went for about another hour.

I told her that I had proven her security to her, and that she had to overcome this, or it was going to wreck the marriage. I told her that she had to deal with her demons and learn how to give to me or I was just going to shut down. Suddenly, she started hollering loudly at me that "Oh sure the demons are all mine!!" At this point, I was so fed up, so I said, "f**k it", and left the room and went downstairs. I was just ready to pack up and drive away at that point.

She stormed downstairs and screamed at the top of her lungs that it was over, that we were finished, and that she would give me a legal separation. She said if I was saying, "f**k it", I was really saying "f**k the marriage" and "f**k her".

I said she was absolutely right, that was exactly what I was saying. So she said she was sick and tired of it and that we were done. I agreed with her that we were done.

I said, "If that's what you want, no problem, we should end it." I also told her that this was going to shipwreck my life because now I would have to give up on SDSU, on all my research work, that I would just move away to nowhere and be nothing for the rest of my life. But I said OK, if that's what you want, I would rent a truck and move you wherever you want to go, and sell the house and give you all the proceeds.

She then said she did not want it to end. I said I didn't really either (mostly because I am not ready to have to go through the hassle of moving and all). But I did tell her that she had to show me closeness or I would just shut down.

I told her the secret to me is just hugs and kisses. I just need hugs and kisses – I don't even really need sex every week. She hugged and kissed me and I put her to bed.

I honestly do not know what to do. I do not want to end up in a separation and divorce, but I am convinced that it will end up that way. I am just absolutely convinced that this will end badly. I have tried everything I know to do to try to help this woman see that a man needs love and affection, but she just does not get it. I am convinced that in a day or two she will revert to her old self – just as she always does, and we will be back to square one. I guess all I can do is to try to keep things going until my doctorate is done. Then she and I can go our separate ways. I really need my doctorate, though, and I cannot get it by living here in

California on one income. If this ends before my schooling does, I will have to move and live in a slum shack near the University I guess. I only have 9 courses left! Otherwise I just flush it all down the drain and go get a burger-flipping job. Maybe I should try to make her feel secure by asking her every day what I did to make her feel insecure. I truly do not want her to feel insecure, but I don't know how much more I could do.

CHAPTER TWO – THE
NUMBNESS SETS IN

July 20, 2004, Tuesday – one month later.

Last night the boys were gone and the house was quiet at about 6PM. I begged her for sex, and tried to touch her – she pushed my hands away and said "Later, honey, when we go to bed"….of course, then she got so absorbed in the "Princess Bride" movie she just forgot all about me. That is usually the way it goes. She puts me off until something distracts her from my needs. Then she conveniently forgets.

This morning she had left me a note saying how sorry she was that she had left me hanging (again) and that she could not sleep all night because of it, blah, blah, blah…..she probably masturbated this morning in her bed. I am a loser stuck with a loser, yeah?

Today was Ronnie's Birthday. I will always remember this day as the day she finally killed my marriage. Last night, as we sat up in her room, a roach crawled across her floor. I ran to kill it and she freaked out. I told her it was because Ronnie continued to defy me and eat candy and stuff in her room. I asked her to go tell him that, (as I have been harping for a year now), now that there are roaches in her upstairs room, as I predicted and to forbid him to eat in there any more. She went into his bedroom and she claims she did tell him, but I wonder. I think she talks to him to appease me. She probably just says, "I love you so much honey and you are so perfect and Jesus loves you too," because she does it with the door closed and I can never hear what they say.

Today after he got home from school, I heard him sneaking around up there in her room. So I crept up and stood over him as he, yup, you guessed it, was eating a candy bar in front of the TV on her floor. He jumped when I loudly asked him what food he had brought in there today – he sheepishly showed me the candy bar so I kicked him out and said he could not come back in there for a week. She said nothing when I told her about it when she came home. Once again I am made to feel like anything but a father – maybe an evil jailer or something. I am convinced that she thinks I hate him.

Later, he refused to eat dinner (expensive, marinated chicken breasts which he always loves, broccoli and rice, also which he loves). Instead, after dinner was over and he was standing around starving, he and Pat schemed up a concocted plan to run off to Taco Bell at 8:45PM (this being a school night), when I had just spent $218.00 on groceries that day, and had cooked everyone a nice dinner. I was totally against it as there was freshly cooked food in the fridge (which they had not eaten), but she said nothing when I tried to get her opinion….she just sat there and let it happen without a word, so off they went, and I was left looking like the butler again. I told her I was really pissed about it. She said nothing.

I got even hotter, so I got up and went in my room. I was so angry I slammed the door to my room and shouted that this was not a "F*&king marriage". She came in but I told her to get out. She came in again and said she was going to leave me, but could she wait until the weekend to leave me? (What the heck?) I told her I didn't care if she got the hell out. I was wrong, no doubt about it, I should not say the F word or hell….but how much can a man take? Dear God – how am I supposed to act in this sick relationship?

She tried talking to me for awhile but she just kept crying and saying she can't ever please me, that she has screwed up my life, etc., etc., etc. I told her it was about being a wife, a partner and not about being someone who pleases me. I told her that doing the right thing was way more important than me being pleased about anything.

I told her she does not care about Ronnie and his character, but she insisted that she does. She just went on and on about how it is her and not me…she is an unfit mother, she is an unfit wife – she does not feel worthy – she feels beaten down all the time.

Then she tells me she has decided to send him to live with her Mormon sister's family in Arizona!!!! I told her that this was totally wrong, even if that was her sister – they were committed Mormons – a cult. I told her that she was just giving up on R and that he would amount to nothing if she did not try harder with him and hold him to a standard of discipline.

She was adamant, however, and nothing I said would change her mind. I told her that I am not a husband, lover, or leader to her. I am merely the butler, and that is only what she ever wanted.

I told her I wanted a signed release form from her, as I did not want to be sued or charged with anything as his legal guardian when things went wrong with him over there in AZ.

I told her that I was wrong to get so angry, to shout, to swear and to slam doors. I told her I was sorry, but this is over. I am tired of trying to be a husband to a roommate. I said I am trying to sacrifice my life for her every day, as Christ loved the church. She said I know. I asked her how she was trying to submit to me as to the Lord, and all she could say was "I am having a nervous breakdown" and that she was coming apart at the seams. So I dropped it.

I asked her calmly to admit that she did not really want a husband, a lover, that she just really wanted a butler and a caretaker, but she would not admit it. I told her actions spoke louder than words and that her actions spoke volumes to me. She said nothing. She does not know how to be honest.

I am screwed. She will eventually leave me and go back to AZ. I am convinced. This of course will be a blatant failed marriage and will be my death knell. I will be drummed out of Christian circles. The house will have to be sold (she was talking about that last night), I will not be able to afford to live in CA, and so I can forget about my nice lab at SDSU in San Diego. I can forget about finishing my doctorate. Where will I go?

Saturday, July 24, 2004

Last night we sat on the new couches (that I spent $1200 on recently) and watched TV. She tried sitting close to me and tried to get me to hold her hand and touch her. I did not cooperate much – I am just so tired of the herky jerky and inconsistent "love" from her. Today we pretty much stayed away from each other. I did help her cook dinner, though, but we ate in silence and later we walked in silence. Later she made popcorn and watched a pretty sophomoric movie on the Disney channel. During the movie, she sat close to me and started rubbing my leg. When it ended, she asked if we could go upstairs and fool around. I said, "Well, you see, if you started giving me oral right now, then I would say yes, otherwise, I would rather just look at a Playboy and masturbate."

She was shocked I think, and she said "Do you mean you won't have sex with me unless I give you oral sex?" I stupidly said, "Yeah, I need to be excited too – its time for me to have that for a change."

I also said that I would just totally love it too if I just got to lay on my back and someone sucked and rubbed my body parts and then got on me and did all the work (meaning that is the way she expects it all the time). She started to cry.

She got up and said she could not give me oral sex. She said " Do you want me to divorce you so you can go find someone who will do that for you?" I asked, "Did I say I wanted you to divorce me? I just want a wife that is passionate about me." I told her I needed excitement and that I had been trying to tell her that for months, years. That I was bored with her wincing – eyes-closed "lovemaking" and that it was not worth the effort. So upstairs she went after crying out "I'm sorry Mitch" several times. That was at 9:40. I expect her to file for divorce any day now, and I won't resist her. Besides California is a 'no-fault' state, so I have no options. She had told me she would sign a release for me, holding me harmless for anything that happens as a result of her letting Ronnie move to a Mormon home in AZ to live. Tonight I gave her a typed form but she then refused to sign it. She said she needed to think about it for a while. (What??)

Tuesday, July 27, 2004

The weather is finally cooling a bit (thank God). It has been over 100 each day for almost 4 weeks now. On Sunday, I went to SDSU for the day, ran the lab equipment and spent most of the day with Dr. Thomas Paine, my "boss" on the research I am doing. He has to fly back to Australia today, so that was the only day we could go over his equipment issues and photograph his samples.

We talked at length about Terry and what has been going on lately. He was shocked that she was sending Ronnie to live in a Mormon home, that this "was disastrous" (his words), but that I just had to step aside and let it happen in his opinion. He could not believe that she was not listening to me and that she had not asked anyone at church about this. As we talked, I asked him if he thought I should have her sign a release. We agreed that I have probably already lost Ronnie, but that maybe I could salvage things with her if I dropped the release form. So, I called her at 8AM before she left for church and told her I loved her. She sounded happy to hear that. On the way home, I called her again and told her I loved her. When I got home I told her that I still believed that her decision with Ronnie was wrong, but that I was choosing love. I told her I wanted to rip up the consent form I gave her. She cried and cried and said thank you. I reminded her that I still did not agree with her decision, and she said OK. I ripped up the form.

Even though we sat on the couch together Sunday night and Monday night, she made no attempt to touch me, even though it has been 12 days since we have been intimate. She must be regularly masturbating now in her bed before she gets up in the morning. This would certainly explain why she pushes me away so much.

Thursday 7/29/04

Well tonight I made the mistake of trying to force her to see that she was wrong to send Ronnie away. (When will I ever learn? No one changes Terry). I asked her if she had spoken to any Christians about it, she said, "Yes, Dr. Unrhat" who is Ronnie's shrink – and definitely *not* a Christian. (Sue Boltner at church who had a daughter go to him said he is anything *but* a Christian). I asked her if she had spoken to anyone at church like Pastor or our Sunday-School teacher, or Ronnie's Youth Pastor, she said, "No."

I said, "That is because you do not want to hear from anyone at church about how this is wrong." I asked her to tell me why Ronnie is leaving and her big answer was that he does not feel welcome in my home! So the spoiled brat feels discipline from me and he wants to run away. I forced her to call Pastor at home (turns out he us in China this week and was thus unavailable). Then I made her call the Youth Pastor, but he was gone too. So I had her call our Sunday-School class teacher, Chuck. She told him that she had decided for the well being of her son that he had to go to live with relatives in AZ. She would not tell him they were Mormon until I asked her to.

She did not say that his old church is 30 miles away from where he will be living and that he has no ride to church until I made her say these things to Chuck. When I got on the phone with Chuck I explained that Ronnie is allowed to routinely fail courses, is not required to do homework and is allowed to play Nintendo and computer all the time with no restrictions. I explained that he was already thrown out of one school. She was shouting in the background so Chuck told me to go and settle her down. Oh, Chuck – you don't get it – nobody settles Terry down….

It just went downhill from there. She said I was putting words in her mouth, that I was abusive, intimidating, and manipulating. She said she lives in constant terror of my temper and me personally. I always ask for specifics, she never has any. This is really getting bad. If I keep trying to talk to her about *anything* she just gets belligerent and crying mad – worse than ever before. I feel often like I am her father and she is my rebellious teenager.

I told her I would never give her a divorce if she tries to divorce me (thinking it would cause her to stop the silliness.) She said she wants a separation, but I ain't leaving. I have done nothing but serve her, but if I say one word about anything, she calls it abuse, intimidation and slavery. So she can leave if she wants, I will keep the house. She can crawl back to Arizona on her own; I won't stop her. I won't serve her anymore if she stays. She can cook her own dinners, wash her own plates, do her own laundry. I will just stay in my room until she goes.

Saturday 7/31/04

Well for 2 nights I ignored her. I stayed in my room, I ate in my room. This morning I left at 7AM and was not here when they took Ronnie to the plane. So he is gone and I had no say. I came home at about noon, and they were all gone. I fixed lunch and got my dinner ready to grill. She came home and ate lunch and took a nap. She came in and asked me if I wanted her to make something for dinner, I just shrugged.

This morning I had a long talk with Dr. Anne. She said that Terry is deeply afraid of intimacy and that I could not talk about it. I really had to use her words to talk to her, like "I feel manipulated, abused," etc. She said the reason Terry only wants me to "make love" to her minutes before bedtime, and always just lays there and does not open her eyes and interact with me is because she just wants me to get it over with. Dr. Anne asked if her mom was a victim, and I said yes, her husband (T's father) cheated on her and then left the whole family all high and dry. They had to fend for themselves. Dr. Anne said Terry has become her mom and that as a victim-her power comes from making me feel like I am making her a victim. She said, "You need to get a new counselor, one that will actually help you like Dr. Phil would." She said I had to take it real slow and not expect much, as she had not yet really dealt with being victimized by her dad and by Ronnie's father.

At about 5PM I came out of my room and she was eating. I handed some mail to her and went back into my room. Later I came out again and she said she was going for a walk. I asked if she wanted me to come and she said sure, so I went for a walk with her. She has really changed now in exercising! She walks so fast I can hardly keep up! When we finally got home, I asked her why the change. She said the doctor really put the fear into her with the bad cholesterol news. So even though I did not get through to her about her weight, thank God somebody did. I fizzed all the bottles of cold water (9 or 10), then we sat and watched TV in the living room for 3 hours. We talked a little, but not much. At the end she said she had to go up to bed and she called me sweetie and rubbed my arm. I made no advancement towards her and I said nothing. I do not feel close to her, and I am sure she just does not want the closeness. I will just continue to be bland and nice, but sex is over for us. It just isn't worth being controlled by her, so I will be nice but not intimate.

I am really hoping she will agree to go with me to a Christian counselor, so I prepared this statement:

REFLECTIVE ESSAY FOR MARRIAGE COUNSELOR

"It is clear now that Terry does not trust me. I am beginning to not trust her. She already had her paycheck diverted once into her Pacific Coast Credit Union account, so she knows she can do that and run away. She does not trust me to raise her son, so she let him run away. That hurts me deeply because I wanted nothing but the best for Ronnie. He is a quitter, and I now suspect that his mom is too. I am on pins and needles. I am so afraid to say the wrong thing, to let my voice rise up in any way for fear that she will pack up and run away to AZ as well. She has family there who will take her back in a heartbeat, so it is just a matter of time. I have been alone before, but I do not want her to leave me. I am afraid to touch her for fear that she will push me away and make my feelings hurt more. I am afraid to look at her for fear that she will take it the wrong way and feel 'terrified' in some way.

We have been in separate bedrooms since our 2nd wedding anniversary. I feel that T is terrified of intimacy and even deep friendship. Her father cheated on her mother for years and then abandoned the 6 of them and he died an early death some time during her teen years. Her mother was a stoic victim, and never remarried, but she carried the family and even got an advanced degree. Two of her sisters abandoned Christianity and are now Mormons, and one of her sisters has been an alcoholic for many years. I feel that T has adopted the victim mentality as a protective measure. In fairness, I admit that I have shouted at her and slammed a few doors in the last 3 years. I even threw a plastic bowl inside my closed bathroom and I threw plastic bowl on my office floor, but I have never thrown anything at her or directed any violence towards her in any way. There have been 4 such angry outbursts on my part in the almost three years since we have known each other and now she is terrified of me. I have never threatened her, hit her or otherwise laid a hand on her or her son. She does not respond well to confrontation or criticism. She does, however start loud and unsettling crying bouts to the point where she is unable to speak, breathe or see, thus she immediately truncates any confrontation that arises. She has called me intimidating, abusive and essentially her captor, who has entrapped her. The Bible says in your anger do not sin, but to T any anger is a sin.

T not only withholds affection, but she cannot give freely. Lovemaking (average every 7-10 days, 30 times in the last 180 days) often must be just before she falls asleep (usually after she has taken her sleeping meds) most always in the missionary position and usually without much foreplay. She always has her eyes closed and just seems to want to get it over with. When I try to touch her, she often pushes me away, saying she feels like a piece of meat, so I have given up. She admitted that she has masturbated "three times" since we were married, but I believe that it is much more than that – even weekly. This would explain why she pushes me away so often. I have given up on intimacy and no longer seek her out for sex.

T's son R, was born out of wedlock while she was in a violent relationship. He has ADHD, but has been off *Ritalin* since May 2004. He has constantly struggled with school since he got here and then had some trouble in school in AZ, as his report cards reflect. The most common complaints from his teachers are that he fails to do the work and fails to turn in homework. He flunked all his math courses (he was in several in 2004) and got a D in English and a D in biology. So he had to take summer school. He ended up going to Arcadia High for Summer School since he missed the deadline for enrolling in Duarte High. He has an addictive personality, and can spend 14+ hours playing video games and computer games. One time he played a new game for so long and hard he vomited and was dizzy for a day. His eating habits are poor, often eating only sugar or complex carbohydrates over proteins and vegetables.

He was caught breaking into my office on 2 occasions, once on videotape as proof to T when he lied several times about it and after she did not believe me. He never responded well to my discipline and often just walked away or ran to his mother. In frustration, and because it was driving a wedge between T and I, I gave up trying to work on him after a year. Her best friend's husband, who kept him in AZ for the first 3 months of our marriage, told me he gave up on him in 2 weeks. My three adult sons live productive lives and all freely interact with me, so I know how to raise sons, and I have proven myself as a capable father. I predicted one year in advance that he would flunk school and would be sent back to Arcadia High School and it came true. Because I did not gush over him, he convinced his mother that I hated him and that he could not survive here. She is convinced that he is not welcome in my home, which is not true. Anarchy and rebellion are not welcome in my home. Nevertheless, she decided without discussing it with me (or any Christian for that matter) that she would send him to live with her sister and brother in law in Mesa, 30 miles from his friends and church in Phoenix. Her relatives are very active Mormons, and I was angry and hurt over this decision. I tried to fight it, but it turned into a raging battle, so I surrendered and he is now gone. I feel that these actions say to me that I am an unfit father and husband and that she has chosen her family over her husband. I firmly believe that she will be moving back soon, as she has complained about living in CA ever since she got here.

Because T drives 100 miles a day, leaving at 4:30AM, I do all the grocery shopping, bill paying, and 95% of the cleaning, washing, kitchen, etc. etc. etc. I do this because I love her and I appreciate her sacrifice, and because it is the least I can do. Recently I quit making her bed and doing her laundry and other little things. She tells me she feels unworthy, insecure in our marriage and a second-class citizen, all because I point out things that should be corrected like leaving hallway lights on and doors open when the A/C is on, etc. She says I have too many rules and that she can never please me. It is all I can do to concentrate on my doctoral program keep the house running and work my research and other jobs. I know she feels that she is the main breadwinner, but she is not. As of August 1, she has earned $25,000 (deposits of $15,200) and I have earned and deposited over $45,000.

Right now, we are suffering from broken trust. I love her and want to keep her and I want her to learn to trust me, but I do not feel that she ever will. I hope she does not run away. I wish she would give me more than a token peck on the cheek and handholding."

Monday, 8/2/04 – her day off.
Today she woke up early (6) and had her own coffee and breakfast. She did not seek me out. I got up at 7:30 and sat with her on the couch for a while, but soon got to work with laundry, research and other chores. She basically ignored me and sat and watched TV and dozed on the couch. I asked her what she wanted to do today, and she said ironing, cleaning her

bath and some other things. I went up and scrubbed her tub while she did her bathroom counters and mirrors. I had scrubbed her toilet earlier last week. She did not thank me.

I started to reach out to her at about 10 and asked her if she wanted to do something fun. Of course, eating out is her big thing, so we went out to eat. On the way we were discussing the budget. I told her I was going to have to work hard to pay for the things she wants. She mentioned that she was hoping to send Ronnie money in AZ. I asked her, "How much?" She did not answer. I waited 5 minutes, then said, "You never answered me." She said $50-60 per month room and board. I told her it was really hard for me to have to do that now since she had made the decision to send him all on her own. I had no say in it and I was now being asked to pay for it. I told her it was like I decided to start scuba diving and spending $750 per year without asking her. She actually said Ronnie was not on vacation and that it was different. (Vacation???) She said that she had to do what was right for her son's emotional well-being. I dropped it because she was starting to cry. I am certainly no husband and father especially for her brat.

During lunch I said I feel like we need to go to a counselor who was Biblical, and a Christian. She said Condant was helping her. I said he is not helping us. She said he had a degree from Fuller Theological Seminary. I said that meant he was a liberal and not a Biblical Christian. She cried and asked, "Why do you do this to me in public?" So I gave up on that. I think that was her plan anyway.

After lunch I called our Sunday-School teacher Chuck and asked if he was available. I asked T if she would go with me to Chuck for counseling, she said she only wanted to go to a counselor who was trained in marital counseling. I emailed Chuck and asked for a referral.

I cooked dinner and she ate, but I mostly left her alone for the afternoon and evening. I do remember she watched about and hour and a half of a Barbara Stanwyk movie called "Clash by Night", which had lots of loud and angry shouting in it. Funny how she can watch a 40's movie with men shouting at their wives, but if I shout I am a criminal. Go figure.

Later we went to an outside Dixieland concert in LaVerne and came home and watched a movie. She kissed me goodnight and went upstairs. Her light was on from midnight to 12:30.

If she ever asks me to go upstairs again I will say, "No, dear, you have rejected me so deeply, you rejected everything I stand for. You rejected who I am. I will be your friend, but I will never again be your lover, you broke that."

I worked up a short budget and it revealed that currently, she contributes well under the $2343 monthly share she should pay for this marriage. The Arcadia PD says I am under no obligation to pay for Ronnie's costs in AZ. Yup I actually called them.

Wednesday, August 04, 2004

Well yesterday she woke up with a hangover. Apparently, the coffee she drank while we were at the Dixieland concert wired her up, so she drank lots of wine to get sleepy. I guess that is why her light was on so late – she was up drinking. I pretty much left her alone while I worked and got a rock done. She lay around on the couch. I asked her if she would go with me to see Chuck at church. She said, "Not anytime soon." I said how about after lunch, she said OK. I set up a 3PM meeting with Chuck. Then I cooked her a hot lunch and she ate and then slept on the couch. We went over at 3 and met with Chuck. She was reluctant to talk, so I laid the whole thing out to Chuck (per the reflective essay above). My willingness to serve her hand and foot, her problems with my authority, her pushing me away all the time, our total lack of any intimacy at all, Ronnie's bad behavior and grades, how she and he decided to ship him off without asking me, my anger and shouting – I laid it all out there with no sugar coating. When her turn came, with lots of sobbing and about 25 Kleenex's, she blamed it all on me. I am authoritarian, I am negative and sarcastic, I do not love and encourage, I hated Ronnie by saying he was not my kid, and that he could not come back if he left, etc., etc., etc. She took responsibility for nothing, basically – she had to save the life of her damaged kid by sending him away (even to a Mormon family). Chuck said, "You are a dear, sweet woman". I about puked and thought, boy has she got you fooled. So, it is over. I will be her slave, I will kiss her and hug her, but this thing is about as broken as it can get. I will send her punk kid $50 per month, but I will bury myself in my books, research, etc. My two new sentences are, "Whatever you want" and "Where do you want me to send the money?"

But there will be no more romantic getaways, certainly no more lovemaking….she broke that. Chuck called me later last night (while I was out walking) and asked me to have coffee with him. I was sorry I missed his call and I emailed him back, but I thought that was interesting. I wonder if he thinks I need real fixing. He did say one thing, and I am really going to have to think about this….he said Jesus knew what Judas was going to do the whole time, but for 3 years, He was silent about it. I don't think

Jesus was married to Judas. He certainly is not married to Terry. Now I know why no one else would be.

Saturday, August 8, 2004

Well, I have pretty much not touched her since 7/27, which is the last time we were intimate, 11 days ago. I am still very hurt by her stabbing me in the back with Chuck our Sunday school class teacher. I generally have been sitting with her and being nice and gentle and sweet. I allow her to hold my hand when she wants to, but I do not reach out for her.

Today, I left early for SDSU and ran the lab equipment. When I came home she was home and she had had her nails done and had spent about $100 on gift cards for Ronnie and her family members that just got married in MN. I did not avoid her, although I did not reach out for her. At one point I was laying on my bed and she came in to cuddle with me. She started kissing me pretty passionately. I kissed her back and she was pulling me onto herself. I was hurt and told her I could not make love to her because I still felt like she had stabbed me in the back. She cried for about 30 minutes and then we talked about it. She said she needed me to have listened to her when she kept telling me that Ronnie was not happy. I told her I still felt like she lied to me about the whole thing and that she had stabbed me and that I could not make love to her. I know she was very cut by this, but she has to know that she just kills me when she goes behind my back like that. It completely depresses me – makes me feel worthless and not a part of this marriage or her life. Later I reached out for her and we were intimate. She had a raging orgasm. So I caved in again, didn't I? I am her slave really. I have no backbone. I will not act lovey-dovey towards her, or so I tell myself – and usually after 2 weeks I am needy and I give in. I will hold her hand if she reaches out to me, but I will not seek her out for sex anymore. But I have no will, no resolve – I am a shadow of a man. I'm a loser. God please take away my libido!

8/10/04 I have to leave for Palmdale College today and service 50 lab instruments. I will be gone overnight. Yesterday I took the Inter District Transfer from Arcadia District over to Duarte HS and got Ronnie enrolled again, even though he is now living in AZ with his Mormon family. The school gave me his registration packet and I left it on T's placemat on the kitchen table. When she came home she looked at it and asked me how it got there. (What kind of a question is that?) I told her they mailed it and that they would sign his IDT by next Monday and he could register on 8/25. Later we talked a little about Ronnie and I said "We can't solve our problems by running away from them." I also mentioned to her that he would know no one at that school in AZ and that she was forcing him to start from scratch in the middle of high school – something that could mess him up worse than being here where he already had friends and knew all the teachers. But I dropped it when I saw her start to get frustrated with me telling her the truth once again. The ball is in her court, but she won't budge. I could make a fortune if I could bet on her attitude and actions. If I could manage her and sell her to a foreign government she could destroy entire regimes.

I decided to come home tonight instead of staying out near the college, and she said she was glad I did because she had convinced herself to go off her diet and go to Taco Bell. I cooked her a nice lo carb dinner. She is now on a Statin drug due to her high cholesterol.

8/12/04 Yesterday I had a long talk about Ronnie and Terry with Patrick. He told me that she had asked him pointedly if anyone from church had asked him about our problems. I guess she is paranoid about her fake reputation at church. He told her no. She told him to tell her the truth if anyone from church asked. He said, "The truth is that my Dad busts his butt for you and you do little or nothing around here." I would have loved to have seen the look on her face on that one. He was kind of shocked at the third-degree she was giving him, but he held up under pressure. Good boy Patrick. Welcome to my world.

I told him that I really did not miss Ronnie and that as much as I was enjoying him gone, he really belonged here. I am sure Ronnie has read my letter that I sent him 9 days ago. I wrote him to encourage him and to tell him that he really belonged here. But I have yet to hear anything from him or his mother and I don't expect to. I will not miss R pounding on the stairs, slamming doors, making messes in the kitchen, eating food all over the house, sneaking in my office, playing video games all weekend long, not bathing regularly, etc. Pat also said that he was convinced that she was going to leave to be with R in AZ. We will see.

Saturday, August 15, 2004 Last night she slept downstairs in my bed. Pure snoring, open jaw, and plenty of no touching. How wonderful is it to sleep next to a snoring woman when all you want to do is to be close? To feel love? To be able to give physical love and connect with another human being? God my torture is too much!!

Tonight she is back upstairs in her own bed. Oh well. Better than being tortured all night again I guess…

Ronnie left a phone message tonight at about 7PM….seems he does not have the phone number for the Oringer's who are supposed to take him to church tomorrow…. Nothing like waiting until the last possible moment. I rest my case. I found out that her Mormon sister faxed Terry a copy of the August 3 letter that I mailed to R. She has had it since August 9th and has said nothing to me about it. The silence and paranoia continue. How bizarre. The one time I write to him and express my desire to be his Dad, to have him here where he belongs – she can't even speak of it. Maybe it destroys her little fantasy that "I hate him." I live in the Twilight zone.

8/16/04 Today I got a call from T's old Pastor in AZ, Paul Keown. He called me back because I pelted him with emails and phone messages about R and T and what had gone on in recent weeks…I found out from him that in the 3 weeks that Ronnie has been in AZ, no one from the church has seen hide nor hair of him. I explained things to him much like I told Chuck, our Sunday school teacher here at church. He acted very coldly towards me said he wants to hear both sides of the story, I said great. He asked me to ask T to call him. I sent her an email to that effect, but I am not going to hold my breath. She won't call him. She will lose control of this marriage if she does that. Paul – did she ever call you and confess how she lied to your face during our "pre-marital counseling"?

When she got in the car on her way home, she called and said she had gotten my email, and just exactly what did I tell him? (More concern about her fake reputation I guess). I said we could talk about it when she got home, but I never broached the subject after she got home. Funny, neither did she. But what does it matter what I told him? She does not trust me. Not to raise her son, not with finances and certainly not as a Biblical husband. And she won't ever contact Pastor Paul….why should she?

She has been depositing at least $150 per month from her paycheck into her own checking account for months now. She never told me this. Even though she is a signatory on the whole dang Wells Fargo account (the main business checking account I have had since 1992), and even though I have given her blank checks that she can use, she does this to me? Hiding money? I consider it lying and cheating. We do not have a marriage, because she cannot trust me. I could lay down in front of a bus for this woman and she would never trust me.

I guess I have to enact long-range plans to protect myself. She will eventually start having her paycheck go completely into her account. But I will not be stuck with this house payment. The loan is in her name, so I can just walk away. I am on the title, however, so if she decides to sell it, she will need my cooperation. The car loan is in both our names, but it can go into default, because I will not pay it if she keeps all her pay. I will call the bank and tell them to stop taking it out of my account. All the utilities are in my name, and I will simply and summarily have them shut off. She can pay to have them all turned on again. All I am responsible for is my credit cards and I am going to keep them paid off. If I have to go rent a room somewhere, she will have to be removed as a signatory from the Wells Fargo account and I will have to cut off her bank card. What fun this is. I have also decided that I will never go to AZ to see her family again. How humiliating would it be to have to show up at her in-laws as the evil stepfather who "did not love his stepson?" What kind of a message has she sent? The message is: "Mitch cannot be trusted, so to protect her kid from me, she has to secretly send him to live with Mormon relatives in another state."

Tuesday, 8/24/04

I am getting numb. The distance between us does not bother me anymore. I made a real mistake marrying a woman with baggage, a woman I barely knew. If you are reading this and you are contemplating marriage to a 45+ yr old woman, do yourself a favor. Ask her to live with you. Test her in every conceivable situation. Raise a dog with her. She how she disciplines it. Take her to as many different restaurants/bars/movies/plays/parties as you can. Take her to the snow – take her to the desert – take her to the ocean. Write everything down…. Kick her out when you know you are incompatible. T and I are incompatible. I knew this in January of 02. I told her this in January of 02. She bitterly cried then, and I let it go. What a mistake that was.

She loves heat, I love cold. She loves to sit in front of the TV and stare at it for hours. I like to cuddle and talk. She does not need intimacy – I cannot live without it. But as I said, I am numb now. I don't call her at work anymore. If she calls me from the car on her way home, I say, "Uh hello, how are you?" I never call her back if she leaves a voicemail. I don't go out to help her come into the house. I sit and eat dinner with her, but I feel no need to talk. I walk with her after dinner, but I feel no need to share. I use my mind while we are sitting or walking in silence to review schoolwork, research projects, bills that need attention. I sit with her as she watches TV – she picks the channel and holds the remote. I usually read or write or find something else to do with my mind while I am sitting there. From time to time I get up to go do something. When she goes up to bed, I let her kiss me on the cheek, but it is not me she is kissing, it is the vapor canopy of my self…I left a long time ago.

On the weekends I occupy myself with research projects, studies, paper writing. Sometimes I just go into my room or I do work with some of my lab equipment. I am in a perfect cocoon. I don't need anybody – least of all her. And so my hurt has turned to thick, cuticle covered scar. She may leave for AZ for good. In fact she is driving there over Labor Day weekend to be with her son and her family. If she doesn't come back, I have my plan…it is failsafe and insulating. She cannot hurt her incompatible husband.

8/26/04

We have not been intimate for countless days. I am no longer touching her except to hold her hand when we pray over dinner and to allow her to kiss my cheek before she goes to bed. (Yeah, I know – I still pray with her over dinner. I am a mouse. She actually *insists* on praying the same exact prayer every single time… "Father God, I love you Lord. I thank you for this food and I ask you to make it *very* nourishing to our bodies, in Jesus name." I say, "Amen," and then she lets go of my hand. She recites this exact same prayer at every meal and she has for years. I bet God gets all warm inside when He hears that prayer.

She seems as happy as a clam that I have moved to the dark side of the moon emotionally. I wonder how long it will take her to move away herself?

12/16/05 Wow. Over a year and no entry. What a difference a year makes (not). I printed and saved this email that she sent me at the start of last year…
"Tuesday, January 4, 2005, 8:34PM
Subject: Me
Mitch,
I now realize that I am what you have been telling me I am for a long time. I am not a wife, just like you said. And although I think I need a husband, it seems I do not and that makes me what you have been saying all along. I feel that I have become what you have said I am and I do not

want you to have to live with that. I will move out, separate from you or give you a divorce, whatever you want.

I am SO very sorry that I have hurt you in all the ways that I have and desperately wish that I could turn back time so that you could have found someone other than me. Please do not think this is me saying, "I am a failure, I am bad…" – it is NOT! I am facing what and who I am and it is what you have always been saying about me. I am not good for you in any way.

I will do whatever I can to make this as easy as possible for you. I DO only want the best for you but, it is not me.

Thank you so VERY much for all that you have always done for me. I will Always be grateful for that.

I love you and I wish I could have been what you needed.

Terry."

I just had no words at the time to even reply to that.

I started teaching full time in a local Christian school in September. She commutes 4 hrs a day. I see her when she gets home at about 5:30, I feed her, we may go for a walk in silence, and then it is the TV and opposite ends of the couch. I have had a fever for the last 3 days and tonight after sitting through numbing TV, and her doing her constant crossword puzzles, I happened upon a Bikini show. OK so I am a man, and am curious. She just storms off and up to bed without a word. As if she had something going on here to protect, huh? I am so over her, I hardly hear her when she says, "I love you" on the phone anymore. What does that mean?

My ex-wife is destitute and about to be thrown out of her place. I invited her to come live here. I told her I would give up my bedroom and all. This could be fun. Haha. I am ready to watch Terry have a real-time drama. Oh, by the way….Terry's son did not last long at his Mormon Aunt's house in AZ. By Christmas last year (after 5 months) they were so enraged they wanted him gone. We talked them into keeping him until school ended for the year in May. So he is back here now, doing his normal things with even more skill than before he left. What a mess.

Monday, February 06, 2006.

What is different? Two months – two millennia what does it matter? We had sex twice in the last 40 days. Good thing I wasn't fasting – I'd be dead. She is still very much not in love with me; I am still very much over her. I am starting to email strangers online. Maybe I will find a real friend there. As I said, I began teaching full time in September. 180 7th and 8th graders. The only plus is I come home so tired I barely notice how indifferent she is to me. The ex-wife decided to move to Texas. Life sure is fun.

4/27/06

Well, we have settled into a pattern that does not disturb her. God forbid she should be disturbed…I quit my teaching job and now she worries all the time about being the sole breadwinner. Again, as mentioned several times in this saga, I made more than her last month just servicing lab equipment. She lives in a delusion. She works and comes home. She calls me 15 minutes away and asks me to turn up the spa heater, which I do. I go to the van and meet her and bring in her bag (I have no idea why I started doing this again – I am such a loser). She goes up to her bedroom to change. She either eats or drinks a Slim Fast. Then it is either a 45 min walk or hot tub (for her) or she sits on the couch and does crossword puzzles. But eventually she ends up on the far side of the couch while she watches shows that she generally picks unless there is nothing else on – on those times, she hands me the remote. If I do not purposefully sit next to her, and grope her I get no affection at all. If I want any touching I have to touch her because she definitely won't touch me. She finds something harmless to watch on TV. At or near 7:10 she asks if I want fruit. I say yes. She makes me a bowl of fruit from the jars of fruit in the fridge and goes back to crossword puzzles. At 7:45 or so she is begging to make popcorn. At 8:30, "I need to go to bed" pops out. I go upstairs and sit on the bed watching TV with her; until she starts to snore then I come down to my room, with a large glass of wine and drift towards sleepiness. Between the sleep meds and the alcohol I get a decent buzz and fall asleep. Next day? Just like the last day. I am a freaking drone. Friday nights she is up till 1AM – I go off to bed around 11. She usually imbibes way too much wine on those nights too. Every other week she asks me to hide the wine from her, and every other week she begs me for the wine. Saturday, she sleeps in and unless we have somewhere to go, she sits and watches TV, maybe does laundry, checks her email, etc. If I act particularly needy in my actions (i.e. constant fondling, repeated requests for sex, etc.), she finally breaks down and says, "OK, we can go upstairs." How romantic. Generally, I last a few minutes and then I rub her until she comes. As usual she is winching with her eyes closed. What else is new?

Then she is worthless for the rest of the day, because she had such a good orgasm. Sunday she gets all holy and smiles and chats at everybody at church. She raises her arms up to the ceiling during the singing and sways to the music. She uses 4 Kleenex's to mop up the joy off her face. Everyone thinks she is a sweet, sensitive, loving wife. Men are jealous that I am married to Mary Magdalene. I should hide a video camera and tape the real her, but what is the point? Nobody cares anyway. Nice life – I need a girlfriend.

5/1/06

Yesterday after church she said she wanted to talk when we got home. When we got home we sat on the couch. Out spills "I think I am losing my mind and that there is something terribly wrong with me." Copious tears and sobs follow. After I ask her a few probing questions, she goes on about fearing the loss of her job, her memory, etc., that she is basically worthless and descending quickly into chaos. After about an hour of this I finally got her calmed down and convinced her that she is basically worrying herself into a frenzy and that "Everything is going to be all right." It seemed to work because she was happier the rest of the afternoon. We watched Star Wars with Ronnie (recently back from his failed venture with his family in AZ) until 9 and then she fell asleep. I need a girlfriend.

6/14/06

What's new and different as we travel down this road together? Nothing. We have gone on a couple of trips so far this summer. We went to St. George UT for a few days – paid for by SDSU to take part in some geology meetings. Then last week we flew to SC and took part in a Research board meeting. I think we had sex in St. George mostly because I was about to explode. I lasted less than 2 minutes. I don't believe I took care of her. Then 2 weeks later we had sex upstairs on her bed. She got on top. I was so needy that I finished while she was on top – something that never happens to me. Again I did not take care of her. So, how pathetic am I? She has trained me well.

That was about 3 weeks ago, give or take a few days. She shows no interest in me. Even in SC, she was content to just lie under her covers and ignore me. Monday, she was off all day. We did the grocery thing and ran some errands. We were home alone for about 3 hours before Ronnie came home from school. But nothing. Not even a "Honey, I think you are a nice man." I really, really need a girlfriend.

6/18/06

Well Ronnie has one week of school left. Oh, then he has to go to summer school (3rd summer for him here in this school district). This weekend is the last weekend he could work on a painting project or he is facing an F. That is why he has been grounded for weeks and weeks. We have spent hours talking with him, his teacher, his principal, etc. Ronnie is a lazy person and will not do anything unless his back is against the wall. So the whole weekend goes by (Father's Day weekend) and on Sunday afternoon, after he has partied and all with his friends, watched TV, gorged himself on Nintendo, etc. all weekend, I ask his mother why he has not painted at all and why has his painting just been sitting there. Turns out he never brought home any paints from school. He basically lied to me at the start of the weekend when he came home with the artwork and no paints and told me he was ready to do the work. I was so mad at him I started yelling at him (I know, I know – stupid, stupid me). He tried to make excuses and say that it was "just an accident". This pissed me off even more. I shouted back that it was a DECISION that he had made and he was back on severe grounding. His mother started sobbing, but she doesn't do a cotton pickin' thing to try to change him. I told him to get dressed that we were going to Home Depot to get paints but his weeping mother says that I am too angry so she was "going to take my son" to get paints. I almost had an aneurysm. Here we go with "my son" crap again. I am so over this woman and the way she drifts into mediocrity with her kid. I am sick of being the bad ass. I am seriously contemplating finding a girlfriend who can take care on my emotional and physical needs. How bad off am I? This marriage is buried and is already rotting in the grave. I cannot wait until he moves out.

6/19/06

We didn't speak by phone today. Tonight she was cold when she called me from the freeway off ramp. I helped her in from the parking lot anyway (Why? Why do I keep helping her??) We walked in silence on our walk (Why do I keep walking with her?) She went straight up to her sanctuary of a room when we came back. The second happiest day of my life was when I realized I would not miss her when this thing finally ends.

6/29/06

It goes on. R is in summer school for the third year. She took him off his grounding because he convinced her that he got all good grades at the end of the school year. I am not holding my breath. I will wait until the official grades come. We barely talk. I am just so sick of what a cold, frigid, self-absorbed prude she is. She doesn't love me – heck she doesn't even like me. She doesn't honor or cherish me (or obey me – any of her marriage vows) – she basically just tolerates me. She never initiates anything romantic or even a half-way deep conversation. She sits way over on the other side of the couch and does crossword puzzles. Every now and again she will ask me a question to help her solve the puzzle. This is not a marriage and she is not a wife. I won't ever marry again. I'll just find a girlfriend or two for a little closeness from time to time. I wish I could find one now. I am probably going to hell. I have written these things in this diary so many times you must be completely bored and I must be mad.

7/3/06 Last time we were intimate? 20 days ago and counting. She has been off for three days and she still does her little distant thing.

Well Ronnie did actually get passing grades, as he told us. I am amazed and pleasantly surprised. He does not seem to be studying much for summer school, however, but who the heck am I to say a word? Today, Monday, he failed to put out the trashcans, so I had to do it. That is basically his ONE standing chore. Every now and again he will be asked to vacuum or to empty or load the dishwasher – that's it -if you can believe that. He should be scrubbing floors in my opinion. So today when he came home at 2PM, in his usual style, he was rushing to get out the door because his mom was off work and home. He was telling her that he was going to leave for the rest of the day. From my bedroom, I hollered, "You aren't going anywhere for awhile…" long pause, "That's what happens when I have to do your chore for you." He went straight up to his room and closed the door. She came and stood in my bedroom doorway and sobbed how he just forgot, etc., etc. blah, blah, blah. I asked her when she was going to become a parent and teach him that poor decisions have penalties? She sobbed that she is a good parent. I asked her what would happen if she just "forgot" to record the personal miles she uses on the company van over the weekends….... She said nothing. I told her she would get a warning letter in her personnel file that if she did it again she would be TERMINATED from employment. She walked away crying and went up to her room – left the TV and everything running downstairs. That was 1.5 hr ago. We will see what kind of a fun night we have and 4th of July tomorrow. OH, by the way, I just took her this afternoon to a $62.00 lunch at Benihana Japanese restaurant. She never even thanked me.

I can't wait to tell her that very soon she will have to choose between him or me.

7/4/06

Well, as predicted she spent the rest of the night in her room. So did I. She did come in and ask me if I wanted fruit and popcorn, and I did let her fix me popcorn. Today she sat on the couch from about 9AM to 9PM. She watched 3 movies while I grilled BBQ chicken, and 2 flank steaks and got lunch all ready. She woke up R at 11AM. Then she flipped channels after lunch from 1PM to 5PM. I worked in my room and we ignored each other. Later I fixed myself a salad. I watched TV and she sat on the other end of the couch ignoring me from about 6PM to 9PM. She went up to bed at 9PM. Ronnie was out from 11:30AM to 10:15 PM. I took off my wedding band. I don't want to begin to hate her, I mean she does bring in $3600 per month, right?

7/6/06

Typical night. She calls when 5 minutes away. She says, "Hello honey", I say, " Hi Dear." I walk out to the van and bring in her bag (Why? Am I a zombie?) She changes, eats a few bites of dinner, plops on the far end of the couch and opens her crossword puzzle book. No words from her to speak of until at 7PM I ask, "Are we going for a walk?" She sighs and complains, so we walk pretty much in silence for about an hour. We come back – she makes my fruit and plops on the couch doing her CW puzzles. I leave the TV muted a lot and a few times she un-mutes it. Round about 8:15 she asks if she can make popcorn. We eat in silence, again I mute the TV. Every now and then she makes a short comment. Round about 8:45 she announces it is her bedtime; she closes the CW puzzle book, and goes into the kitchen. On her way upstairs she asks, "Are you coming up?' I say OK and I go upstairs for about 15 minutes. (Why? Am I a zombie?) About the time she starts falling asleep I just go downstairs again. Why do I have to go upstairs and watch her fall asleep? Does this meet some bizarre need in her? How boring to do the same thing every night. I took my wedding band off 2 days ago because this is not a marriage. She hasn't even noticed. By the way, when on her computer, I found child porn searches that her son did on her computer.!!! I wonder how she will react when I tell her that wonderful perverted tidbit. I wonder if the Feds are now tracking child porn into my home??? Just the kind of excitement I always wanted…

I am in so much pain here!!! What do I do to get out of this cereal-box relationship?

Well I told her about Ronnie's porn-and she blamed me. HA! *This is my fault*!! She said that because I watch "Friends" and "That 70's show", Ronnie is driven to download child porn (she is the one that controls the remote – not me). So it's my fault!! She did ground him again though. Our relationship has been really frosty ever since, as if it could have gotten any colder. The other day I was ragging on her about leaving lights on and throwing away good food. She got up and just walked away from me – went upstairs and shut the door. It was about 7:30 and she never came back down. I put my ring in an envelope and wrote on it "when you walk away from me you are walking away from our marriage." I put it in her coffee cup. She hand wrote me a note that said, "The hurt is killing me." She wrote, "It is a FACT that I cannot do anything without making you angry." She said I do not have to put my ring back on and she will do the same. So I emailed he and said that I should just give her freedom since all I do is hurt her all the time. I said, "I know you want to be rid of me and back in Phoenix anyway"…later she emailed me back and *agreed*. I was right all along. Why do I open my mouth? I emailed her back and said, "Whatever."

7/20/06

Ronnie's 18th Birthday. Well things spiraled out of control tonight. I believe we were inches from her just walking out. Yesterday, I located and then called Ronnie Linton Sr. – the man she became pregnant with Ronnie by. I called him, introduced myself as Ronnie's step dad and Terry's husband, and asked him a few questions about T. He said she was controlling and stubborn (and that was 18 years ago – long before she became a "Christian"). He did not sound particularly bright, but he was very cordial. He stated that he wanted to speak to Ronnie and so I promised to give Ronnie his number, which I did last night after T went to bed. Tonight she got home and completely ignored me – did not even stop to say hello when she walked past me. On her way back out the door she said she was taking Ronnie to Starbucks, and that was all. She stormed back into the house about an hour later, came into my room and demanded that we talk – I said sure – well she just went ballistic – completely shouting at the top of her lungs and accusing me of going behind her back and stabbing her in the heart by contacting Ronnie's dad – she kept yelling and crying and glaring at me and stating that she could not believe I had done that. I tried saying, "Now you knew how my heart was ripped out when you went behind my back and shipped Ronnie back to your Mormon sister in Phoenix two years ago!" I also reminded her about the time she stabbed me in the back when we went to talk to Chuck at church. Didn't help much and it drew fire from several quarters: "There you go again dredging up all my old faults-and rubbing it in my face", and "You brought back one of my old monsters into my life" – and of course, "behind her back." "You don't care that he almost killed me." She just kept saying she could not believe that I had done this. It was the worst I have ever seen her. Then she launched into a diatribe about, "you just do not want Ronnie around," blah, blah, sob, sob, *anger*. (By the way, Ronnie's grounding for downloading porn onto her computer lasted ONE WEEK – that is all). He spent all day Friday 7/21 out (because I could not stand him slamming around the house and told him to go play), he spent the night Friday night out, he returned about 11:30 Saturday morning, took a shower and left and came home at around 8:30PM. We were on a walk, but he tracked us down and begged to go to the movies! What kind of discipline is he learning from her?)

So I found her breaking point and she is at it. This gravy train is about to crash if I go any further with basically any criticism at all – anything directed at her – anything at Ronnie, I must become a mute and "Accept her" as she is – even with all her faults, "As my church family did in Phoenix," or it will end. What the folks in Phoenix did was mess her up badly. They let rebellion and control grow in her unchecked, they never called her on it (why?) – and I inherited it full blown in her. This woman is not to be crossed, that is unless you don't want her around (or her work benefits)

I am now convinced that she is psychotic. Her parents were second cousins and there is a messed up chromosome here somewhere – or she was sexually abused by her father or something. She spent the next hour saying it was over – (Oh, and also that I am the most negative, mean, hateful, critical person she has ever, ever known.) She had to have a separation NOW – it had to be so because "I am killing" her. The woman seriously cannot take a milligram of criticism. Apparently when I try to rebuke or correct her on something, I am "blowing up." (Course, during her shout fest, I could not have accused her of that. I have never shouted at her or carried on like this in front of her, but man she can sure can dish it out when she wants to. Oh sure I have shouted 4 or 5 times over almost 5 years – but *nothing* like this! What if I just got in the car and drove away like she does?)

She also said she knew that I had been talking to Ardith and Annie (PSU friends) about her (purely to ask for advice from them) but I had been honest with her about that a long time ago. So she had 20 questions for me about that – a real inquisition. I tried to explain (again) that I needed a woman's advice about what I could possibly be doing wrong in this marriage – why it was not working, and the only 2 women I knew were Ardith and Annie. But she was seriously pissed about it. I got the grand lecture about how "they don't know me," and "who do you think you are," and "who do they think they are," and "what if I was always calling an old husband (yeah right – you have one of those???) all the time?" She very much behaves like a control freak that becomes instantly paranoid when she knows the cat might be out of the bag. I asked her to be honest with me and tell me how many people she has talked to about me, and who has she asked about how she should deal with me? She said ONLY ONE – her friend Eddie in AZ. I asked her again "So there is no one else?" and she said no. She is a liar because I have emails from her computer sent to several people in AZ complaining about "what kind of a man" I am and trumping up some sort of dirty laundry (obviously a plan to get into everyone's good graces there before she runs away and moves back there). But that shall remain in the file in case this sucker goes to court.

2/12/06

Almost Valentines Day. Yesterday afternoon, she came to me as I was working in the office to ask me if I wanted to "go upstairs" (for sex). I said, "No thanks." She, incredulous, asks "Why?" (After all she has kept me deprived for weeks.) I say I don't want to talk about it. She presses me relentlessly for 5 minutes; so I say, "I am over you," and explain that since it is evident that she does not want a lover, but a roommate, I will serve as roommate, only let's drop the charade because it is a joke already. She cries for a few minutes and starts making excuses, like "I hate my body" and "I'm afraid you will ask me for oral sex," crap like that. I haven't asked her for oral sex for 18 months. I tell her, "Sorry, I can't help you." She then wants to know if she should divorce me, move out, what? I state that she has nowhere to go, so why the bother? She wants to be a roommate, so that is what I will be, only just don't pretend that you want to be lovers because I know it is not true. Tic Toc – what will happen? I am quitting my job teaching these annoying kids because it is killing me. Plus I make next to nothing doing it. I can make much more in the lab equipment business and I don't need t grade 180 papers each night. She is all upset because I am "quitting the real job."

We did talk everything all out to her apparent satisfaction after a couple of days (never my satisfaction of course), and I lied telling her that I am OK with how things are working out. I give up. It's not worth it. I need a girlfriend.

I realized that I had pushed her too far, at long last. I realized that these benefits of hers were about to fly out the front door, so you know what I did? I became a mouse. Yup, I said "I am sorry" about 20 times, I cried (convincingly) – I caved. I told her that if she chose to leave I would not stand in her way, but that if she stayed, I would no longer be critical to her or Ronnie in any way. I would be a sponge.

She *owns* this relationship AND ME now, and she knows it. She sternly lectured me and severed away my manhood. And you know what? I really don't give a rat's ass anymore. She WILL NOT be forced by me, by the Bible, by any Pastor or anything or anyone to give me any attention or *any* affection, or to even consider what I have to say. When she wants to give me pity sex 30 seconds before sleep rolls in, she will ring Pavlov's bell and I will snap to attention to do it on demand (although I have just about abandoned the whole physical side of our pathetic relationship). She is nothing to write home about, trust me. She WILL NOT be forced to go outside her comfort zone for me except for her job related things. That is it. I know this now.

Interestingly, the three things she mentioned that I AM doing right are:

-running the house ("and it is a lovely house and if it weren't for you I would be in a poor and crappy studio flat")... no kidding.

-"you have taken me some places I have never been and would never have gone to and I like that a lot!" AND FINALLY...

-"you are really trying to cook us nice things and new recipes I have never tried before."

THAT'S IT FOLKS – THAT IS THE SINGULAR IMPRESSION I HAVE MADE HERE. That is all I am worth after 5 years of a relationship and putting up with her controlling behavior and her bratty idiot son.

She will not be coerced in any way – *nothing* works – it just makes her angrier, and honestly, I need her benefits for at least the next 5 years to complete my doctorate and dissertation. I have to steer her towards a nice climate (for me), a campus town with lots of house bang for the buck, where I can be happy and teach, or do research, and be on my own. With her at work during the week, I can work at home in my boxers and do what I want. That has to be worth something, huh? Even if one has to be a piece of Melba toast during the 3 hours of face time each night, and weekends, right? I can handle that, can't I? I just hate weekends now because I have to sit around with her as she watches TV and ignores me. (Case in point, Saturday 7/22 – she sat and watched about 5 Star Trek episodes, then after lunch, more Star Trek, then a 2 hour nap – then the Maltese Falcon – [finally I talked her into getting her fat rump off the couch to do a short walk], then the Miami Vice Pilot. Promptly upon completion of that – she stood up and said goodnight and walked upstairs.)

So, friends – my new motto is: "Just shut up about it" *Just shut up!* If I have any dreams of getting my doctorate done and getting into a career where I can later drop her like a hot piece of you know what, I have to eat crow for the next 10 years and be silent as I choke it down. Be silent about her kid, be silent about her, etc., etc.

SO, I GOT MY ANSWER AFTER FOUR YEARS OF WRITING THIS DIARY…. I have had my testicles removed by her. I do not rule the roost – no, no, she does that. And I am to be Mr. Positive from here on out. Butt kissing will become a highly prized art form in this home.

So I am signing off folks…thanks for listening. Look for me in 5 years – I will be free of this psycho and will be teaching at a local college near you. Sayonara.

OH Yeah! I just put my wedding band back on (even though she has removed hers) – now for the next several months, I must convince her that I am truly sorry for doing something so stupid as to take it off…

ADDENDUM: 8/15/06

Last week she drove to Phoenix for 5 days to see her niece's wedding and to be with family. I, of course, cannot jeopardize my health by exposing myself to 115-degree heat and monsoon 45% humidity, so I did not go. I did make the stupid mistake of writing out some Bible passages for her to read and I put them on her purse (one another passages, wives and husbands stuff – etc.). I had made some lab equipment appointments for the day BEFORE she told me she was leaving, so imagine my surprise when she decided to leave a day earlier. So, I was not here when she and Ronnie left, I was out working. She called me generally twice per day while she was gone. But usually only after she had had a blast with friends and family (Sunday she did not call me until 2PM). But here is the crap kicker. The verses I gave her? She underlined parts and filled in parts and made them *about me*. When she came home she just handed them to me. For example Romans14:13 she underlined "stop passing judgment on one another". Over and over she underlined "being gentle, being kind, bearing with one another", etc. As if I am the one who has not completely swallowed his tongue around here.

1 Thessalonians 5:11 she actually underlined "build each other up"! How in God's name does this woman build me up? And how can she not see the hundreds of ways I build her up? I am mystified….!

1 Peter 3:8 and 1 Peter 4:9 she really camped out on. She underlined "all of you live in harmony" and "offer hospitality to one another." She says those were important because I am not loving Ronnie. She actually made this *about me*! While in AZ, her brat went to Hooters Bar and Grill and he also drove a car over there (without a license). AND SHE DID

NOTHING – oh, I'm sorry – she "talked to him". And she is pissed at me because I am not a doormat for him.

I told her Jesus also said "wipe the dust off your feet when your message is not received" and "don't cast your pearls before swine" – course, that made her cry for an hour. I will not do it. And no matter how many times she says "my emotions are all tied up with sex", I will not ignore her kid's transgressions just so daddy can get some. I would rather dry up my testicles.

Finally, and even though I swore I was done writing about this crappy marriage and this psycho woman – I just have to include this….In 1 Cor 7:3-5, where it talks about the "wife's body does not belong to her alone" and how she "must fulfill her marital duty to her husband", etc., I had omitted the passage "In the same way, the husband's body does not belong to him alone but also to the wife." The reason I did not include that, I think is pretty obvious…I am the one always begging for sex and she is the one withholding it. I told her that I can think of only three times in our marriage where I actually said no to sex, and that was when I was so pissed that she had ignored me for weeks that I wanted to just hurt her. So I don't think *I am the one withholding the body here.* Yet here is what she said, "you only made it about the wife," (I made it only about the wife??….isn't it GOD making it about the wife?), " and so you made me feel like a piece of meat." Yup – it's all about me and what a large turd I am. Even when I try to point her to Scripture, this woman makes it about me. So I repeat what I said above… She will not be coerced in any way – NOTHING works – it just makes her angrier. The end the end the *end.*

CHAPTER THREE – WHY
AM I SO STUPID?

9/2/06

OH, OK. So I'm a jerk for not ending this diatribe. Here is a recently sent email:

"Terry, I have to tell you that I am very troubled and disturbed that Ronnie is trying to access My Space to "chat" with his friends. Who knows what other places he has been and what "friends" he has? I don't-do you? His computer is locked with a main password (according to Patrick) and no one can view what he is doing.

As we discussed, some of these "social" networking sites are loaded with smut, porn and images that are probably illegal, as are other websites such as the ones he went to in the past.

I made it clear to you and to him that I will not tolerate, under any circumstances, Ronnie downloading anything objectionable into my home, including child porn. The reason the computer has a filter is because I asked Patrick to put one on it when they were building it, since Ronnie has done this in the recent past and denied it until I found a problem with his testimony. I am sorry if you think I am judging Ronnie, but he has judged himself with his actions, so I have to have some form of protection here.

I was glad when you yourself asked Pat to put a filter on before Pat delivered the computer, but tonight has demonstrated to me that Ronnie is going to push to get his way when it comes to what he wants to see on his computer and that you can give in to him. He actually got you to use Pat's password and change the filter, and then you saw some of the crud on My Space.

I did not want Pat to give you the password because I believe that you are too impressionable by Ronnie when he wants to get his way. Pat told me that you changed the filter back to where it was before, so Ronnie cannot access photos and My Space on the web and I am happy that you made the right decision there. But it bugs me that you did not talk to me about this tonight, because I have a huge stake in what Federal laws Ronnie may have broken in the past.

I wanted Pat or myself to have the password to his filter, so that the filter could not be changed by you or him, thus it would stay in place and he would not be able to download anything objectionable. Pat agreed to keep the password to himself. I do not apologize for any of this or the rest of what I have to say in this email to you because too much is at stake. I also wanted to send a copy of this to a third party, showing that I have communicated to you clearly on this issue in case I am forced to take action to protect my reputation. I will not play games here, Terry, because there is too much at stake for me. I have sent Dr. Paine a copy of this email.

I want the filter password changed to something that neither you nor Ronnie knows. This point is non-negotiable. Pat can be the only one who knows the password if you do not want me involved, but after the way Pat was treated tonight (he does not want to be in the middle of it), I doubt he will agree to do it again. I also want R to give you his main computer password, so that together we can look at what he is doing at a time when he is not around. If you cannot agree to these conditions, I will turn off the DSL at 5PM and it will stay off until he is gone the next day to school.

It is as simple as that. I will not give in on this one T. If he wants to live a certain way, he is 18 and he is free to do so, but not in this home.

So, I hope you will read this email carefully and that you will agree with me that under the circumstances, this is the best policy for now.

With love and sincerity,

Mitch"

Well, just after she read the email at home, the water works and the shouting came out and once again she was leaving me and going back to AZ. 45 minutes later she had calmed down, but only after I said: "If you abandon me, I will sue you for divorce and I will own 50% of your paycheck and 50% of your retirement for the rest of your life." Well that shocked the crap out of her I think. Needless to say, this has not been a romantic weekend.

10/14/06

Well the torture continues. She has made no attempt to fill my previous requests about Ronnie's computer, so I ignore R as much as possible and the same with her until it just becomes rude. We have not had sex since a week before that last entry – about 8 weeks. Heck with her. Just keep going to work and bringing in the benefits. If I am not here, check my girlfriend's house. Man I need a girlfriend!

10/24/06

Eleven weeks since we had sex. Does she care? Evidently she does not – she is happy as a lark with her crossword puzzles and inane talk about work and people on her vanpool. What a load of bull crap. I hope to be able to introduce her as "my companion" soon. Wonder how that will go over....maybe..."Honey, I'm your wife" to which I will reply "Honey you are no wife....wives are interested in meeting their husbands needs. You are interested in not being changed."

At times I get angry and even teary and wistful when I think about what kind of a marriage we could have. But then I remember....no one changes Terry. She even said to me during our last fight "Don't try to change me." I doubt I could if I tried. So keep going to work, keep helping with the mortgage, Terry-I'm looking for a girlfriend (I wish).

Her kid came home with another F...and she wants me to put him through college? It will NEVER happen. He now has to go to night school, in addition to regular school just to graduate in June. Here is my prediction: she will try to get R admitted to Pasadena City College next summer. I will, of course, refuse to pay for it. She will then pack up with him and drive away. I had better find a divorce attorney now, I guess.

10/26/06

No change. She remarked tonight that I must be going through menopause, (probably because I have not asked for sex in months???) I said, "No, Terry, my sex drive is still as strong as ever." This had the singular effect of icing over the rest of the walk. Stony silence for the remaining 30 minutes. Before I unlocked the front door to get back in the house, I quipped, "Well, I can see that my comment pissed you off, so are we going to have another frosty night? She moaned, "Why would you say something so mean?" I said, "You know T, I am not going to pick a fight with you. You just seem to want to fight all the time." I continued with, "I will say one thing however, go upstairs and read 1Cor 7:5. Then come down and write a letter to Pastor and explain why this verse does not relate to you."

Basically the night was chilly after all. She did come back downstairs and watched TV with me. She leaned over on me and I wondered what it meant for her to do that. I asked why and she said, "Just cause I want to be close to you." We'll see....

10/30/06

No change, no sex. Sunday night I got out my Greek Bible and turned it to 1Cor 7:5. I circled the word "deprive" in the Greek. I looked up its meaning in the Concordance – "defraud" and I wrote defraud next to it and left it open on the counter near my coffee pot. Last night, she came home and asked to speak with me. I said OK. She sat next to me and said that she had read the Scripture I had left on the counter from my Greek Bible and that she was not trying to defraud me of sex. I let her talk for awhile and she said she was sorry, that she was trying to work through things I had said and trying not to withhold affection from me. She said she really wanted me to be patient as she worked through this and that she would be with me again soon. I thanked her for talking to me. I told her that the passage says, "come together again so that Satan will not tempt you," I told her that Satan was not tempting me with lust, but with bitterness and hatred towards her. I told her that if you stop watering a plant, it will die and at some point you would not be able to resuscitate it. Why the heck do I keep trying to fix this dead relationship??

11/22/06

Well, things are once again worse. Last night Ronnie showed up at the door after sunset with some (big) kid I have never met before. Before I knew it, he and his friend were running up the stairs to his bedroom. T had told him when she answered the door it was OK for his friend to come in and did not even *look* at me to see if I was OK with it – and I was sitting right there as if I was a piece of furniture or something… I just could not believe it! I told her we do not do that – we don't just throw the door open to anyone her kid shows up with and the caca hit the fan. She cried and yelled and shouted that "I need to be away from you Mitch…. everything I do, is wrong…I am ruining your life and am going insane because all I do, all I say all I think about is how I always do everything wrong….you just want to manipulate me and keep me under your thumb…I have to leave and set you free and be separated from you because I am going insane….I cannot please you in anything I do….One of these days I am going to kill 12 people in the van because of it" (the implication is that she would drive off the road with the company van she drives and it would be my fault)…she also said that she has been begging me to go to counseling (yeah right!!)….and so forth. The gist of it is that I am not pleased by anything she does or says or fails to do or say, and so she wants to run away. I reminded here that in a relationship, people talk to each other, they work through problems *together* and they develop a set of guidelines to live by *together*…that she spends night after night on the couch doing her crossword book and IGNORING me. I reminded her that she had once told me "I have never had a good relationship with a man", and that she still did not…I asked her why she never read the books on intimacy I bought her, why she NEVER wears the hundreds of dollars in jewelry I bought her ("because its too fancy for what I wear" – what does *that* mean?)…I told her she has never loved me and she would never love me because she did not know how to have *a relationship*. She said she would never stop feeling that I manipulate her and keep her down and that she would never change – that things would never get better between us. I said, "Can I ask you one question?" "When Ronnie stood at the door and asked if this stranger could come in, did you even think that I might have an opinion about it?" She said, "I assumed that you would not care… and there, do you feel better now? I was WRONG again!!!!" Followed by more tears and shouting and that she had to leave and we had to separate because she is ruining my life and killing herself.

I walked out and went for a walk. She was upstairs when I got back at 7:30PM and that was it for the night. I went into my room, mixed a martini and stayed in there for the rest of the night.

1/25/07

She let R ride a bus to Vegas over the holidays to stay with friends (who??) Now he wants to quit school and move to Vegas. Of course she won't talk to me about it. R rarely speaks to me anymore. He comes home from school, goes to the bathroom and is back out the door from 3:15 to about 9:30 PM. Then he plays Nintendo or watches R rated movies in his room. His room is a nuclear waste dump. I only found out about the Vegas thing because I read one of her printed emails to her friend Eddie in AZ. Eddie (God bless her) told T what she needed to hear – that R is a hooligan and that she is going to ruin his life if she does not get him under control, but I am sure R will bail soon because nothing has changed. He is probably failing in everything in school again and has to start night school soon. That will be Mondays and Tuesdays from 3PM-9PM, oh joy. Grades come out next week – what fun awaits us.

1/27/07

Any time I get into an argument with her, she descends into "I need a divorce, I am losing my mind, etc., etc." So I do my best to not engage her any more. Sometimes I cook, sometimes I don't. Sometimes I shop, sometimes I don't. I mostly just do it for me since I know she never would. She can abandon me, I don't give a crap. I will get 50% since this is a community property state.

I haven't really spoken to her in days. She still calls me "honey" from time to time. Whatever. Monday I was gone all afternoon and evening and finally came back with groceries at about 8:15PM. She was already upstairs for the night. The last 2 nights she has stayed down on the couch, but I get up frequently and find things to do.

1/29/07 Sunday night.

R has been away 3 nights. I guess he thinks that bothers me or something. She kept trying to talk to me tonight...I kept ignoring her. She realized I was packing for a 3-day trip to San Diego and she asked if I would call her daily. I said, "I'll try". Like that is going to happen. There is barely any food in the house. Her life is about to get worse.

Thursday, Febuary 1.

What a crap head I am. The long and the short of my ongoing attempt to change Terry and have a real marriage have once again resulted in a crash: She offered to take a loan out against her retirement and to pay down all the debt, including my tuition AND she said I could sell the house and keep ALL the proceeds – wow, I would be a fool to not take her up on this....huh?

Like an idiot, I believed once again that I can change Terry. *No one changes Terry.* She is an island unto herself. Any attempt I make with her is met with a vicious attack in reply. She is *going to walk away* and destroy my lifestyle. She is so willing to walk that she has agreed to PAY ALL OUR DEBTS and to *give me the house proceeds* and a legal separation!! Tonight I begged like a school child and prostrated myself. I am not even sure I talked her out of it. She did agree to go to godly men to discuss this but she said, "They will all know the truth about you Mitch." WHATEVER,

I have nothing to hide. My conscience is clear. I have laid it all down for this psycho narcissist....it is all here in this depressing book for the world to see.

WHEN WILL I LEARN? DUDE – you lost this battle 4 years ago. She owns you. If you want to keep your lifestyle – accept her kind of marriage – you are her butt slave and nothing you desire is of consequence to her. Make her dinners, watch *only* the TV she wants to watch. *Be silent* and be content or tomorrow you life changes dramatically.

I even told her that her offer was enticing – who would not want *all* $250,000 proceeds from the house? Am I crazy not to take it and move on? I would have *no debt* and $250k in cash.... Well in one last foolish desperate act, I am going to try to hold things together, for as long as I can. Then if she really wants to leave, I will accept her offer and more.

My counter offer if need be:

-We do this in the presence of church leaders

-All debt (including Honda and all credit cards, Sallie Mae) paid by her retirement.

-I get 100% proceeds from the house and we do not sell until I am ready to sell, period. In fact I really want to refinance under her credit before she leaves so I can afford to live here. But this house is really a tomb – am I sure I want to still live here after this? Live with the ghost of this so-called union?

-She can legally separate and write a notarized letter making me look like the biggest servant of all time. NO DIVORCE.

-She must be willing to appear before religious leaders and personnel and make it clear this is her idea and not mine, AND that I was a model husband, etc., etc.

-She goes away with no claim on me whatsoever.

-She alone pays off her retirement loan.

-She never contests the decision on the sale of the house.

Saturday, 2/3

Well it has been a couple of frosty days. Yesterday I did talk her into going to the Getty Museum with me for a Science Society function. She seemed to enjoy herself. I took her to a famous steak place afterwards near LAX and she enjoyed a top sirloin. I dropped $125. She had the leftovers for dinner tonight. She never thanked me today for the amazing artichoke/sun-dried tomato pasta with garlic chicken I prepared yesterday. She was up in her room most of the day...the phone was ringing a lot, so I was getting paranoid, thinking she was arranging for someone to come and get her and take her away. Well that didn't happen. She actually came down and fixed me a salad while I grilled some fish. We ate in silence on the couch while she guffawed and swooned over 'Air Bud'. I was doing laundry while I was eating, so I had lots of excuses to get up and get away from the boredom. At about 7, and since there was nothing good on TV, I suggested we order a pay per view. She went through the whole list while I snoozed for 40 minutes on the couch in boredom. She gave up. Finally I picked 'The Devil Wears Prada', so we watched that. At the end I made some stupid comment about how perfect Meryl Streep was for the role. She said, "Well, I guess I better go to bed; tomorrow is church" – got up and walked upstairs.

2/4/07

She is convinced I have access to her computer and actually I do. I have read all her backstabbing emails to her family and have printed off most of them. She is so manipulative – people can't see it. I emailed her the following after she left me a note complaining :

Dear T, I know it is hard for you to look at personal things at work, and I *do not* want to disturb you in any way, but I did get your note. Thank you for writing me the note. Terry, I do not have "access to whatever is on your computer" as you say, I would not even know where to begin first of all, and my life is too short with everything I have to concentrate on with work, school, research, Board activities, etc., etc., etc. It just wears me out at the thought of it. (I know-I lied through my teeth). So, no, I have read nothing on your computer. Yes, we are agreed that if this cannot work, we should proceed with separating. As I said, the terms would have to be negotiated a bit from what you suggest. I have accepted all this to the core of my being, and am resigned to whatever may happen. You are wondering if things won't just become too much for me if I truly stop trying to change you. You are fearful that I am too old to change and that we will just be back where we were. Here is my reply: I accept you as you are. I will no longer try to change you. I accept our marriage as it is. I will no longer try to change it. When I lost Judy and still had Patrick and Jay at home with me in 2001, I was deeply hurt and wounded. I cried for weeks, but I had to accept the reality of the way things were and I had to face the future in order for my boys to turn out OK and not hate their mother or God. I resolved to be their friend through it all, and today, they respect me and they have no bitterness. I have done this before and I will do it again, you can count on that. However, if at any time you believe that you cannot stay with me, you are free to go, of course, with a bit of negotiation on the terms. I hope that helps you today. I want nothing but the best for you – I hope you can believe that. Mitch

P.S. T, also PLEASE do not think I am comparing you to anybody-most of all what Judy was for me for 23 years before she walked out. PLEASE do not think that. I am only sharing with you how I was able to change and be a certain person for the people in my life-that is all, OK? I accept you the way you are. (Boy what a great liar I am).

Wednesday Feb 7, 2007

She has not called me from the vanpool for weeks. She just comes in the house without any help or contact with me. We have spoken little over the last 3 days. She basically says "Hi" and then goes upstairs, then comes down to eat and sit on the couch for about an hour. Then she goes upstairs. The last 2 nights she actually thanked me for dinner and said good night. Tonight she did neither. I think her real self is finally coming out. The faux façade of "really caring" has been stripped away. I have not made an effort to reach out to her other than to offer her help with dinner. Tonight she did make my fruit, so I probably should not complain. But she is definitely punishing me. I wonder how long this will go on.

Sunday 2/11/07

Thursday night "Survivor" was on. I made an effort to come out of my room a few times while she was on the couch and reached out to her. I touched her and asked how she was doing. She did not respond. Then I came out after turning off my room light and sat on the couch about 5 minutes before "Survivor". Within less than a minute, she said "I am falling asleep here I have to go to bed", got up and walked up the stairs. She was ¾ of the way up when I meekly said "good night" and she responded in kind from the stairwell. That was at 8PM. 50 minutes later, I could see the lights on in her room. At this point I was convinced that she was simply now lying to me each night, so I walked into her room. She was lying under the covers, on her side facing the TV. I walked between her and the TV and she jumped and said "Uhhh, I guess I fell asleep…" I started to walk away but then (stupidly) I went back and said, "So now you are just lying to me…". She asked several times, "What does that mean?" but I just said, "Nothing, forget it." Friday night she came home in tears, well at least she was in tears when she walked into my room, which was closed up. She had just seen R's new report card with a fat, fresh F in Economics (which means now he definitely will not graduate). She was crying and started babbling about how she didn't understand why I had said she was lying, etc. I said, "Terry, all I know is what you tell me and how you behave. You told me you were falling asleep and that you had to go to bed. Then you went upstairs and watched TV for an hour, what am I supposed to think?" That sort of cemented the evening. I made her a smashing pan of stir-fried shrimp with broccoli in teriyaki sauce. She did say it was very good, but we sort of went our separate ways after that.

Saturday I drank coffee with her on the couch, and then I left for most of the day. I met with several different people and got home before 5pm. I cooked my own dinner (she had already eaten). We watched TV until about 7PM, and then, you guessed it, "I have to go upstairs". Crud, woman, it is only 7PM and you are already dumping me for the night? This had gone on all week. Therefore, today, after church and lunch and our Bible-study group, I went straight into my room, closed the door and spent the afternoon and evening working. She was up and down the stairs and watching TV, but my door stayed closed. At 6:15PM, she came in and "I have to go upstairs". No goodnight – nothing. I think I just grunted or something. Later at about 7:30, I went up and knocked on her door. I said, "I am going to take a chance here and wish you a tender goodnight." I hugged her and kissed her neck. I said, "No matter what happens, I will still love you," and weeping, she said she loved me too. I said, "It is hard not to be close to you." To which she replied something like, "I am working through this and I need more time, blah, blah." Bottom line is she doesn't act like she is going to run away -at least not tonight. So I sucked up real good on that one. What an ass I am.

Saturday 2/17/07

It has been an uneventful week, mostly because I have not interacted with her. Ronnie continues to ignore me and walk right past me into and out of the house. I have mostly worked in my room whenever they are home, doing rocks. I have made $2000 this week alone. I should have done this years ago. Who knows how fat my savings account would be now? Yesterday, I drove to Ventura early and had breakfast with Annie, my old friend from PSU. She said T does not want to put her issues down specifically because then she would lose control (I would have something to correct which would leave her alone needing to correct things.) By keeping things nebulous and me in the dark, she is in control. Whatever. I know she spent about 30 minutes on her phone with Eddie last Monday. She gave me a card for Valentines Day-I gave her a bar of chocolate. Last night she ate about half of it.

2/22/07 TONIGHT WAS HORRIBLE!

It was pouring rain when T called me from the van, but I was somewhat happy that she did – she hasn't called me from the van in over 4 weeks, so this means she is not going to run away right now anyway. I asked her to beep when she drove by so I could come help her in. I got my rain gear on and went out to the road, and she never beeped, but I said it was OK and I carried her stuff in the rain. I had turned on the furnace to warm up the house a bit for her, and then I warmed up the food I had cooked for her while she went upstairs and changed. A long distance phone company bill just came in the mail and I opened it just as she was coming back down. She went into the kitchen to fix a plate of the delicious shrimp and broccoli that I slaved making for her.

I noted that there were about 20 long distance calls to Las Vegas on the bill, one even for 23 minutes, which came as a total shock to me. I quietly and meekly went into the kitchen and asked her if Ronnie had made all these calls. She seemed a bit stunned by it. I asked her if she had authorized him to call Las Vegas, and she would not say. She would only say, "I will talk to him about it." I quietly commented that I did not think it was fair for her to not tell me in advance that he was doing this and asked if she had allowed him to make all these long distance calls. She said that he would only call his girlfriend over there for a few seconds or so but I pointed to some very long calls.

She took the bill from me and said she wanted to look at it. I meekly and humbly said that it would be a lot different a response if I had done that to her and she went ballistic. She said that I do that all the time and made it all about me instead of about R. I took back the bill and said forget it, and to just please drop the whole thing because I did not want to fight. She put her food away and ran up to her room and closed the door. I put the bill out in my office and wrote a check to the phone company. Two minutes later she was down in my room demanding the bill. I calmly said to just forget it and I did not want to fight. I went out to the office but she just kept hounding me for the bill and crying and carrying on. I kept saying no and that I did not want to fight with her. I asked her why she wanted to fight me and she yelled and hollered that she was not fighting and there I go again trying to control her and beat her down! This went on for an hour and she said she could not do this anymore – that she was leaving – that she had seen a lawyer, etc, etc. She said it was going to be good for me because I would get the entire profit from the house, but I kept saying I only wanted her. She actually then said that I had married her for her money! I reminded her that I already had a good job at the university when we married, that I had no plans to give up that job, and could not have predicted that they were going to terminate me 3 months after we married. But she said "No, you have schemed and plotted the whole time, for five years just to get my money." I reminded her how many times I had told her she could quit her job and I would go straight into the "real" workforce. But she claimed I never said that! I have said it multiple times. She is so completely warped in her thinking that she believes that I married her for her puny salary. She had less that $25,000 in her retirement then and now, with my careful strategy the fund is over $75,000 in less than 2 years.

T cannot tolerate even the most benign criticism – especially about R. So I have to just shut up and let him get away with anything. Even racking up long distance bills to Las Vegas. I wonder when he will start stealing my credit cards? I am so sick of being a mousy milk toast. For 60 days I have kept my mouth shut about everything, and I probably should have just not said a word about the phone bill as well. But it is not enough for her. Walking across burning coals would not be enough for her. She doesn't even notice that I have become a complete milk-toast and that I don't offer advice or make suggestions or try to anticipate problems and deal with them early on. I say nothing about everything! She said she has seen no changes in me! But R is out of control -he knows now that he can rack up large phone bills and nothing will happen to him. If I even look at him wrong she starts ranting about a separation. Maybe I should just send her packing and move away myself.

He came home at 8:30 and went into her room to talk to her. I heard them arguing. Next thing I know he is back on the phone talking to Las Vegas girl. I am going insane!

Email I sent her the next day:

"T, I apologize for bringing up the phone bill last night. I had no right to be upset about it. I will remain silent about R's calls to Las Vegas."

I finally put the vacuum cleaner away after leaving it in the hallway for 10 days. No one caught the hint. The floor was finally too filthy even for me, so I vacuumed.

3/10/07

What the heck is the point of further writing? She is only happy if I ignore every wasted plate of food, every burning lamp – every spill on the floor) oh yeah, and whatever crap R may pull. I dutifully throw away, turn off and clean my way into her happiness. And her happiness includes no physical contact or banter to speak of. The last time we were in bed together was 69 days ago. The crossword puzzle book is almost exhausted and it is almost time for another one. She was watching a Billy Graham crusade on TV while I was working on the taxes tonight at the kitchen table. He mentioned that "God designed sex for marriage." I laughed and said, "If you want to eliminate sex from your life – get married." I think she ignored me. WHATEVER. She has gotten so fat from not walking for the last10 weeks that I have no desire for her anymore – only resentment.

3/20/07

79 days and no intimacy. She is an idiot – I must be too. I did marry her for her money I guess – that is the only thing that makes any sense to me now. I really never loved her I guess – I was only looking for someone to support me. What the crap kind of a person am I? Did I ever really love her and want to give to her and make her feel special? God only knows inside my personal hell. Who can remember and know anything in this torture chamber?

I'm curious about R and his Las Vegas girl, so I decided to buy a recording device. I can record his calls to her now without him knowing – should keep me entertained, God knows she does not; sitting with her crossword puzzles every night. She comes unglued every time someone on the van emails a bad report about her. What the heck? Who cares what people think about you as long as you are doing your job correctly? She comes home hating the world.

3/23/07 Friday

Things have taken an ugly turn here with R. I now genuinely fear for my safety; so much so that I went to the police this morning and met with two officers and disclosed the things that have come to light over the last several days. Last night I think I slept 2 hours and had to lock my bedroom doors in order to feel safe enough to sleep. I have been so rattled that I have not been able to concentrate on much of anything at all.

The police said that I might want to consider having R evicted under a temporary restraining order, but that I would have to go to court to do it.

He is becoming uglier and uglier towards us and is now physically challenging me in some ways – standing in my way – acting in a threatening manner towards me, being openly insolent, etc. His deportment towards T is deplorable. I bet she fears him too. He has been lifting weights for months and is physically intimidating.

He gets on the phone every night to Las Vegas to talk to this girl there and the things I have heard through the walls and door of his room were alarming to me. Apparently this girl is in a drug-dealing family where her mother died (I am not sure how but it seems violently) and where the girl was attacked in a knife fight during which time her friend Justin was knifed to death! She has the scars to prove it. It is also apparent that if her dad does not come through on drug deals she is required to do things to compensate (that she would not disclose on the phone, but I suspect it is sex for drugs), so she is suicidal about it all and says she thinks about killing herself daily.

I decided to start the recorder on the line the other night and was shocked at what I recorded. What follows is a truncated transcript of the exact words I have on tape. *I warn you that some of this is shocking and graphic.* YOU HAVE BEEN WARNED.

I had come home late on Wed PM after the Home Owners Association Meeting, and after T had gone to bed. The porch light was off and both outer doors were locked requiring the use of two different keys and I was fumbling a bit in the dark, but got in fine and went into my room. I noted that R was on the phone already so I turned on the recorder. I was in the kitchen and T showed up looking sleepy and asked me if I had been knocking on the door, and I said no I had fumbled a bit in the dark but got in OK. I said she should go back to bed. I did not wake her or yell or anything – in fact I was surprised to see her come downstairs, as I was trying to be very quiet.

Here now is the transcript from the recorded conversation:

He: "Mitch's on the phone now...hold on a second. I think I hear Mitch on the phone – this phone... Oh, I hate him."

127

In response to her question about how was your day, something about "I was in fashion but I was on the computer so I got in trouble, so I was laughing" …. "I think Mitch woke up my mom… I think Mitch woke up my mom!"

She "Why?"
He: "hold on a second"
After a few moments…."Oh my God, " (said very slowly)
She: "what?"
He: "I swear to you I am going to beat the shit out of that guy before I leave"
She: "what?"
He: "He woke up my mom to yell because the porch light wasn't on."
She: "Are you shitting me?"
He: "and he couldn't open the door"
She: "are you shitting me?"
He: "No I'm not, I swear – beat the crap out of this guy"
She "No let me do it!"
He: "why?"
She: "cause I want to"
He: "I want to too! Like really bad"
She: "Oh, I can't stand him."
He: "Me either"
She: "What is his deal?"
He: "I don't know"
She: "Why is he such an asshole?" (He laughs)
He: "I don't know, he always complains about his past and stuff, it's like, it's bull crap – it's a long time ago"
She: "that's why he's an asshole because of his past?
He: "no – he's also a scientist, and like, I don't know. He just makes up so much excuses. He's like 12 in his own world." He yawns.
Later on…
He: "She's dumb. "
He: "my knee hurts, that lady – she doesn't know how to drive. I was so mad at her. I think I scared her." (who, Danny's Mom? Kyle's Mom?)

He knows he cannot use his computer to go online but he has figured out how to use his Sony hand-held PSP to do so, here he is complaining into the phone about his PSP and draws me into the conversation:

He: "C'mon PSP. Access point was not detected, my ass. Damn you little faggot – Oh! I'm gonna kick his ass. Now he disconnected my wireless router" (meaning me and *my* wireless router).

He: "Fuckin knee"

He: "Fuckin shoulder"

She: "My whole reputation is ruined because of one pathetic little kid"

He: "who?"

She: "Luke"

He: "I swear to God I'm going to kill that kid, I swear"..."does Patrice know anything?"

She: "no and she never will"

He: "You need to get out of that school. I can't be here anymore, I need to be out there now."

I know he walks around with a knife and has been in fights at school. As I say he is acting worse towards me all the time and I don't want to end up in an altercation – what do I do???

The school called last night and set a mandatory Saturday meeting with R and T to discuss his academic standing. I know that he will not graduate. I later asked T what she was going to do if he did not graduate. After a long pause she said, "I do not know."

I am trying not to overreact here but when I explained all this to the police they said I would be wise to do something. It seems like a ticking time bomb to me.

Saturday 3/24/07

Ronnie is gone. She made him move out last night and took away his keys. When he came home at 3PM yesterday, I locked him out. I came to the other side of the locked security door and told him he could come in when his mom came home. He stood at the door shouting obscenities. It upset me so much; I had to lock every window and door in he house. It is 6AM Saturday, it is 63 degrees in my room with the fan on high, and I have been sweating all night – that is how stressful this has been for me.

As I thought, he twisted things to his advantage with her on the phone before she pulled up in the van last night. He plays her like a fiddle on fire. She was extremely cold and hostile towards me. When we got in the house she demanded to know why I had treated him so dastardly, I gently explained that things were so serious I had met with the police and filed an incident report. She became enraged and demanded to know if I was looking up his "record" her "record", (apparently she has one), his emails, her emails. I denied it all because she always tries to turn this into an "I hate R" routine.

I explained to her that things were serious, that the police knew about it and that things were going to change and that I fully hoped that we could work this out as a family decently and in order and patiently without involving the authorities. For an hour she pressed me relentlessly to demand what he had done. Finally I told her he had threatened my life. I told her had heard him through the wall and door of his room shouting obscenities and death threats on the phone to his friends and the LV girl. I told her I had to be safe in this house and that I was not afraid of him but I was afraid of what might happen if I had to defend myself. I told her I would wait until after the school meeting but that soon something had to be done.

Amazingly, after that she (while crying heavily), did the right thing! I was dumbfounded, but for the first time in 2 days my heart stopped pounding in my chest. She made arrangements for him to live with the people he has hung out with for 2 years...

Today at noon he will come over to remove most of his things. Then at 1PM they have an appointment at the school to determine his fate. T talked to me openly last night – she knew all about the drugs, the sex for drugs, the stabbings, murders and rapes associated with this girl (yet she was encouraging him to go and have a relationship with her!) T was even emailing the girl herself! I printed off some of their emails and put them

131

in my stack. I told her we should be telling R he was heading into hell and that he was going to lose his life, not encourage him to go there. This morning I found that she had gotten into my closet during the night and drank about ½ of the cooking wine I had stored there. Guess my fatherly advice did some good, huh?

Later that day....3/24/07

Well the school told R and T today that he is failing in 2 other courses and may not graduate if he does not start doing the work and pronto. Amazingly he is doing well in the night school class, but mostly because they make him sit there and complete a self-study work text as they watch over his shoulder. They also said he has enough absences already to be expelled for that reason alone. If he does not stop missing school they will flunk him out. The option of summer school is still open to him, but at this point, who knows? He came and went several times today "getting stuff" and stormed in and out each time. T has had diarrhea and stomach pains since last night. She did spend time with me today however and after a nap, we went out and had a nice Chinese dinner and then we shopped for a desk calendar for her, so I am just trying to support her and encourage her. I don't speak, I mostly just asked her how I can do things for her and help her. So I don't think she is going to pack up and leave. However R is still just across the street, basically, so who knows how this saga will end.

5/14/07

Same old crap. She had been ignoring me pretty much right up to our anniversary. In fact, she actually marked the wrong date on the calendar! I corrected it with a smiley face so she would not say, "You think I am dumb, stupid, I always do things wrong," etc. etc., etc.

I only got intimacy from her twice in the six weeks leading up to the anniversary, so I bought her a card and some chocolate. She bought me a DVD and was angry to not get a gift. So like a moron I broke down and bought her some crystal earrings.

In 20 weeks since January 1, she has graciously allowed me to have her 8 times. That's once every 2 weeks. What a loving wife.

Last weekend I took her to a nice Italian lunch. Yesterday I took her to a $75 lunch again, Italian, for Mother's day. She hasn't offered to buy me any lunches lately with her bonus money (How much was it? She never told me), but she did manage to spend $170 on a plane ticket for R to go see his freakish girlfriend in Vegas. I am just mystified as to why she fosters that sick relationship between her idiot son and that druggie groupie in Vegas – even after she admitted that she knew everything about what was going on there.

R is probably flunking out of school because she has to use the car tomorrow to once again, go see the counselor at 2PM with him. So it goes. I also looked at some papers in her purse. She actually wrote last year that she had decided not to be intimate with me because of the jokes I made about sex, women, death, etc. Really, practically any joke I make (which are incredibly not offensive in the least – believe me) she bristles at. And I made, what….3 jokes all last year? She finds them coarse and objectionable. Well, it beats listening to the crickets while she sits on the couch and does her crossword puzzles. I should just stay in my room and type. I thought about planning some weekend vacations with her, and even talked with her about it at lunch 2 weekends ago, but why? Might as well just plan to go off by myself. Least the company will be nicer (me, myself and I.)

She really does not want to be with me. I think she is only staying because I told her I would sue her for divorce and take half of her retirement.

5/17/07

Well a notice came yesterday that Ronnie's graduation is on hold. Course, she would not tell me that, and when I asked about the meeting they had with the counselor, I got the usual silence. I called the school to ask, and he has 2 F's and a D-. He basically has 3 weeks to bring them all above a D or he does not graduate. So it goes.

5/24/07

Earlier this week she told me she was terrified of me and was even afraid to tell me that she was afraid! Even though I have never laid a hand on this woman, she is terrified of me. I have been a humble floor-sucking butler to her over the last 5 years and particularly the last 18 months. She also said she felt I was caging her in and choking her life. I do not for the life of me know how I am doing that. Yesterday I had to hit the road so I called her from the car, so she would know I was on the freeways in case I died in a fiery wreck and all. I only got her voicemail, so I left a nice encouraging message. So I get home safely and I call her to tell her I am home safe. Once again the voicemail picked up. Tonight I ask her if I did anything this week to cage her in or frighten her. She said, "Yeah – you kept calling me yesterday, making me feel like I was under your thumb"... Will somebody please explain to me how this makes somebody feel like they are under my thumb???? Dear God help me.

I called my friend and former co-worker from the university, Dr. Annie and explained what had been going on of late. She was very quiet and after a long pause, she asked, "Mitch, why are you still with this woman??" I had no answer. I have no idea why I am still here. My life could be so peaceful and stress-free if I were to just pick up and leave. There is nothing for me here and I am so tired of beating my head against this steel wall called Terry. Can God fix this? Does He even care? I am thinking He does not. I should just leave. Will He punish me if I do?

I took about two hours to write out a list of things that could be terrifying her. I wrote on the top of the sheet, "Mitch terrifies Terry when he...." And then I listed every single behavior that I do around here, including all the ways I cook and clean and straighten up and shop and bill pay and plan for her and our household. I listed everything – all the ways I would love to be intimate with her (including kissing, hand holding, cuddling, having sex – but nothing bizarre or out of the ordinary) – everything I could possibly think of that I say, do and accomplish around her. I then gave her the list when she came home and asked her to circle the things that terrify her so that I could work on my behavior. I absolutely do not want to terrify anyone – least of all the woman that I want to love and be happy with! She started crying and said, "Oh Mitch – the list is so endless I could never come up with a complete list of all the ways you terrify me." What does THAT mean? I spoke to my friend Annie again and she said, "Terry doesn't want this conflict to be resolved. She wants to keep things nebulous and undefined because that is how she controls you." Man oh man, I am so utterly stupid.

5/30/07

We were watching a program about Japanese folks walking barefoot in the snow. I said, "Wouldn't it be cool to go to a snowy place next year and walk barefoot in the snow just to see what it is like?" Silly me. Here is what I got back, "Oh yeah, so then I could get frostbite and have the doctors amputate my toes and then my feet and my life would be over, blah, blah, blah." I said, "You aren't going to get frostbite Terry for just walking barefoot in the snow for a few minutes." She counters with "I'm already getting frostbite at 50 degrees from sitting in this house." It was 76. I waited for a minute and then I said "I hope God punishes you someday for the way you treat me." Well the tears started flowing and the cries for, "It will never be different, I will always screw up with you – it is always the same, etc., etc." She started to make the run for her bedroom….I gently asked her to not let the sun go down on her anger, but to work it out with me…she said no it takes too long and I have to get up early and I this and I that….more tears and the pulling away – no goodnight…nothing…she just walked up the stairs and closed her door. That was at 8:28PM.

6/10/07

The more things change the more they stay the same….We spent last Wednesday through Sunday in Phoenix. I was at the Research Board meeting there, and she pretty much spent all day Thursday and most of Saturday with family and friends. But I was committed to giving her a carefree time away with her loved ones, so I happily wished her fun and put no restrictions on her whatsoever. I did try to do fun things with her while she was not already committed to be with her friends and family, but she resisted me at every turn. No, she would not go to Cork and Cleaver with me on Wednesday night because it was "too far away," (3 miles??), so we ended up at a crappy restaurant eating cold food. No, she would not go to the Botanical Garden with me on Thursday morning "I'm too tired" (even though we were married there over five years ago and have not been back since.) Her friend did not get to our hotel to pick her up until almost noon on Thursday, so we could have gone from 7:30 to 11AM in the cool of the day. It would have been fun. No, we could not have sex, even though it has been one time in the last 21 days since we had sex. (Nevertheless, I begged and begged her and finally got my way. How romantic.) No, she would not show off the beautiful 3-carat garnet birthstone ring that I gave her (when I purposely stopped under a Palo Verde tree – her favorite tree) and we got out of the car at the AZ border on the way to Phoenix from California. Course she cried and hugged me then, but no, why show it off to the family that hates me? No, we cannot have a nice lunch in Phoenix on Sunday before we have to drive back home across 400 miles of desert (once again I coerced her and she just glared at me mostly during my lunch.) No, we can't spend any time together on Monday even though she was off because she has to cut off all her hair again and take R to the doctor. So it goes.

I did make sure that I performed one task I had promised myself I would do at her church in Phoenix, over that weekend however. Remembering the wedding ceremony video that I had at home and the different vows that her

Pastor Paul had used on her versus the ones he used on me, I pulled Paul aside after his sleepy little church service and asked him, "Pastor, why did you have Terry recite 'Love, honor and *obey*' when you had me first recite, 'Love, honor and cherish'?" He thought for a second and said, "Well that was just a traditional set of marriage vows I used – it didn't mean anything in particular."

Uh, huh. Yeah right. I think I figured it out now....Pastor Paul *really did know* Terry from the start – he knows her as the manipulative conniving witch that I now know she is. He was looking to get rid of her from his church. That is the only logical explanation! That is why he never got involved when I cried out to him for help over and over – he didn't want to fix her – maybe he had tried and failed miserably – much like I had. Maybe he wanted her gone for good.

In fact, one story about Terry that they kept repeating to me at North City Baptist Church before we were married (and I guess they thought it was endearing and all...) was that the church had to keep several sets of her keys distributed among several members because she was constantly losing her keys. I am now confident that this is a positive, "funny" spin on the antics of an out of control woman whose church was probably sick of her...She was probably causing all kinds of dissention there...so when Mitch, the sucker comes along – Paul sees a good thing. He sees Mitch as someone who can lift a big problem off his hands, so he tells me, "Mitch – in this woman there is no guile." He knows that if he, her Pastor, gives her the Good Housekeeping Seal of approval, there is a greater likelihood that stupid Mitch will take her off his hands...Boy did I get played. I got stuck with his rebellious progeny and her pathological lying son and he got some peace at North City Baptist Church.

It really makes sense to me now. Paul *knew* that she is a narcissist. He knew her kid is a rebellious punk who had to be drugged up with *Ritalin* just to function in church and at school and at home. He knew if he could pull it off I would move his problem church member and her bratty son far away from him and his sweet, sleepy gig. I am now sure that is why he never answered my emails and phone calls – and why he was so cold to me when he did speak with me. He had successfully rid himself of two sickos and didn't want them coming back to him. Well guess what Paul? I am convinced that these two sickos will be back in your sleepy little fold before too long. Better you than me. Haha – you enjoy having them back, OK?

Sunday night after we got back was a disaster. I was flipping channels after we got home and knowing how much she loves Cary Grant movies,

I asked her if she knew the one that was about to play on TNT with Cary Grant and Ida Lupino. She says, "No!!" and frantically starts looking for a tape. I found her a tape and started taping it. For some reason, she was spouting off about something she wanted and I said, "Well the whole weekend was about Terry, wasn't it?" It was stupid of me, I know.

She came unglued…started crying heavily. I said I was sorry and "Let's please just enjoy the movie." I tried to placate her and she seemed ok. The movie was about Cary and Ida divorcing, so I went into the kitchen. Next thing I know she is hollering and crying about how she cannot watch such a movie and she pounds up the stairs. I beg and plead with her to come back down and to work this out – let's not end our lovely weekend on this note and all. And she says, "No it is ALWAYS about me". I beg some more and she comes down. I gently tried to explain how I worked hard to give her a nice experience in Phoenix and again the waterworks started and the shouting. I went into my room and she locked herself upstairs in her room for the night. That was a 7:15PM.

Monday 6/11/07.

Today I stayed in my room all day. I locked my doors so she could not come in. When she came home from cutting off her hair and doing whatever with Ronnie, she went straight up to her room. About an hour went by and she never attempted to say anything to me. Then the phone rang and apparently it was, my ex-wife. Suddenly Terry was banging on my door and trying to get in. I didn't answer. She slipped a note under the door saying Judy was on the phone and I ignored it. She banged some more and called my name but I was silent. Then she slid a note saying Dan, my son would call me when he got off work. I text messaged Dan and found out there was a Father's Day BBQ for me. I waited ½ hr, and then I dressed and left the house. I purposely said nothing to her. I came back at 8PM, before her bedtime because I was feeling guilty but she stayed locked in her room ignoring me. So it goes.

Tuesday. She went to work as usual today. I spent the day on the freeways doing lab equipment work. She emailed me the following:

"M–

Just wanted to let you know that I will be home later tonight as I have errands to run with Ronnie.

T"

I emailed back and said "OK, LU" meaning Love You. I got no response. When I came home I made a very tasty dinner of garlic chicken.

She has always said she likes it. I stayed in my room, doors closed but not locked. At 7:30PM, she comes in the house and goes to her room. Then she comes down and bangs around in the kitchen. I can hear her making her lunch for tomorrow, then her dinner and fizzy water. Then she goes upstairs; I suppose to eat by herself. She never says boo to me. I went out to the kitchen at 9:15PM and saw a note from her on my coffeepot "M- Thank you for making this chicken. We have not had this for awhile. I am glad I have some for lunch too,-T." How lucky am I? Nice loving note, huh?

Wednesday 6/13/07.

I left at 3:30AM for my lab in San Diego. I left my cell phone on all day, but no call from her. When I came home, no note, nothing. She never called from the van to tell me she was on her way home, surprise, surprise. But she did drive in from the direction of where R is staying, so she may have been meeting with him. I left my door open by about a foot but she came in walked right past my door and went upstairs. Then she came down and served her dinner from the food I had on the counter for her. Still nothing. I opened my door up all the way and went out into my office–lights blazing. She acted as if I was not even here. After scanning some forms for Dr. Paine I sat at my computer in full view of the doorway. She walked out of the kitchen, one foot on the stairs and said over her shoulder, "Thank you for making dinner". I said, "You are welcome," and she went upstairs to eat. I closed my door in humiliation. She brought her dishes down after awhile and promptly went back upstairs. Am I supposed to move out or something?

I wrote a note and left it on the stairs…it said, "Can you please tell me what I am supposed to be doing? Are we completely ignoring each other now? Am I supposed to speak to you? Do I wait until you speak to me? Am I supposed to cook and pay bills and act like we are a happy "Christian" couple? If this is about who can outlast–you win. I am afraid to speak to you because I do not want to start a repeat of Sunday night.

Am I supposed to say I am sorry for saying that "The weekend was all about Terry"? Please tell me. Have you decided to leave me and this silence will just make it easier? Am I supposed to say I am sorry for not answering the door on Monday? I am afraid to speak to you! Please tell me."

She came downstairs and picked up the note at about 8PM and just then Ronnie called. She came to my door and knocked. I opened the door. She asked, "Is it OK if Ronnie comes over for a minute?" I said, "OK, whatever", she walked away and never came back down. I got no response from my note. I found the wine in my closet and started drinking. I had 7 glasses. For the first time in 29 ½ years as a Christian I was drunk. I went into the kitchen at about 8:30PM. I got on my hands and knees and scrubbed the kitchen floor, which was filthy. I was pretty upset and was talking loudly about how the floor had to be clean for the queen. I felt ashamed and stupid, so I went to bed.

Thursday

This morning a note was by my coffee pot. It said, "I cannot live with you any longer. I am in full fear and terror of you. I beg you not to hurt me. Please allow me a little time to arrange a place to stay. I will make it as soon as possible." I called her voice mail at 5:30 this morning and explained that I did not understand…what had I done??? I told her that her pulling away from me was killing me and that I was depressed. I begged her to reconsider. I told her I had resigned earlier this week as Small Group Leader at church and that I was going to Pastor for help. I have little hope that they can save this marriage. I emailed her and told her I was very sorry – that I would like to come and take her out to lunch so we could talk things over -she sent me this email:

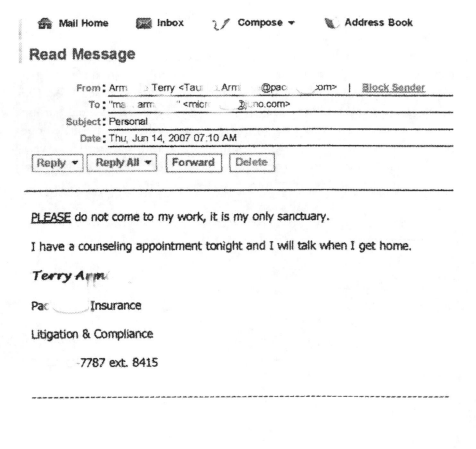

Read Message

From: Arm ⋯ Terry <Tau ⋯ .Arm ⋯ @pac ⋯ .om> | Block Sender
To: "ma ⋯ arm ⋯ " <micr ⋯ @juno.com>
Subject: Personal
Date: Thu, Jun 14, 2007 07:10 AM

[Reply ▾] [Reply All ▾] [Forward] [Delete]

PLEASE do not come to my work, it is my only sanctuary.

I have a counseling appointment tonight and I will talk when I get home.

Terry Arm

Pac ⋯ Insurance

Litigation & Compliance

7787 ext. 8415

Please note her comment that work was her "only sanctuary." Isn't church her sanctuary? Why has she never made her husband and her home her sanctuary? Of course, we never talk when she gets home—she walks right by me and IGNORES ME. She will never talk this out. She will never open up and share her hurts, frustrations, desires, goals, dreams, etc. with me. Terry won't do that because she loses control.

Friday 6/15/07.

I stayed in a motel last night. I cleaned out my bedroom at home, so that she could see that I was willing to honor her desire to be away from me. I left a note saying that ….well I can't quite remember exactly what the note said. I know I said I was ashamed for drinking, and that it was the first time in 29 ½ years that I had been drunk. I said it really doesn't take away the pain does it? I said, "I only ever wanted to take care of you and that I guess our meeting online and marrying wasn't a 'God-thing' after all." I know I said I would only come in on weekdays to get my things. I left it next to her note from the night before.

She had a counseling appointment after work and then she went to the grocery. She never called my cell phone. Finally at 7:45 I called and asked if she could talk. She was really upset—even shouted at me. It was not a pleasant call. I asked her if she had diverted her check because I had to pay the mortgage the next day. She was upset that I even asked her, but no she had not diverted her check

She said that I was a fool to leave the house because of my business. I said her comfort was more important to me. I said that if she was leaving me my business didn't really matter to me anymore. Then she really shouted—"You are putting your burdens on me!!! When you say that or that you will do anything to make me happy, like move to Phoenix, you are placing your burdens on me—you have been doing this your whole life and I can't take it anymore. When I was in Phoenix, I had a wholesome and healthy life! I can't carry your burdens any more!!!!" I am still trying to understand what that means.

This morning, I woke up at 5, packed and left the motel. I started to drive home. I wondered if I would see her because it was her normal time to leave for work. I decided to drive up Foothill Boulevard towards home, knowing that this was the route she normally takes. I saw her van parked by the side of the road where Anya lives. We looked at each other in the early morning light. I drove on. I am not sure she noticed me, but I bet she did and she thinks I am stalking her.

Saturday.

Yesterday morning, I basically came home. I washed my sheets and blankets and remade my bed. I vacuumed the room. Later in the day I left her a voicemail at work asking her if I could have permission to come home. She emailed me this:

M-

I don't know but, it is your home too.

I am still frightened so, I will not be able to talk to you much.

After the phone call last night, I had horrible sleep so, I just want to come home and relax in my room.

I must go into another meeting now.

Terry

So she came home and I cooked her filet mignon and grilled shrimp. She did love that and we talked a bit. I told her I was so ashamed of drinking the other night and that it would never happen again. She sat watching TV with me but only from the other couch. Out of the blue, she says she wants to ask me a question. I say sure. She asks why I mentioned the guns last night during our fun phone call. (??!!) Now I am really concerned. I said nothing about guns and she is convinced I did. I told her I was drawing a blank and even showed her my notes from the conversation, which included her replies. Nothing about guns. Nevertheless she was acting weird and very frightened, so I went around and collected all the handguns and put them out in the trunk of my van. I come back and she asks about the rifle...so like a dutiful slave I remove the rifle from the house as well. (I wonder if she plotted this actual event just because she has been afraid of all the guns all this time but was too afraid to tell me??) She also asked me if I have software that "sees" what is on her computer.....She has become completely paranoid. I lie skillfully and convince her that I cannot see a thing on her computer–nor would I want to. After the movie "Marooned" she went up to bed. This morning I got up at about 7:30, made coffee and sat on the couch. She did not come down until close to 10. I tried to interact with her but she was stiff and cold. She just went upstairs and was holed up on her bed. I turned on Christian music on the TV. I made it loud enough to go through the house but not too loud. After about 30 minutes I went upstairs and meekly asked if she would like to go look at kittens and get some info about them–you know, and then do something else fun like Red Lobster? She says no. She was up in her room most of the day ignoring me. I took it pretty hard at first but started letting go. When she came down we interacted a bit. I made a sandwich and she made some food and took it upstairs to eat it. Finally at about 5PM, she came down and made herself a salad and actually ate with me downstairs (again on the other couch). That was only her second meal down here in 7 days…

I asked her if we could talk. She said OK. I explained to her that SDSU had told me that I had until October (I figure August) to move out of the building with my research lab since they are closing the department and moving it to Dallas. I said I could have my lab in Dallas and "commute" or I could do the same for northern AZ at the Research lab there. At this, she piped up a little bit, but then said that she would never leave her job, and if she could not post and get hired in Phoenix, she would probably move closer to work—get a small apartment, room with somebody in Irvine. She said the house could be sold and "we" could buy a manufactured home in No. AZ.

She is still planning on getting rid of me. I think she says, "I love you" only after I do to humor me. I say it to keep her from walking out. She is gone. I am sure she wants R to move back in with her and so she can enable him the rest of her life…

We decided to watch a pay per view—one she liked. I asked her to please sit next to me and she said no. I said OK. We watched the movie and she said she really liked it. I said yeah. Then she went up to bed. That was 8:25PM.

What are the positives here? She hasn't moved out yet. She has not made me move out yet. But it still could happen in a matter of days, I am convinced. So, shut your pie hole brother. And keep it shut. You warned yourself last time and you ignored your own advice. This time you will not be so lucky.

Sunday–Father's Day–6/17/07.

This morning, she got her coffee and cereal while I was in the shower. I had to make my own coffee, which is no big deal. I did not see her until ½ hr before church when I went upstairs to iron my shirt. She was all bundled up in bed. I asked if I could come in and iron my shirt. She says OK. I meekly ask if she is going to church. She tearfully says no. I came over to her by the bed and knelt down. I said then maybe I will stay home and comfort you. She cries and says, "No you are putting that burden on me." I still don't know what that means. Then I said OK and I got ready and went to church. When I came home she was upstairs. I made a couple of hotdogs and sat down to eat in front of the TV. About 30 minutes later she came down looking haggard and dressed to go out. She is keeping her new purse upstairs with her I notice. She says "I am going to gas and wash the van"–I say OK with a smile. She came back about 2 hours later. I was in my room doing rocks. I waved and smiled when she walked past my door. She poked her head in and asked if we could go to Red Lobster later. Shocked, I smiled and gave big thumbs up. Then she said she is going up to nap. I ask, can I give you a backrub? Again, no. So I say "Can I pray with you?" She says yes so I prayed for peace for us both and for her to have a great nap. She said thank you and went up to bed. Later we went to Red L, and she chatted me up. She did not sit next to me, but it was still fun, I guess. We came home and she sat downstairs while we watched Monster's Inc. We both laughed. Again she was on the other couch, but at least she was there. We smooched a small smooch even. Then she was off to bed at about 8:40.

Tuesday 6/19/07.

Well tonight she actually called me from the van for the first time in what… months? She had to take R to something, but it was nice that she called. He is in his 2nd day of summer school and she says he is doing "smashingly" according to her. One can hope, can't one?

I was thinking that maybe I should invite R to go to the Police band concert with Patrick this Saturday at Dodger stadium. Yup I actually got tickets. And yes, I would give up my $100 seat to encourage him a bit. That should make her happy, huh? All she said was "He probably won't go." Not even a thank you. How ungrateful. And she is still sitting on the opposite couch from me like I have cooties. She also cried and said she could not go with me Sunday morning to visit Thomas Paine and his wife at LAX She said she could not handle being asked how we are doing and "I don't want to talk about moving to KY." Dr. Payne wanted to offer me a research job in KY but I knew she would leave me if I took the job…I dropped it and sat in silence.

Friday night.

Last night she did not call and she did not eat the dinner I made. Turns out she ate before her counseling session, but did not bother to call and tell me. She came home cranky. I was feeling sick and begged her to sit next to me on the couch–she did for 30 minutes and then complained that her arm was hurting. Tonight she did not call before she came home. I didn't ask. She sat on the opposite couch. At one point I went over to hug her as she lay with her eyes closed. I started to speak as I got close to her and she started screaming like I had hurt her. I am convinced she has lost it.

Sunday 7/1/07.

Third Sunday in a row that she has not gone to church. Course I was at LAX last Sunday meeting with Dr. Paine, but she did not go to church then either. I think Ronnie is flunking out of Adult school just as he did High School. He got 2 F's and a D-. She is sad about him constantly. She just will not let it go and let God. I keep praying with her at night and that seems to help, but she is not sleeping because she is worrying….the kid is a train wreck and he does not give a rip about anybody but himself.

We have been closer it seems and I have been careful to just shut up about most things. Last week we had kind of a breakthrough conversation. She said she definitely wants to move to northern Arizona with me so I can be near the Research lab, so this just may work out after all. She is even willing to wait about 2 years to make it happen. We'll see.

Sunday 7/15/07

This girl is one sick puppy. She has not gone to church with me for 5 weeks. Every Sunday morning it is the same–no matter how the Saturday goes–no matter how much I grovel for this woman or smooth out any wrinkles, she is unhappy. Yesterday I took her to see Evan Almighty. We both sobbed. Then I took her for a nice Italian lunch. She scarfed it down. Then she came home and napped. Then I brought out another new video (Narnia) for her to watch because she got huffy when I was changing channels and lingered on TBS–"As good as it gets" for 1 minute. She sobbed and cried at Narnia. At least she thanked me for Narnia, but she did not thank me for the movies and lunch yesterday. She got real pissed, "You just keep score all the time" when I mentioned that today during her 2 hour cry fest.

Here's how it has been for the last 5 Sundays: I get up to start my coffee…there is a note by my coffee pot saying, "I had a horrible night. Please go to church without me…blah, blah." Today, I waited until she came down at 8AM. I sweetly asked her how she was–she scowled. I said, "Please can we go to church?" She made her cereal and said no. I said, "Terry, what is wrong?" She, sobbing said "I will talk to you about it after you get home from church." I turned to the window and she walked away–upstairs to the inner sanctum. 2.5 hours went by. I never got ready for church. She never came down. Finally I went upstairs and sweetly asked her to go with me to the 11:15 service. She "No" and the sobbing started. I sit for 3 minutes in silence and ask her to tell me what is wrong. Another 3 minutes of silence with her sobbing and then the usual, "I don't want to talk about it." This went on for 35 minutes, but I am not budging. I gently prod this way and that. Much sobbing, much "I don't want to talk about it." Finally 2 hours later here is what I got out of her (besides, "This is always the same, you demean me, you always have a come back, this is never going to change, you need to let me go", etc):

-I can't face people at church because you aired our dirty laundry.

-You and I are different kinds of Christians

-You don't respect the way I love Jesus (the last two I still do not understand)

That is the sum total of all the "bad" things I do to her! She is nuts and I am convinced she is only going to get worse. I told her again with a smile that it was over and I gave her permission to leave me. Not only that I would happily move her. After much more sobbing and a little more openness on her part, she reiterated that she thinks a move to Prescott will save us. But she finally openly admitted that she really wants to be back in Phoenix and has almost run away back home many times. She also admitted that I am the best man that has ever been in her life. So who knows? If I shut up and let her talk about whatever, and if I don't ever answer her (see-because I am smothering her), if I don't say anything negative, if I only watch PBS while she is around and don't touch her or anything like that, she is very happy. This is sick.

8/5/07

Well she finally went to church with me. She seemed all cuddly and happy as we sat on the pew. What changed? Maybe the fact that I have been silent for weeks? But when we got home she got very angry because of something I said. You see, during church, she was hunting through her purse for a pen to take notes of the sermon. I sensed her frustration and pulled out a pen from the side pocket of my leather Bible cover. It was a pen from the AZ lab I was working with to move my equipment to. The lab name and phone number was on it. So after I gave it to her she started poking me in the ribs to get my attention. I look over at her and she was pointing to the pen with a big smile on her face. I looked down at the pen and noticed that the last 4 digits of the lab phone number was the same as my birthday—1153. I thought, "Oh boy—she has a sign from God." But I smiled and looked back up front where Pastor was preaching. On the way home from church she was babbling on about how much it was a sign from God and I made some remark about how silly it was to assume that God had the lab phone number rigged to be the same as my birthday so that she could have assurances that my lab equipment should be in this particular lab in Prescott, AZ. You guessed it—the waterworks came on and that was the end of our happiness for that day.

9/22/07

Someone please explain this to me. For the last 6 weeks I have been working to get my lab transferred to AZ because:

A) She told me she would be happy if I moved her back to AZ, and:

B) because she is convinced that God wants it, etc., etc. So I am laying down my dreams and my desires and going into the dry desert mainly for her—cracked skin or no cracked skin.

So far we have driven the 7 hours each way 3 times in the last 5 weeks. Two of the three times we have gone over, she has driven an extra 300 miles round trip from Prescott to Phoenix/Mesa to go see her family. I gladly let her go because I was busy at the lab anyway and it made her happy, plus I am just sick of being around her. So far, I have convinced the lab people to spend $9,000 just to get the rooms ready for the lab systems I have, and I am about to have them spend another $4,000 to have the equipment transported and re-installed. I have hired the equipment movers, the truck, and the date is next weekend. She has had this on her calendar for weeks and weeks and has the time off of work. All because I understood from her that this is what she wanted and she would be happy going over there, etc., etc., etc.

Now all of a sudden, the equipment movers could not get a motel room near the lab (because they procrastinated and waited too long), so I have to drive them back and forth from the lab to a different motel 15 miles away in Jerome when we are there next weekend. So when I got off the phone tonight with the movers, I told her I am sorry and that she may not be able to spend the night in Phoenix unless Marty and Dede at the lab are willing to help with the driving…..what does she say? "Well then I just won't go because I will be bored." WHATT??? It would have been better if she had just shoved a knife into my brain. What on God's green earth am I doing moving to AZ if she is just going to abandon me at the first speed bump? So, like a fool I asked her what she was really saying…..

"Are you saying that if you cannot go stay with your family, you won't be going to AZ like we agreed we were going to do as a couple??? Well, you guessed it–she went nuts. "I'm no good for you" "This won't work" "You always use my words as weapons against me." Now she is hiding up in her room sobbing again. SOMEONE PLEASE EXPLAIN TO ME WHY I AM STILL WITH THIS NUT JOB OF A WOMAN

10/14/07

Yesterday when Terry was out gassing up her van, I decided to write a note for her in her Bible. Now when I say in her Bible I mean on the pages of her Bible. So I opened her Bible to 1 Corinthians 7 and I wrote in pencil, "How convenient that you underline some Bible verses but this one you don't underline because there are some Scriptures you just don't want to obey." I am sure she read it because she has been an ice queen towards me today. I sure am impressed that her Jesus lets her pick and choose the Christianity she wants. I don't think He loves me that much.

11/3/07

If I was a songwriter, this would be my song...
She's really cold. I can tell when her arms cross her chest.
She could snuggle her man, and that would really be best, but
somehow the love seat grew too long.
Her blankets hide her, it's like she's not really there.
She's curled and packaged–suffers like it's unfair.
I see her stooped shoulders, ponder the gritty distance here
somehow the love seat grew too long.
Her view of the TV from here would be clear
but she doesn't think enough of me to be dear
so I'm alone on the east end of the love seat.
A cup of tea, a shiver and a sigh, the body language
says more than a man should buy.
Without affection, her real feelings do show.
No conversation, she's strangely averse to that
maybe a question about who is up to bat
and then stone silence,
somehow the love seat grew too long.
Her view of the TV from here would be clear
but she doesn't think enough of me to be dear
so I'm alone on the east end of the love seat

Thanksgiving Day, 2007

Well we just spent 10 days in AZ. The first full day there, Wednesday, she spent with her kid and family in Mesa. I worked at the lab. Thursday mid morning, she came back to pick me up. We then drove to Tucson where I spoke to a science meeting Thursday night. Afterwards a cozy steak dinner at Mimi's. Friday was a free day, so I took her to the Sonora Desert Museum, the National Saguaro Monument and a really nice lunch in a hidden dive/jukebox 50's diner. Later after a rest in the Motel, we went back to the cliffs at the Sonora Monument and watched the sunset with a LOT of other people. Then off for Chinese.

The next day I checked her into the Sheraton in North Phoenix. Nice breakfast and then off to the Desert Botanical Garden. We bought some cute juvenile cacti to take home, and then a nice lunch at the Sheraton where we had spent our honeymoon night. I spoke two times that night, but we went out for a nice dinner after the talks. We slept in a king size bed at both hotels. Did she touch me? Nope. I didn't make an effort either. Sunday morning, I spoke at a church and we had a smashing Mexican lunch. Then we rushed to the hotel and checked out and drove back to Prescott. She was acting like her usual selfish self and finally that night I told her that she had no affection for me anymore. I tried to walk away from her saying it again. She was shocked, but to her credit came over and hugged me and hung onto me. We made love for the first time in almost 8 weeks. So, yup. I begged again. She held out 8 weeks and made me into a freaking beggar again. Boy do I feel empowered.

Monday I took her to the artsy fartsy mining town of Jerome. I spent over $200 on gifts, food and other stuff. Tuesday I took her to Sedona. The lunch alone was over $100. Wednesday we just hung at the lab. She had said she had no desire to be with her sister for Thanksgiving, so I said, "OK," and we drove home the seven hours on Thanksgiving day. On the way home I asked her if we could stop at the grocery to pick up some Turkey rolls so I can spit roast them. Nope. Then we get home and she got on the phone with her family. She started crying because she missed them. Then she started crying because she got no turkey dinner. She asks me if we can go to the store to buy her a turkey frozen dinner!! Long story short, I made her some cooked turkey, green beans and mashed potatoes with gravy and turkey meat that I had on hand. She gulps it down and ignores me then goes to bed at 9PM, but at least the crying stopped. What a day to celebrate. I sure am thankful, Lord on this day to give thanks.

11/30/07

Today she came home with a yeast infection. I made the mistake of asking her why she had a yeast infection. She took that to mean something sinister to be sure and sat cold on her end of the couch for the night. I got up and went and did stuff–ignoring her. She came into my room at 10:20PM and said she was going to bed. I said fine and went back to what I was doing.

Next day, Saturday, more of the same. I ignored her and did my own thing. She asked me if I was mad at her, I said no but went on ignoring her. Finally she said, "It's because I have a yeast infection, right?" I just stared. She continued," I never want to tell you when I get them because you make me feel like it is my fault that I get them." I felt like saying, "Maybe God is punishing you for never touching me and always depriving me of sex." Nobody *makes* anybody feel anything–but you could NEVER convince her of that. So I said–"This is way beyond a yeast infection….you have no affection for me whatsoever–you ignore my physical needs for weeks." Well the water works came on and basically I was told it was really all about me and the things I say to her that hurt her emotionally and so she clams up, etc. Her emotions dictate whenever or not she is going to be "in the mood", and my words apparently control all that. Funny, I don't remember saying much to her over the last 12 weeks. I guess stone silence puts her out of the mood as well. By the way, have I ever seen her in the mood? Hardly. She made it all about me, (that she can go 12 weeks without touching me). I pointed out that she is cold in the house all the time but she will never cuddle me. I even confessed to masturbating regularly, and she still made it all about me and how I make her feel. How convenient for her to never take the blame. I finally gave up. I keep forgetting that this woman is a frigid cold fish and I will NEVER change her.

So, I will keep ignoring her. Maybe I should start searching for a normal girl-some how some way-someone that I can email and dream about, and eventually, once the house is sold and she pays to move me to my lab in AZ, I will find someone else. This nightmare of a "marriage" to a screwed up woman has to end.

12/21/07

Well, for the last several months, each time we go to Prescott we visit with a Christian realtor and look at land for sale up in the Prescott area (her idea). Yup – we are actually looking at properties together. I know this is probably an exercise in futility, but it humors her in some way, so I go along with it…There are some really sweet deals to be had to be sure, as the bad economy seems to have driven down land prices. She acts all excited at the prospect of buying a piece of property up there–I'm not that excited because I have seen this kind of psychotic behavior before. It seems that her employer had a pension account for her that no one knew about–valued at about $50,000 and they are about to dump it out to her in a lump sum. But do I want to own another property with this woman? I mean, I don't even know if she is going to run away from the one we already own together. For now I will go along with it and maybe she won't take the $50,000 and run away.

So now we go to the Prescott area, once a month, and we look at properties. I often make a day of it with her. I take her out for breakfast or lunch, and then drive her to many communities in and around the Prescott area. We have driven all through Dewey, Humboldt, Prescott Valley, Chino Valley and Paulden. We have talked and talked over all the possible ways we could make our move so that she will be happy in AZ again and how she could find work in the area or even NW Phoenix. I have been really trying to bend over backwards to placate her. But she is still a stone cold fish. She will never love anybody or me–she loves herself too much.

2/26/08 No change. Why even write about it?

3/3/08

We went to the AZ lab over the weekend where I did some new research and taught a workshop. She never touched me. Same old same old. I had to look in my Daytimer just to see how long it has been since she allowed me into the Holy of Holies between her legs. Frankly I had completely forgotten. I don't even look at her when I want to think of nude women anymore. She is about as sexy as a brick. Yesterday a sexually oriented letter came, addressed to Bruce Alexander, a pen name I used on the Internet many years ago. Well, you guessed it–the water works came on and she used it as an excuse to scream and cry about why she never gives me sex anymore. As if I am sitting around waiting for her to give me sex. Dude–I am over you woman! You think I have any desire to have you anymore? Get over yourself. I just sat and looked at her.

3/24/08

Same. I have not been speaking to her. She sat next to me the whole weekend on the couch and we did not utter hardly a word to each other. This woman is an ice princess. I think her heart; if she has one is made from arctic permafrost. She can easily outlast me in this game of who owes whom an apology. I am going to try to make it all the way to our 6th wedding anniversary, about 2 weeks away.

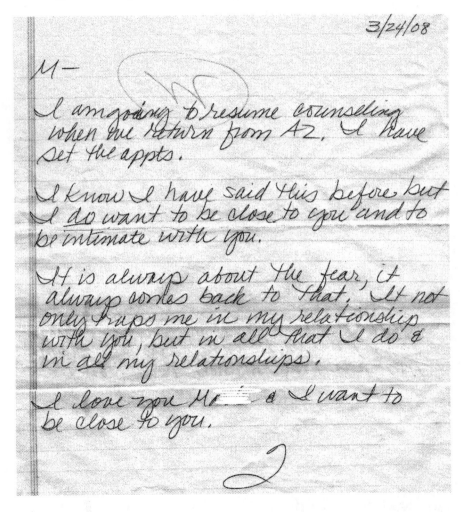

January 1, 2009.

Holy crap: ten months have gone by and I am still ready to jump on the third rail. Too bad no electric trains run through here....

My birthday–big deal. No sex today – no sex in what-a year? No holding no cuddling, no fondling, no kissing. I tried sitting with her on the couch today but all day she just laid there dozing in between the Pasadena Rose Parade and other crap. Then I got up and cooked her veal Marsala with rice pilaf for lunch. She burped her way through it and slept some more on the couch. Then I got up and cooked her shrimp and veggie kabobs on the grill. Once again 'stuff and snooze'. How endearing. Her butt is as big as a coffee table. I hope I get hit by an uninsured drunk driver on crystal meth.

January 4, 2009.

Today's church message from Pastor Gene was about marriage – how wonderful it is and all, from Genesis 1 and 2. How it is just chock full of submission to one another and all that hunky dory "we are so happy in Jesus" stuff – and how the wife does not withhold affection from the man – how her body is his and all, from 1 Corinthians 7. I remember these passages – I tried to share them with her once in the distant past. It got thrown back into my face, remember? She was flipping around madly in her Bible during that part of the sermon today so I am sure she managed to miss it. What a crock. Pastor should make movies of what happens (or does not happen) around my house with deranged people standing next to us just screaming and screaming at the tops of their lungs. Pastor Gene could show it to engaged couples, just to show them how bad their lives could be. I could be a poster child for how to avoid marrying a psycho witch. She is a Frigidaire on nuclear power.

Many couples, and I mean many, went up at the end of the service to look longingly into their spouse's gazing eyes and renew their wedding vows as Pastor led them. It was a thing of beauty – I think 3 single women and Terry and I were the only ones still in our seats in a room of about 300 people. I didn't budge. She didn't either. We just sat there and watched–all the chairs around us were empty. She probably thought up more ways she could torture me as the ceremony went on – who knows? Then at the end, she put her hand on my leg for a minute as if to say–"It's OK honey–we were up there too and I am all happy and all." What a crock.

I wouldn't repeat my vows to her if Pastor held a gun to my head.

Then later that same day I had to lead a small group on how cool Christian marriage is and all. (I had resigned as small group leader a while back but I stepped back up to lead so Terry would start coming to church again.)

I never shared a word during small group about my personal experience of marriage hell and how I am living in a prison from the Twilight Zone. I was wondering how drunk I could get tonight. What was the one thing she shared about our marriage during the group session? That she is so in awe of how committed to the Bible I am. Boy, am I special. I hope I have a brain tumor that is going to wipe me out soon. I need to move in with a crack whore. Then I will be able to appreciate how good my life is...

Saturday, Feb 14, 2009

She came home early from work yesterday. I ran to the store before she came home and picked up a fifth of Gin, just so I could be ready for the horribly long weekend. I should start drinking by 6PM like she does. She now goes through 2 three-liter bottles of wine per week. Well, actually a bit more than that. She'll be out of wine by tomorrow night and then she'll be pretty mad because she is off on Monday. Today is Valentines Day. I was worried that she was going to hand me a sweet card and some chocolate. I had rehearsed my little speech about how I was not going to validate her Twilight Zone love relationship with me. But thank God she ignored me this morning! She didn't even mention Valentines Day!! I was so relieved.

She sat on the couch all day and watched TV. Then she spent about an hour cleaning her room – it was good to have her upstairs and out of sight. But she came down again and parked herself in front of the TV. I worked and finished a rock, then I started a new one. We managed to ignore each other most of the day. But I didn't feel like cooking, and was hungry for Chinese, so we went out to eat. The food was good, the company was detached. No matter – I have finally figured out that she is a narcissist–she is incapable of loving anybody at all. They say that people don't recover from this, so the rest of my life should be fun. But I am going to start listing the good things about being married to her–for example, with her work benefits I can afford to go away alone once a month.

Sunday 2/15.

The aftermath. This morning I woke up thinking I would not have to deal with the whole fake Valentines thing. But I was wrong–a red envelope greeted me on the kitchen counter as I groped for my coffee. Within seconds she had traversed the stairs down to the kitchen and sweetly asked if I had found her sweet little romance card. I am sure it said how much she loved me–I never opened it…Not turning to face her I said, "Terry, I just cannot accept your Twilight Zone romance thing…". She started bawling and crying and slowly worked her way back up to her lair. Geez, this is so friken painful.

After an hour I went up to iron my shirt for church–she was drying her hair, which she has grown out long to please me no doubt (and it does please me greatly–I always tell her that), but she always complains about it now. We exchanged no words. When I finished ironing my shirt, and walked past her I said, "Your hair looks very nice." She thanked me. About

20 minutes later, I exited my room ready for church and she was sitting on the couch with a truly pitiful and sad face. She wasn't looking at me. I was strangely moved to offer her some hope, so I walked over to her and signaled for her to come to me. I hugged her–and she hugged me very strongly. I lied to her and told her I loved her. I drove to church and we held hands. She held on to me all during church. We went to lunch together. I asked her if we could talk after we were done eating and she said yes. I started to gently explain to her how she could not understand how much she was hurting me by being distant. But people starting standing close to us at the restaurant, so I asked her if she would be more comfortable in the car. She said yes, so we went to the car. I explained to her that she was KILLING me. I could not live without intimacy and I did not mean sex.

I asked her to tell me plainly if she felt obligated to give me sex when I only wanted closeness and she said yes. I told her, "It doesn't always need to end in sex. I need intimacy, closeness–I need you to cleave to me." She said she understood.

Later that day we sat close on the couch. I was hoping for sex (since it has been what? Last year?) But I didn't ask and she ended up falling asleep at about 9PM. I made her go to bed.

Monday 2/26/09.

She was detached again today. She did a lot of cleaning in her room and I helped her with her floors. I took her to a romantic Italian lunch, but she just ragged on me when we got home. My hopes are not high.

March 8, 2009.

Back to the WAY WE WERE. Still no sex since last year sometime. When the hell was it??? Same old same old. We were sitting on the couch this morning drinking our coffee and trying to wake up. I told her I would like to go out for Chinese or Mexican later, and she said, "That would be nice."

She had just taken her laptop upstairs but now she wanted to surf the net on something, so she asked to borrow mine. Silly me–when she tried to log on, a sex page that I forgot to close last night popped up with naked couples on it. Course she went into a frenzy of crying and shouting and ran upstairs–I laughed out loud and said I thought it was funny; then sobbing she yelled at me from upstairs landing demanding to know why I had porn on my computer. I said, "Because I was looking at it last night while

I masturbated, dear." That made her even more upset, and she sobbed and cried. (I know, I am going to hell).

I reminded her that she had a nasty habit of always denying me sex – for at least 3-4 months now (I stopped counting), and that as a red-blooded man; I actually wanted sex from time to time. She moaned and cried. I worked quietly on the taxes downstairs for about 10 minutes, and finally she came back down. She said, "Remember when you asked me if I masturbate at night alone in my bed, and I told you yes, and then you told me that was like I was having an affair with someone else?" I said "Yeah." She said that what I was doing was no different and that now she felt that way-I was committing adultery. I explained "No, it's not the same, because YOU never beg ME for sex, and I hardly ever turn YOU down–plus I WOULD never turn you down if you asked me regularly. So if you run off and satisfy yourself it's not because I haven't tried. On the other hand, I beg you for sex, and you ignore me and then YOU run off and masturbate-so no it is not the same thing." That seemed to make her even madder. She started crying and saying, "I can't be the one to satisfy you because you want me to do awful things like oral on you–you need someone else because I can't be that person for you."

I told her that I had long since given up on that prospect, and she had to admit that I haven't asked her for oral in years. I told her that "Now that we are having a frank adult discussion–I remind you that I have begged you, cajoled you, threatened you, read you 1 Corinthians, 7 where it says you are depriving me what is rightfully mine–the one thing I look forward to in life to get by–and I have done everything possible to get you to have sex with me." I pulled out a book next to the couch called "His needs, Her needs" I reminded her that she never read it like I asked her to (or any of the other Christian intimacy books I bought her), so I read her some parts of it–especially about how husbands react when their wives refuse to give them the ONE major thing they need in life. She said, "I'll try to read the book" and took it from me. She never will. This discussion went on for 20 minutes. I told her that I knew she could not stand to take her clothes of or to have sex, and that if she would just hand me a Playboy and at the very least touch me with her hand, that I would be exceedingly happy. That way she would never have to take her clothes off, or get cold, or get messy or be inconvenienced in any way like she usually is. Heck, truth be told, if just got me excited while I looked at sex pictures, I would even finish myself and would be very happy. She said, "Taking my clothes off and getting cold are not why I don't want sex. I don't want sex because

I know that the minute we start having it you are going to ask me lots of questions, like 'do you like this or that? Do you want to do this or that?' I will be before the inquisition."

So that is her big reason?

I said, "You can't promise a man a steak, and then never give him a steak and make him watch steak on the street and on TV and then get mad when he talks about steak when he only just lives to have steak with his wife."

But again I was getting nowhere, and I told her so. I said, "The reason I don't talk to you about sex is because it always comes back on me—I pay for it one way or another. I would like sex regularly. You know that. I even showed you the recent poll of 3000 UK couples who were happily married and how they have sex 3-4 times per week-that is one thing that makes them happy. I bought you all those Christian sex books and you ignored them. You ignored my pleas—you ignored what the Bible says about sex in marriage—how can you be so shocked if I look at free naked women on the Internet and try in some way to satisfy myself without going to a real woman and without spending money we don't have when you just completely ignore my need?? You have robbed me for 7 years and I never left you for another woman. I wanted to every week over the last 7 years—even though you have let your figure go—I never went to anyone else. But I don't even care anymore that you don't want to have sex with me. If you want me to be happy, get some lubricant and start touching me while I look at pictures on the Internet. I won't trouble you further." Well she was quiet at that point and walked upstairs. After about 5 minutes she called out, "So what time can we go to lunch?" Go figure.

Well we went to lunch, which she gobbled down and then we came home and sat on the couch together. I continued to work on the taxes. She complained about having a headache. She never touched me all day—she did her laundry and watched things on TV. At 9PM she stood up and announced that it was bedtime. So what have we learned campers? She is just screwed up in the head. I think I will start masturbating in front of her and hide the laptop screen from her so she won't be offended by my adulterous lovers. Nah, better not. What fun we had today.

March 28

Three more weeks have gone by and still no sex since last year some time. Oh yeah, it was last October 12. Five months. She still acts angry if

I even hint that a gorgeous woman on TV has a nice body. Today we went to a Chinese buffet where I got all protein and veggies and she got tons of carbs. I said, "Why don't you go get some of those tasty deserts they have too?" You didn't have to ask her twice. She stuffed her face with them. By the way–she cut off all her hair again yesterday. Fat + short hair = ugly.

OH, yeah, the book she said she would "try to read"? Still sitting on her bed, unread.

April 10, 2009

Still no sex – no cuddling–no affection. What else is new? Looks like she has read the first 20 pages of the book. That amounts to ½ page per day. She loves me, she loves me not. Did we even wish 'happy anniversary' to each other 5 days ago? Nope. How telling is that? We aren't even excited about our anniversary anymore. This will end badly.

April 21, 2009

Wow I am impressed–11 days later and she is on page 53. (She underlined all the parts that talked about hugging…how easy is it to underline the word hugging. How hard to actually do it.) So 38 days have gone by and she has read 53 pages. That is a blazing amount of 1.4 pages per day. Maybe she started reading more because I went away for a whole week.

Yup! I drove away on Sunday 4/12 and drove straight to the Texas coast. I spent 3 days on the coast swimming, eating fish and just generally being free of her–all with a blasting air conditioner and a cold room. I was in heaven. Then I left and went to my lab in AZ and did some work with the lab equipment. Again, heaven. For one whole week I didn't have to listen to her whining or make demands, look at her crappy short haircut and huge butt or have to cook for her or clean up after her or listen to her inane remarks.

I have to plan more trips away. In fact, I am trying to plan an overnight trip up to the mountains before school lets out, just to have 2 days away from her with no crowds. I am happiest when she is not home during the day and either when she is gone or I am gone and I don't have to interact with her. I hope she never retires.

May 4, 2009

Six months no sex, no touching, no kissing, no hugging. Oh yeah–I forgot–she held my hand as we walked from the car to church last week.

Lucky me. I guess she wanted to show everybody how close and in love we are. She has made some blazing progress on the book. Lets see–24 days and 73 pages…MAN an astounding 3 pages per day. Of course, she only underlines that parts that say things like, "he has to make me feel like a person, he has to act like I really mean something to him, his words have to be sweet all the time." Maybe if she acted like a wife and not the Queen of Sheba putting away a gallon of wine every 2 days I wouldn't be so hurt by her. Please God, keep her strong and healthy so that I can slide into my retirement.

I stopped cooking altogether. I don't do any major grocery shopping any more. I still keep a grocery sheet on the fridge for when she needs toilet paper, wine–stuff like that. We don't go out to eat either–we were going out 2-3 nights per week for salads, but even that has stopped now. She just gets a salad from Wendy's on her way home and she eats in her room.

June 10, 2009.

I met someone. She is pretty, sexy, has a great figure, a great sense of humor – we laugh at the same things–she is a Baptist too… She is available and she calls herself a cougar!! Wow, I would like to be her first meal. I really like her.

I'll never have her. I am trapped in my prison that I cannot divorce myself from. She is going to get snapped up by some lucky guy. My unlucky life will be over before I would ever be so blessed to have a woman like that. We could make each other very happy. Oh, well. My toxic marriage rolls on. Why do I still honor my vows?

Here is a series of emails that went back and forth this June and July. This is over. Time to get the lawyers.

6-15-09, 6:15AM via email,
Terry to Mitch:
Honey,
I have tried so many times to just open my mouth and talk to you.
I'm sure you consider this is cowardly to send you a letter but I become incapacitated when I try to talk to you.
In Pastor's sermon on Sunday, he used this term: "dismal failure" and when he said it, it hit me to the heart. I know I am a dismal failure to you as a wife but I do not want to be, I do not want to be.

I want to be intimate with you and close to you. I wish we could sleep in the same room together even if we can't sleep in the same bed but, how would I not freeze all the time and not have to wear earplugs so that I can sleep in order to get up at the ungodly hour of 3AM?

I want to tell you what wounds what hurts, what heals me but when I try to, the words that come out of my mouth cut you like a knife. It's destroying me let alone what it is doing to you. Am I supposed to be better educated, reprogrammed or something so that I say the correct words that transmit to you properly? I am incapable of separating the emotional part of me from the physical, the intellectual or the mental; I have sincerely & genuinely tried.

I am just not able to watch certain movies/shows with you without comprising the very core of my being. It is the same with other things too. I truly cannot see that I am so wrong in how I live and think-it is what I read in how God tells us to live in the His Bible. If not, then why hasn't He gotten through to me else wise? He always has.

I want to be your wife, and I want you to be my husband. I want to be the best of friends, the best of partners, the best of mentors, the best of family.

I will go to Christian and/or pastoral counseling with you; I have gone on my own as you know but it is not that beneficial when it is just me going.

I love you Mitch and I do not want to live this. It is effecting (SIC) every aspect of my life.

Terry

I felt like saying, "God is trying to get through to you but you won't listen to me." That would have gone over very well. I am so tired now of all this.

6-18-09 M to T Printed and via email

Dear T.,

I waited until today to reply to your email because I did not want to upset you to the point of crying and getting all stuffy while we tried to talk. I felt it was better to reply in a dispassionate way and so you could read this again if need be and hopefully not "read into" what I am saying. I won't be around for a few days, so I think it will be good for you to be alone a bit and just to think on your own without any pressure from me. And no, I do not consider it cowardly for you to send a letter. Communication is communication, no matter what form it takes.

First of all I thank you for being honest. I don't know that I can answer any of your questions though, because after (almost) 8 years of knowing you I'm not sure that I have any answers. It seems that after 8 years we are pretty much still at square one.

So I think we finally have to look at things as adults and realize that neither of us are happy, that we have tried to become happy through various means and that we are just two very different people who can't seem to make it work. I also have to say that we have had this conversation so many times before and I honestly have no expectations that things will change.

I sincerely believe that you mean well but I think you are just not cut out for marriage—this is my belief, so please don't take it personally.

Some people dive headlong into marriage and others just don't know what to make of it. So I am not faulting you, I am saying it's just not your cup of tea. I am powerless to bring about any change (and as I said I have little to no hope that things will). You have emotional needs that I simply cannot meet and I have physical and emotional needs that you can't meet. We end up frustrated time after time trying to meet needs that we just cannot seem to meet. These are just the plain facts.

That being said, where do we go from here? One thing is certain and that is, if we rush angrily or emotionally into a "solution", we will only hurt each other in the present, and possibly into the future and we will generally make a big mess of things. There is no sense in that.

We seem to be good at meeting each other's very basic needs for security, safety, food and household, and some entertainment things, etc., although you have said that many things on TV, etc. offend you. Because of that it seems to me that we should stay the course for the immediate future, try to find common ground where we can, and maybe seek recreation in the separate areas that interest us.

You work hard to bring in a decent income and benefits for the present and the future, I work hard to bring in as much (or more) in cash, but I don't have a retirement plan or health benefits. We have a little sanctuary of a home and you know that you have a safe place to unwind, relax, and decompress after work. You know that you don't have to come home and slave over a hot stove. I know I have a place that I can work in every day, study, write and do some research. So as I say, it makes sense to stay the course in these areas because they work pretty well for us.

You get to work with a company that you love and have been dedicated to for 18 years, (although the last few weeks have been rough on you). I have the freedom to pursue my passions in research and publishing. I am content to live here in Southern California, but you are not.

We simply have to both be honest and say that you have essentially hated it here since you came in 2002. No one is faulting you for that—it is just not your cup of tea.

But you have the goal of retirement ahead of you in about 5 years or so. I don't know if that helps you or not to know that you will be back in Phoenix (or somewhere in AZ) in 5 years. But I am sure, all things considered, if you could get back to Phoenix quickly without messing up your income, benefits and future, that would be something that would bring you peace.

I want a passionate, sexy, fiery relationship with a wife who will fondle, touch, caress, etc., on me all the time, and that is just not your cup of tea. No one should be faulting the other here—it is just the way things are. You feel guilty every time you think about it and that is killing you because you think you have to be someone or something you are not. So why not be adults about this and just accept the fact that "housemates" might be a better definition for us than the miserable married couple we have tried to be.

I think that because you have so much vacation time available to you, it would be wise for you to spend it on yourself, doing what brings you the most happiness-that is being with friends and family in AZ for extended periods of time. I think you should plan a week-10 days or even 2 weeks away—we can rent you a nice car and you can turn it in at some point when you get over there and re-rent to get home, and that way I wouldn't be stuck driving the van. Since I cannot take that much time off in one block, I might just take an overnight trip somewhere (inexpensive) here or there – maybe to the beach, since I love the cool air, water and seafood so much. Maybe that would help the both of us not feel so much pressure to perform or be something we just can't seem to be.

I know you have said in the past that you don't want to seek out other men, but it may not be a bad idea for you to consider before you get much older. You are still young enough that you might find someone who is really more what you need, and to be honest with you, I would not be hurt or offended if you went out to dinner or a show with someone like that if it made you happy. There is no harm in going to dinner or a show with someone if that is something you would like to do. But I am not pushing you to do anything, Terry, that you are not comfortable with–I am merely stating the obvious.

Clearly I have no such person in my life that I could go on such outings with, and to be frank, I will never marry again. It would be such a black mark on my career in ministry, but who knows what the future holds? Of course, if I never re-marry, I will never have the fiery, sexy relationship I have longed for. So who knows?

Also just as obvious is the divorce issue, if we do decide to divorce. It is not something I am looking forward to, inasmuch as it might just completely wreck my standing in the Christian community. So if being married on paper is the most expedient thing for us to do in the immediate future and for some unknown length of time, then I think I would rather keep it that way, and work out a separation if we need to, between us somehow that would include finances, living arrangement, etc.

So, again—where do we go from here? Well I would say that to continue to do what we have been doing and to expect a different result is madness. So let me know what you think. I don't want you to be unhappy but I don't want to completely shipwreck everything as well.

I hope you know that you are welcome to come to the hotel on Saturday. There are 2 rooms per suite so you can have your own room and I will not bother you. I am sure Diane and Beverly will be happy to have you here, so please feel free to come.

With love,

Mitch

6-18-09 T to M:

Dear M,

I appreciate your kindness in why you waited to reply to my letter, Thank You. But alas, due to my weepy nature, that's exactly what I am doing now as I write this...

Yes, it would be nice to see Diane & Beverly again and I would love to come to the hotel just to be out of the daily rut but, I cannot guarantee that my weepiness wouldn't take over.

Your letter has so very much for me to try digest, it will take a while, I am sorry. It's that pondering thing I do. Please allow me time to do that. As a favor to me, could you email your letter? It is helpful to me when I 'ponder' what is on my heart to be able to consider what I am pondering in portions. If that's not do-able for you, I will understand.

Right now, I need to tell you something about my stress at work and I ask that you do not "read into" what I say, (as you asked of me). The 'stress' is not really that I am under any more stress at work-the job we do is always stressful-it is simply the nature of the work we do. It is because of my own inability in that I cannot separate what is happening with you & me from my ability to perform well at work so, my performance at work has really fallen down to the point now that my boss is having others take up the tasks I should be doing. I envy you because you can totally separate certain parts of your brain so that you can shut something out and perform just one task at a time well! I can't separate anything I do from anything else I do so, "multi-tasking' really is not; it is an oxymoron! It's all a house of cards in me and if you remove just one, it will all collapse.

For now if I could please ask of you just one thing I need to know (even though I didn't ask it as a question in my letter):

"Would you go to Christian and/or pastoral counseling with me?" I will respect and accept your answer.

Please wait to reply to this email until after I go to work since I will want to check my email to see if you replied. This will help me not to fall apart again right before I have to go to work.

Love,

T

About three weeks went by and then this:

7/10/09 T to M

Dear Mitch,

I ask that you do not interpret the method of my replying as 'mimicking' yours but, I felt it best so that I also reply in a dispassionate way, and little further 'reading into' things is likely. I really don't know of another way without my emotions interfering, causing me to not act like an adult which only creates further ado. I ask for your compassion and understanding in all that I have said here.

I have italicized my input in my responses to help distinguish your statements from mine. I have also pasted below the short communications we had in addition to the original one for easy reference so, you can disregard them if you like.

‒ ‒

‒ ‒ ‒ ‒ ‒ ‒ ‒ ‒ ‒ ‒ ‒ ‒ ‒

...marriage is not your cup of tea... *and I too understand that being married to me is not your cup of tea.*

I am not faulting you... *and I too, am not faulting you.*

I am powerless to bring about any change (and as I said I have little to no hope that things will)... *as am I powerless to bring about change and although I always have hope, I do understand you have little.*

You have emotional needs that I simply cannot meet and I have physical and emotional needs that you can't meet *Yes, I do have emotional needs that you are not able to meet and I too also have physical needs that you are not able to meet. I acknowledge that I cannot meet your emotional and physical needs.*

...rush angrily or emotionally (*I agree*) into a "solution", we will only hurt each other in the present, and possibly into the future and we will generally make a big mess of things. *I do not want to make a big mess of things either but, I need to retain a semblance of dignity & security.*

...meeting each other's very basic needs for security, safety, food and household, and some entertainment things, etc., *And we also know each of us can meet those needs on his/her own.*

...you have said that many things on TV, etc. offend you. Because of that it seems to me that we should stay the course for the immediate future, try to find common ground where we can, and maybe seek recreation in the separate areas that interest us. *There does not seem to be much common ground though, does there? Outside of some similar Biblical views we have, this is increasingly difficult to see.*

You work hard to bring in a decent income and benefits for the present and the future, I work hard to bring in almost as much (or more) in cash, but I don't have a retirement plan or health benefits. *Yes, we both work hard and my benefits and retirement require a great deal of my income and they are vital & priceless.*

We have a little sanctuary of a home and you know that you have a safe place to unwind, relax, and decompress after work. *Mitch, please know that I truly see that this home is really your sanctuary and it should be-it is your career site where you can work & do your research in an obliging atmosphere, an atmosphere over which you have total direction.*

You know that you don't have to come home and slave over a hot stove. I know I have a place that I can work in every day, study, write and do some research. *I do not mind cooking but, because my time & energy is robbed from me it would just rob more from me and, my cooking is not at the level that you have been blessed to attain.*

You get to work with a company that you love and have been dedicated to for 18 years, (although the last few weeks have been rough on you). *Yes and PL has been good to me because I have been an ethical, moral hard worker.*

I have the freedom to pursue my passions in research and publishing. *It is only right and good that you should have that freedom, now and into your future.*

I am content to live here in So. Cal., but you are not. *Yes, it is true that I do not want to live here beyond retirement.*

We simply have to both be honest and say that you have essentially hated it here since you came in 2002. No one is faulting you for that – it is just not your cup of tea. *I truly do understand why you feel I hate it here but, I do not hate it. You are correct that it is just not my cup of tea. And I too, do not fault you for not being content to live in AZ.*

But you have the goal of retirement ahead of you in about 5 years or so. I don't know if that helps you or not to know that you will be back in Phoenix (or somewhere in AZ) in 5 years. But I am sure, all things considered, if you could get back to Phoenix quickly without messing up your income, benefits and future, that would be something that would bring you peace. *Yes, you are right and correct- I do have the goal of retirement for which I feel awesomely blessed to have and if I could get a position in Phoenix without a drastic reduction in pay & likewise my benefits, I would. Again, you are right in that I do feel it would bring me peace.*

...we can rent you a nice car and you can turn it in at some point when you get over there and re-rent to get home, and that way I wouldn't be stuck driving the van. *Please take this into your consideration: renting me a car is a nice idea however, once I got there, I would have to turn it in, leaving me without access to a car for visiting & getting around thus, having to impose on others for transportation while you have access to two vehicles here; this doesn't seem fair and reasonable. I think you can understand that whether I am taking a trip or just running errands, having my own car is a genuinely reasonable request . (It probably would have been a good idea to have spent the money to repair the Tercel so that I wouldn't have had to then and never have to now be stranded & captive without transportation).*

I want a passionate, sexy, fiery relationship with a wife who will fondle, touch, caress, etc. on me all the time, and that is just not your cup of tea. *Yes, I do see that that type of relationship is vital to you as is the type of relationship that I want vital to me. Just as your type of relationship is not my cup of tea, my type of relationship is not your cup of tea, we just we have different ideas about this.*

...just accept the fact that "housemates" might be a better definition for us than the miserable married couple we have tried to be *Yes, sadly, we are. Mitch, I do think we both know that for me to function in an even somewhat productive manner on a day-to-day basis, I am not able to live with you as a housemate or roommate; it is just not within my capabilities.*

...seek out other men... There is no harm in going to dinner or a show with someone if that is something you would like to do. But I am not pushing you to do anything, Terry, that you are not comfortable with – I am merely stating the obvious *Knowing what you know about the way I believe the Bible shows me to live Mitch, I believe you truly do know that I am not able to and cannot contemplate this, it is not possible for me. I respectfully ask that you do not suggest this again.*

...but who knows what the future holds? Of course, if I never re-marry, I will never have the fiery, sexy relationship I have longed for. So who knows? *I truly do understand how critical this is to you and thus not healthy for your well-being if you did not have hope for this in your future.*

...continue to do what we have been doing and to expect a different result is madness... *I do not think it is madness, but continuing like this is most definitely not healthy for either of us.*

...yes I am not opposed to going to pastoral (or other) counseling as long as it is productive. *Would it really work for you to try this? Please consider that by placing a condition on the outcome of counseling, it would almost predestine it to fail or at the very least only provide limited beneficial results. I note that you will go to pastoral or other counseling but not Christian counseling. I am truly not faulting you here but, please remember when we went to Live Oak counseling, you made the same condition and only went once or twice and I know that you thought it was not productive.*

I don't want you to be unhappy but I don't want to completely shipwreck everything as well. *I too, truly do not want you to be unhappy but I think you and I both know it is already shipwrecked; truly, don't we?*

So as I say, it makes sense to stay the course in these areas because they work pretty well for us. *While I truly understand how it seems sensible to you to stay the course as you feel it works well for us, it does not work well for my all-around stability.*

...if being married on paper is the most expedient thing for us to do in the immediate future and for some unknown length of time, then I think I would rather keep it that way, and work out a separation if we need to, between us somehow that would include finances, living arrangement, etc. *Yes, I think that being married on paper is the most prudent & reasonable thing to do. For me to retain some sense of well-being, stability and capability, and by extension how I perform at my job, and in my day to day functioning, please understand & accept that I need to work on making financial and living arrangements apart from you. I respectfully request that I be allowed to stay here while I work it out; it may take a little while, so I can set a deadline to work toward. I have done some online research and found that there are various ways of dividing liabilities and assets through legal separation by filing on our own which would be beneficial to both of us without involving attorneys. I sincerely & genuinely do not want to create any problems for you in your ministry career so, I will make whatever adjustments in arranging what is needed to keep up appearances for you in the public's eye.*

So let me know what you think. *My thoughts are as above and I hope that I have been dispassionate and adult in my responses.*

Again, I ask for your compassion and understanding in all that I have said here.

I deeply thank you Mitch,
T

Notice that the "love" was dropped at the end of that email. Also notice that she characterized her benefits and retirement from her company as "vital and priceless." Does that sound like a person who is dependent upon God for future sustenance? She doesn't trust God for anything. She only trusts her own ability to provide for herself and her future. Notice also that although she states, "although I always have hope, I do understand you have little," yet she is resigned to the fact that things are shipwrecked and she asks for time to find another place to live so she can work out a separation. She has no hope – she never will.

She also matter-of-factly admits that she wants to move back to Phoenix. So this exchange began with her lies on 6/15 that "I want to be intimate with you and close to you. I wish we could sleep in the same room together even if we can't sleep in the same bed…" and within 3 weeks she is asking to be separated. Can you see why this has been vexing to me? Terry is a lying conundrum. She doesn't know what she wants but she still lies anyway.

The next day I typed this up and left it for her on the stairs…
7/11/09 Dear Terry,

How can you say that my being married to you is not MY cup of tea? I have made every attempt to lay down my life for you in every area I can think of. I have tried everything I know to do to try to compromise what I want (not touching you because it 'makes you feel like a piece of meat', not begging for sex, not talking about sex, not joking about sex, not watching things on TV that I want to watch, letting you watch anything you want to watch, making you the meals that you like—being silent when it came to Ronnie, being silent about everything really…..taking you to Phoenix every month, praying with you at 5 each morning, leaving you little love notes, buying you books on Christian intimacy and hoping that they would make a difference, trying my best to keep the house warm enough for you, talking to you gently about how you are killing me over and over and over and over and over and praying about it with you and waiting and waiting and waiting…..etc. etc. etc.), yet the only way I see that you have tried to make marriage 'your cup of tea' is that you moved to CA and you are working a hard job with great benefits.

Have you really worked at this marriage? HOW? List the ways you have rolled up your sleeves and tried to make this marriage work (besides going to a job every day).

Marriage is about finding out what is important and essential to your mate and then doing everything you can to meet those needs. Other than working a job that produces income, Terry, how have you met my needs?

You now have all kinds of hurts due to things I have said and done in my attempts to fix this relationship (might you have a problem with forgiveness? Do you hold grudges for years?), but please remember that my hurts go back to almost day one. I *predicted* that this was going to happen years ago—even before we married. But you threw a crying fit (your first one) and it floored me into backing off.

I *predicted* that you were going to make me fall out of love with you because of the direction you were headed. I *predicted* that I would not want to reach out to you, to pray with you, to do all the little things with you that I used to do. I warned you that you were going to kill this relationship by your refusal to give to me and meet my needs, so you should not be surprised at the depth of your dismay—I told you it was coming but you ignored my warnings.

Think back Terry—how many times in our almost 8 years together did you bring me a book that explained the way you feel a married relationship should be? Never. Yet I have bought you book after book after book, and as far as I can tell you have never even read them—you have never come to me and said, "honey, this book really meant a lot to me and these are the ways we can change". Think back Terry—how many times have you initiated showing me Scriptures that explain the way you feel a married relationship should be? Never. You always come back at me with "your" Scriptures after I show you what the Bible says about how the wife should treat her husband, but only in response to my tries to show you the Bible—never because you have a heartfelt desire to make our marriage the best possible marriage it can be. Never that. And I have shown you Scriptures many times, as you know.

You say you have physical needs that I am not able to meet. What physical needs? The need to be at 90 degrees all the time? The need for fizzy water every 15 minutes? The need to eat all the time and sit on the couch? The need to drink a lot of wine each night to dull the pain??

You seem to have no needs to touch, cuddle, kiss have intercourse or any of what I would consider to be 'normal' married physical needs....you never have, really. I think sex is scary and dirty to you.

You call this home my sanctuary, and 'over which you have total direction'. Yes, I have made it a sanctuary, but we shopped for this place TOGETHER. This is the place YOU really loved and wanted. It is decorated and painted pretty much the way YOU wanted—it has a $7,000 spa on the back porch which you 'needed' (and which you never use), the new kitchen is decorated according to the color scheme you wanted—(although we did agree except for the paint color until you showed me I was wrong), so why do you make it sound like this is sort of 'my place' that I let you live in?

You say you don't want to live in CA beyond retirement, that you have the blessed goal of retirement, but then you say you want to get a position in Phoenix 'without a drastic reduction in pay & likewise my benefits'...???? So which is it? Do you want to move to Phoenix and get a job, or wait until you retire and then move? I think you just don't want to be here and that if your company had an office there you would already be gone.

I am happy to spend whatever we need to spend for you to have a car the whole time you are in Phoenix. No one is leaving you 'stranded & captive without transportation'. Better yet-just take the Honda. I will manage somehow with the van.

You make a big issue over what things I sometimes watch on TV, but I have bent over backwards in the last 4-5 years to let you decide what will be watched. I might complain and ask if there is nothing else on, but since we have had HBO and Showtime -you have watched your share of R rated movies. Even when I am not in the room you do this, so I don't think you should labor over this point too dramatically.

You say 'for me to function...I am not able to live with you as a housemate or roommate'. Really? What do you call the last 4-5 years? It seems to me you live as a roommate very capably. You never really wanted me to be involved in Ronnie's growth and development—isn't that something that a roommate would do? You are pretty much content to let me do all the housework, bill paying, shopping, etc., isn't that something a roommate would do?

When is the last time we had sex Terry? The Bible says, "do not deprive each other except by mutual consent." Have you had *my consent* to deprive me? Do you even wonder if you are depriving me? I bet you do not. The Bible says you should have my consent—and you do not. You talk about how the Bible shows you how you should live, but you pick and choose the passages you will follow and you ignore the ones that command you to give me your body.

When did we last have sex? How many times have we had sex in the last 6 months, 12 months? DO YOU EVEN KNOW? I do and it is beyond depressing to me. And how does just laying on your back and letting your husband 'do his thing' meet a husband's need for intimacy? It is almost like you are tolerating the gynecologist's examination–how exciting for me!

You cannot answer these questions because you have a serious intimacy problem. You need professional help because you are terrified of intimacy and you are CONTENT to live like that, so please don't tell me you are not able to live with me as a roommate–YOU DO THAT VERY WELL.

I NEVER said I did not want to go to Christian counseling. I have told you repeatedly that I would do that. And how can you twist the truth of what happened before in our counseling sessions? I stopped going to counseling with you because you cried bitterly each time I was there. You just cried and cried and cried and cried and cried. How productive is that? You repeatedly chose to go to an ungodly man–Dr. Unrhat, when I told you he was ungodly and women from church told you he was ungodly – yet you kept going. Then after I counseled you to go to a Christian, you finally did. You were going on your own and telling me that you were learning new things and that you were changing. But you never changed (except maybe to draw further away from me) and then you quit going altogether. And now you say, "Would it really work?' and "it is already shipwrecked." Are you are revealing your true feelings? It seems to me that you really don't want this to work and maybe you never have. Your words, "I have never had a good relationship with a man" ring louder than ever.

How can you NOT place a condition on the outcome of counseling? Are you saying you want to go to counseling but you don't want anything to change??? What is the point of going to counseling and not putting a condition on it (that we should be reconciled, or that you should want to learn to meet my needs for intimacy or that we could both understand what a Biblical marriage is all about?) Isn't the point of counseling to HAVE a condition that things can improve and that is why we go and talk about it? That's like saying, "let's repair the car and get it working but let's not expect it to be fixed and drivable."

Lord knows I have tried everything I know to lay my life down for you as the Bible says, but nothing works. You are terrified of intimacy. You are content to live as a roommate – you are content to just carry on as if nothing is wrong.

You also won't seek the counsel of godly people, and I believe that it is because you can't trust. You can't trust me – you can't seem to trust anybody. Could you trust these email exchanges to Pastor or his wife? I wonder.

So I guess I really don't know quite what to say. Once again, you have dropped the "I'm leaving" bomb on me.

I never know if you are just going to drive away one day because you have told me so many times that you are leaving. Imagine how that affects my security, Terry. So I guess I will just quote Jesus here and say, "what you do – do quickly." You can look that one up for yourself. I wish you the best—I always have.

Mitch

I got no reply.

7/15/09

She made the comment to me (again) the other day, "You only married me for my money." How deluded is that? We have discussed this so many times! I came up with the $20,000 for the down payment on the house, I have always plunked down cash for her to have a nice car. I have always made more money than she has (and dumped it all into the general account) since we married. To prove the point, I went through the period 6/15/08 to 7/15/09 and tallied up all the deposits. Hers: $32,842; Mine $56,744. Then I reminded her that she has her own separate checking account with her own "stolen" money in it and she walked away from me…

7/22/09

She drove away to Phoenix on 7/16 for a week to get away. I think she comes back in two days – Friday or Saturday. I have had such a peaceful, productive time. She called me only once on the 16th to say she got there. I didn't answer the phone. I emailed her Pastor's email address from the church here. She seemed shocked that I was expecting her to set up counseling. This is it folks. This needs a miracle or I am going to a lawyer. I will rip everything in half as is my right under community property laws: the condo, her retirement – everything. Only Pastor stands in the way of me doing this now.

Chapter Four – Fasten
your tray tables

8/4/09

On 7/24 she came back home. She called me ½ hr away and said she was getting gas and "Was there anything else needed?" I said no. She locked herself in her room all the rest of the day Friday, all day Saturday. Saturday afternoon I went to spend some time with a friend and then I picked up my new student Enoch from LAX. He came to do an internship with me in AZ. We got home at about 11PM and went to bed. Sunday morning we drove to the lab in AZ and spent all week at the lab. She emailed me and asked when I was coming home, I said Sunday August 2. On the 1st I drove Enoch back to LAX and then went to the beach to think. I went home after midnight on the 2nd – she was sleeping downstairs on the couch. She thought her bed had bedbugs or something, and wanted to know if someone had been sleeping in her bed while she was gone to AZ!!! She was completely freaked out about it….I said that was ridiculous. Who on earth would have been sleeping in her bed?

She did go to Pastor while I was gone to Arizona, but refused to say anything other than "I can't be what you want…sob, sob." How about freaking being what you said you would be when you made your freaking vows???? I wrote her a letter and said my heart was cold and that even a miracle probably couldn't change that now. She got up Sunday morning and was again locked in her room. I could hear her pacing back and forth. Then at 9:05 she came down and announced she was going to church. I was still in shock from the night before and had not even unpacked, so I was certainly not up to going–especially with her and her whole psycho "everything is fine" behavior at church.

After she left I finished the letter and put in on the stairs along with a response to her earlier stupid email (see above). Later, as she was walking in the door, I was getting dressed to go out and run some errands. Then as I was walking out she asked, "Are you leaving?" like I had some big reason to hang around. I said yes, and I went to lunch and ran some errands. By the time I got home at 2PM she had packed her bags and was walking out the front door. She did not say a word to me, but wrote a note saying she was "staying with a friend to sort out things over a few days."

Last night she emailed me the following:

8/3/09

Mitch,

I agree that I don't think there is anything that will change. I agree that we should settle on an option. None will be easy, I know. The 3rd option is something that we can try to work on. (By this she meant my suggestion that we continue to live here as the economy improves and then sell the condo when the price is back up to snuff again).

I think a legal separation might provide the best possible result for both of us. It looks like it would be the most economical and could save money on attorney fees. I want to work with you on separating our income and dividing the bills. Since the economy might take awhile to recover, maybe we could check out the prices of units in our complex and see if we could sell the house in the near future without too much of a loss. I hope we can work together as much as possible even as our lives separate. Please let me know what you think. Thank you very much, Terry

Today 8/4, Tuesday, I emailed her the following:

Before I reply to your email, Terry, tell me "What do you want?"

As far as I can tell, your needs are to be left alone, to work your job without any interference from me or anybody, to be in a warm home, to have the wine and foods that you like, to be able to watch Cary Grant movies and TBN, to go to church on Sunday and to go to Phoenix every month as I have been faithfully taking you for many years. Other than that, I cannot think of any other needs you might have.

Now that you have moved out on me and have left me-"What do you want?"

Mitch

So folks-here is my plan: I will try to lure her back to the house – I will get her to keep depositing her paycheck and then I will stop paying bills without telling her. I will then amass as much cash as I can, put it into a separate checking account and when she finds out that the bills are not being paid (in about 2 months or so), I will walk away and leave it all in her lap. This is what she deserves for screwing me over for nearly 8 years.

Will Jesus love me just as much as her after I do this? I sure hope so but I am not hopeful.

8/9/09.

Well she came back on Thursday. Apparently she had failed the carpool van driver's medical test and was told she was no longer a driver. Her blood pressure is up pretty high and she had blood in her urine. She was home from work on Thursday and Friday trying to get things sorted out with her doctor. This alone drove me about insane. On top of that she was convinced that her bed had bedbugs in it and that she had bites all over her body "from the bed bugs". So I had to set off bug bombs in her room, which stunk up the house. She sat around Thursday, Friday and Saturday on the couch watching TV for over 14 hours each day. Turns out that all the bites she has were from fleas all over the many pets that her sister in Arizona has. She must have been bitten like crazy when she was there late last month...

I tried to get work done but with her blaring the TV it was not easy. Sunday she announced she was not going to church and she locked herself away in her room all day, watching a Carey Grant marathon on TBS.

I hope I can start to amass enough cash to just walk away. But I will be doing just that. I will be walking away from her retirement, from the equity in the house, from any hope for a stable life over the next few years. I will have to live in a crap apartment or room somewhere. I don't know what I will do with all my equipment upstairs in the in-home lab that I have set up.

Or, I could just keep my mouth sewn shut and be a silent butler until death parts us or she walks away again. I just don't know if I can actually do that though. Why is this so hard??

So I am blackmailed into this bizarre relationship–if I try to talk about this loveless, sexless, dead marriage, she walks away and all I have worked for is lost. If I smile, act like all is well in her dungeon of horrors, I get to keep my nice lab, my nice house, my nice lonely life. So I am blackmailed. What a "Christian" marriage this has been.

10/7/09–Final entry.

Yup, I'm finally done with this whole diary thing. For the last 8 weeks, she has been locked in her room. She comes home, grabs a bite to take upstairs and stays in her room each night. She stays in her room all weekend. She does not go to church. Course, she reads her Bible, (at least it seems like she does because I can see it on her bed through her open door each day). So God must be very happy with her. She actually ordered 2 copies of Pastor's sermon, "Husbands are to be the leaders in the home," but I would bet anybody $500 that she has not listened to it. It was a good sermon—maybe she would learn something….

I am slowly pulling cash together and I am trying to pay down my credit cards. I go out every weekend to do my own thing. I have met some cool people and have been having some fun—it helps me not to think about the dead, lifeless ghost living in the upstairs of this house.

10/14/09

The tenth week she has been locked in her room every night and all weekend. Today she emailed me from work and said there had been "some new developments" and that she needed to talk to me. When she came home I was eating a salad and watching TV. She went upstairs and after about 15 minutes she came out her bedroom door and asked me from the upstairs landing if now was a good time to talk. I said fine. She came down, sat on the opposite couch, started to cry and sniff, and proceeded to tell me that her company had decided to disburse all employee pension funds in a lump sum before the end of the year. She said she had gone to a free legal office at her work and was told that I was entitled to 50% of the net gain in all her retirement funds since the day we got married (no duh…). She said she wanted a divorce and that she wanted to work through this and divorce me and move away. I explained that we had little equity in the house (maybe $30,000 after agents fees, costs, etc.). I also explained that with the tuition loan, credit cards, new spa on the back porch, car loan and kitchen remodel costs we had debt of about $50,000. So our debt exceeds what we have in equity, which means—she does this and we both hit the street with basically nothing. She looked shocked.

Like a silly fool, I asked her, "So what really went wrong?" I said I believed I did everything I could to be a loving and serving husband. She said, "I was hoping that this was going to be amicable." I said, "Yeah, in other words be silent Mitch…". She said nothing.

I also made the mistake of saying that it seemed to me that she had no good advice from anybody I knew -especially not from anybody at church, and that I also knew she was intent on doing this. I said "to quote Jesus, what you do—do quickly." She said, "Oh yeah – you have said that one to me before." Too bad it never stuck. Then she went on saying, "It's me, it's me-it's not you."

So this plane is coming in for a crash landing. I hope I survive it. Way to go Mitch – a marriage for the record books.

10/20/09

I prepared a sheet for her outlining our debt. Including upcoming property taxes it amounts to $59,000. So I was almost $10K off by my guesstimate. I think it shocked her even more, as she has been locked in her room again over the last 6 days. But somebody had to pay for her 15-18 trips to Arizona every year, her new cars (2), her new kitchen and all. She did tell me that she would like to use her retirement and whatever equity exists to pay down all the debt. She also wants to refinance the house so I can afford it on my own. Uh, huh – like that's gonna work…

10/26/09 Monday

Well tonight she came home with a green company form that was essentially a waiver of all my rights with respect to the $51,000 pension that the company is about to pay out in a lump sum. She is still behaving as if the divorce will go through with or without me (this is a no-fault divorce state after all, so I am powerless on that). I am of the strong opinion that we should jointly roll it over into the main retirement fund and lose none of it. I told her I would look it over, which I did and then I left a post it note on it after she went to bed. My note asked simply, "What happens if I do not sign this?"

10/27-Tuesday.

I have been sitting here reflecting on all the ways T has thrown temper tantrums to get her way and to control me. I am wondering why I should just sit by and let this foolish woman rip my life in half by walking away from the condo (and probably destroying my chances to keep it), by destroying the retirement funds (and probably paying huge penalties and taxes to the IRS), and generally running roughshod over me yet again? So silly me, I typed up a 2 page letter and told her I was not going to make this easy, that she was in rebellion against her husband – THE authority God placed in her life and that according to 1 Sam 15:23 rebellion was as the sin of witchcraft. I said I had never told her to obey me but that I was now doing so, and to submit and stop this nonsense. I gave her the letter when she walked into the house. SHE WENT JUST ABSOLUTELY NUTS! I forgot the cardinal rule once again – NOBODY changes Terry.

The screaming and yelling was unbearable. I am serious – it was just shocking. She waved the green form in my face and screamed that if I did not sign it, my half would become a "death benefit" meaning, I would never see the money since women outlive men by at least 15 years in America. So once again a tantrum was levied upon me. I told her I was leaving and started packing. She begged me not to go but I repeated over and over that she was in rebellion and so I was leaving. She said she had not had time to divert her paycheck and could she have some of it and I said, "I'll think about it." She kept shouting that she could lose her job as a result of me not cooperating. What a pathetic ruse!

I packed 3 suitcases and several boxes. I took 2 lab systems and all the research rocks and my van. Before I left I gave her the $1400 mortgage bill, the $362 new Honda bill, insurance bills totaling $3500, and the HOA fee of $238. Haha – I am sure that shocked her. Dear God, I am not paying out for this nightmare any more! I also gave her the Honda key.

The next day (Wednesday) I paid down the electric bill and put a shutoff order on the account (since it is in my name). She can have it turned back on in her own name. I canceled her debit card on the main checking account. I dropped her and the Honda from my auto insurance account – she is on her own for car insurance. I did not turn off the phones (obviously my business would suffer) but I did change the voicemail passwords so she cannot delete any voicemail messages that I might receive. I turned off her cell phone (that she racked up 400 minutes on last week.) I checked into a motel and ignored her for 3 days. I did however, sign, date and had notarized the green form that she had waved in my face. I put it on the stairs Wednesday before she got home. I also asked her for the gas cards since I am carrying all that debt.

This woman is going to feel some pain for a while. I cannot stop her nor will I resist her – she can cash it all out, dump the condo and crawl back to Phoenix. She can't possibly pay for all that on her salary so she is going to lose some real sleep for a change.

By about Friday I emailed her and told her that wasting precious money on a motel was pointless, and that since I had nowhere to go I was coming home on Sunday after church and small group. My next-door neighbor (the LA County Sheriff) told me, "Don't you vacate the house under any circumstances." My behavior doesn't warrant that I move out so I am going back.

Saturday, 10/31/09

A little history before I make this point: Terry has never been one for sports. Ronnie did play some soccer when he was 10 or 12 in Phoenix but she has never encouraged him in any sports here in California at all. She does love the Olympics, so every 2 years she has to watch all the coverage non-stop for days, and I have to either sit there with her or find something else to do. I don't watch a lot of sports either, but I have always followed my beloved Florida Gators football team, having gone to college there. Tim Tebow grabbed my attention during the 2006 football season because he was such a great athlete and because I thought it was so cool that he was so open about his Christianity. The Gators beat Ohio State in January of 2007 to become National Champions for the 2006-07 season. Terry began getting into the Florida football games each Saturday then and even more as I fanatically rooted on my Gators. Although the Gators did not win the Championship in January of 2008 – we both enjoyed watching the games every Saturday and were thrilled when the Gators beat Oklahoma this past January for yet another National Championship. Well the Gators played today–against Georgia–a huge rivalry for me, and one that I remember vividly when I sat in Florida stadium (the Swamp) as a student. Now the game is played in Jacksonville but in any event–a huge game was on TV. So I was watching the game in the living room and Terry was locked upstairs in her room, as usual. I could hear her TV on–she was also watching the game and I could hear her cheering Tebow and my Gators on. It made me so angry I went upstairs, threw open her door and told her, "How dare you cheer for my team. Don't you dare cheer for MY Florida Gators!" I closed her door and did not hear one more cheer from her during the rest of the game. I know–pretty rough huh? I don't care any more.

Sunday, 11/1/09

Well it got down and dirty again tonight. She once again laid into me about cashing out the retirement funds and the divorce. I stopped her and said, "I think we should have this conversation in front of a mature Christian–someone who knows us." I suggested a few folks from Church but she kept balking about that. Finally I suggested Patrick and sobbing and screaming she agreed. I made her call him and in 20 minutes he came over. She was sullen and barely talkative when he came. I made her start over and she did, but she started skewing her story a bit. I kept saying, "Pat don't get played" to try to keep her honest but again she *openly lied* that my only option was to sign my rights away on the retirement funds. I said, "No, the law allows me to roll it over. We should roll it over–take a breather period and go from there." She would not answer Pat when he kept asking her if it was possible to roll it over. She's out of control when it is just me, but sanity returns when someone else is present. I said we needed to go to our own Pastor for counseling. She said, "No, because he knows you too well." Huh? What does that mean? He knows me too well?? Isn't that the point? Don't you go to a counselor who knows you well enough to help you with your marital problems?

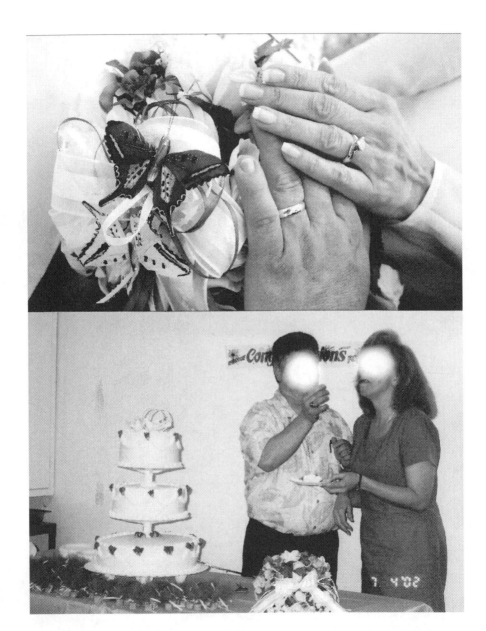

11/2/09

Monday she brought home a huge packet on the pension and sure enough it had a whole section about the option to roll it all over, tax-free into our main account. I knew it and she had been lying through her teeth. I put a note on it that said, "so this is possible?" and she replied overnight, "You can do that with your portion." My portion!! There is only OUR portion in my mind – but she wants out and this is her ticket to run.

Patrick told her she had to go to counseling, that she had no Scriptural reason for divorce and got us an appointment with his Pastor, Don Sythfor of Upland Mountain Church. It would be just one appointment because "he does not counsel couples who are not in his church"....perfect. Now she can go and cry and cry and cry and never have to go back... But if he does not counsel people like us, why is he counseling us? That made no sense to me and it also put me on edge.....was I about to be asked to leave my church of over 10 years?

"You make this all go away; you make this all go away; you make this all go away, I 'm down to just one thing – I'm starting to scare myself. You make this all go away, you make this all go away, you make it all go away – I just want something I just want something I can never have, I just want something I can never have."

Words and Music, Trent Reznor, Nine Inch Nails.

Wednesday November 4

Well we both showed up at the counselor's and I was shocked that she came. We spent a few minutes talking about our backgrounds and then he asked her a difficult question. She started crying and clamming up. Like an idiot, I offered to leave the room, and Pastor Don said, "Yeah, sure." I waited about 40 minutes and then finally he called me in. I am sure she lied through her teeth. I am sure she told him that I am Satan on steroids. I doubt she told him that she would lock herself in her room and stop gong to church for 20 weeks if I dared to be honest to our small group about our struggles. I doubt she told him that she withheld sex from me for a year. I doubt she told him that she has been dropping the divorce bomb on me for over 5 years. I am sure she played him like Nero's fiddle.

She was gone from the room when he asked me to come back in. I assumed she had left and gone home. He then proceeded to hammer the crap out of me! According to him, I was responsible for my first marriage ending in Judy getting cancer and now I am responsible for all Terry's problems too. (What??)

He asked me what I had done wrong in the marriage. I admit I felt backed into a corner at this point, so I did not do well in answering that question. He then said I was the most defensive person that had ever come into his office! Really? You don't even know me.

Then he invited poor, dear, sobbing Terry back into the room. I said that the only reason we were actually there was because I pushed hard for it and that she was determined to do her thing and divorce me no matter what anybody said. He said that neither of us was walking the walk and that against his better judgment he would see us again, but only if we did some homework. Her homework–read Romans 8 ten times.

My homework? Go buy an obscure counseling book and read the chapter on humility and service. Then I was to write down the top 5 pride issues in my life. So I can see where this is going….poor, sad Miss Terry–how you must have suffered at the hands of this angry, mean person who does not love you…. When she got home later I asked, "Is there anything I can help you with?" She ignored me and walked upstairs. Why do I bother? What fun.

11/5/09

Today I emailed her and asked her if we could go out for a salad or Chinese. She took two emails to decide and finally said no. OK the heck with that-I then decided I would try to answer Pastor Don's question on what I had done wrong in the marriage. I figured it would be a good bet to go with: anger, resentment, bitterness, discord–things like that. I can eat crow–what the heck? If it keeps her from destroying my life, I can play-act all sorry and repentant. She won't change and I will be out of the house doing things with other people anyway, so whatever. So I typed up a very contrite email to Pastor Don and said my anger had prevented me from being honest with him last night. He emailed me back and said–good–now read it verbatim to T and ask for her forgiveness. OK……..

I am still wondering when she will have to come up with her list of things she has done wrong and confess it to Pastor and me and ask me for forgiveness? Probably won't happen because NOBODY CHANGES TERRY. And let's not forget, she played him big time with her tears last time she was here. It's what she does. Academy of Motion Picture Arts and Sciences, are you reading this?

So tonight when she walked in the door, (and by the way, I turned on the porch light and left the outer door unlocked–did she thank me? *No freaking way….*), I asked her if we could talk for a while. She immediately started in with the excuses and walked away. I said "Terry I want to confess something to you." She came back and sat down. I read her the email I had sent to Pastor in which I admitted to my anger, discord, resentment–I read it slowly and very contritely. I said I was sorry and asked her to forgive me. She immediately and coldly said, "I forgive you" and stood up, went to her room and locked the door for the night. She doesn't forgive–she only mouths the words that need to be mouthed to move on to what she really wants.

So I am already to split–I have some friends in Ocean Beach with a big house near the ocean. It has lots of room for all my lab stuff. It is tranquil and peaceful there. I can have a life away from here and all her bull-crap. She can get hung with the house-all I will have to deal with are the credit cards–about $24,000 in debt including my tuition bills, but I will live very inexpensively with some very nice people who really care about me as a friend. I will survive. That is my backup plan–if this attempt to bring her in line fails, I am set up and good to go. I did finally find Don's stupid book–I called at least six Christian book stores including several large ones in Pasadena–turns out I had to drive 45 miles – all the way to the bookstore at the large Grace Church in the San Fernando Valley just to get it–but I did–after all it was my homework.

11/11/09 Pastoral session #2.

Tonight Pastor Don spent about an hour talking and using many large "John MacArthur" words. He read many passages and expounded on them expertly and with great aplomb and emphasis. I felt like I was in a classroom and not in a counseling session. The whole time he was looking at me rather sternly–he made facial and vocal emphases towards me about 90% of the time and he rarely looked at Terry who sat and sniffled and cried the whole time, although she did take a few short notes. Then he proceeded to state that I was the one responsible for the bad quality of this marriage and that I had "driven this poor woman to this." He even stated again (like he did last week) that my previous marriage ending in loss to cancer and Judy walking out on me and my sons was completely my responsibility as well. (Wow–can someone actually accuse you of that?)

He basically said that since the husband is the head of the wife (Eph 5) that I was to blame for it all because I am the head and the buck stops with me. The whole reason we are in this horrible mess is my responsiblity..,.. Is that what that verse really means? And when have I ever been Terry's head? She has ruled this household by tantrum from day one–before day one in fact. For the last 5 years I have been silent because my mentor Dr. Paine advised me to be so. The only reason this whole thing has blown up since June is because I called her a liar when she said she was "really, really trying to love me." She had been manipulating me from day one, and I finally dragged up the stones to call her on it. Now I am paying for my stupid mistake of being honest with her and calling her out.

I did my best, however to remain open and teachable and to stay calm and humble as I sat through one verbal pounding after another. I wrote down what he said–I silently prayed for God to keep my heart open and to speak to me through this experience. Don told me several times, "This is going to hurt you," and to be honest it really did. Still, I sat there and kept a cheerful look on my face and trusted that God was in this some how.

Several times during the session I said that I was trying to be an open book. I said that I knew that I had mountains of pride and that I had confessed that readily and openly and that I was committed to working on my pride issues. I praised the book he asked me to go buy, as being a real eye opener for me and very practical. OK, I was stretching things a bit, but I did learn some interesting things from the book. I said that I could actually see both Terry and I in the pride chapter–and that is true. I saw the same old pride issues that I had always struggled with but I also got new insights into her issues of pride and how hidden and masked they are. She is skilled at playing people and hiding her pride. But she has tons of it and NOBODY ever calls her on it because of the waterworks and the sad victim game she plays.

I had done my homework quickly last week and had mailed it to him right away. (Terry turned hers in tonight and he put it away without even looking at it [!!!!]). By the way-he made absolutely no comments about our homework. I found that odd.

I was honest about myself and did not make any "buts" about my behavior. I took full responsibility for my hurt feelings my feelings of anger, etc. But still he pressed relentlessly on me. At one point I said that I felt he was being unfair, that this door swung both ways and that T bore some responsibility for these problems too–of course he used that as an opportunity to smack me down again as being prideful and haughty and "Unwilling to be broken before God," (does he mean *him*? Must I have to cry to make *this guy* believe that I have sincerely tried in this marriage???).

He said that my stating that the door swung both ways was one of the worst examples of pride he had ever seen. Wow–this was a whole new form of counseling to be sure. Why were we there?

So needless to say I started feeling that (once again) Terry (that poor dear crying woman) was the victim and that I was the sole aggressor and generally mean husband. Same story as so many times before in front of so many counselors. Mitch has to be completely and utterly sacrificed on the altar before Terry can even be expected to change–her behavior is understandable and expected–mine is an abomination to God. He made such shocking statements about how despicable and horrific I must be to have caused these problems. I swallowed hard, fought back feelings of anger and tried to listen with an open heart. This went on for about 2 hours. I definitely got the feeling that he was trying to make me cry or something–he even said, "I have to break you – I have to *completely* break you, because you are an idolater," like I am some new project for him or something. Wow, Jim Jones anyone?

He made a diagram that had CONTROL on one side and COMFORT on the other. He said, "Mitch wants control and Terry wants comfort,"–he is right about that. She does want to run away and she has always acted that way (wow you got that one right Don). I said, "You are right I do want control and I have spent 8 years letting go of control and allowing her to run roughshod over me." He said, "You obviously want control right now–even though you sit here and say you are trying to let go – you are still a prideful and haughty man – you seek control over me as well. You are only trying to preserve YOUR rights when you say anything about Terry. You are trying to justify yourself – as you did in your previous marriage and you are still doing it now." What??? He also said that when I told him about my accomplishments (my publications, my patent) last week (because he asked and wanted to know about me), that once again I was trying to control him. I said, "Pastor, you don't know me... you don't know my life–you know nothing about my previous marriage and Judy's cancer–how she walked out on me. And yet you make such judgments on such little knowledge of me?" He just glared. What a mean guy. Dear God–is this kind of person really a reflection of you? For a long time after I said that, he stared at me and sternly said that he had the right to say those things to me because he knew me and that he wondered if I was even saved. Wow–I kid you not. I started to feel hot at that point.

Then he actually accused me of not being a Christian!! He wanted to know evidences for how I knew I was a Christian–I told him my conversion was radical-that I went from a 2 pack of cigarettes a day and heavy drug user to a cleaned up person, no drugs –no smoking since the day I was baptized. He said anybody can quit drugs and smoking cold turkey(!!!) He said I could have done all that by my own strength (wow – it really started to get to get me then.)

Finally, I said I knew that it was only the blood of Jesus spilled for me that I was going to go to heaven – that I clung to that and I was only saved because of that. He wanted to hear more about my works (what??!) I am now convinced that this Pastor is a works oriented legalist. He is a pompous authoritarian who loves to hear himself talk and who likes to exercise strict authority over people. I did not find him to be loving towards me at all.

Terry did admit to him that she was fearful and that she was trying to work on that, and that she knew she had a victim mentality, but she spoke very little and he hardly questioned her at all. I was on the hot seat all night. But when Pastor asked her why she was here and not at our own church with our own Pastor getting the help we need, she actually told him that our Pastor *knew me better than he knew her* and that she was afraid that he would just side with me. I waited for Don to call her out on that–to tell her that she was just manipulating the system and refusing to go to our own Pastor of over nine years. You could have heard the crickets burping. He just shook his head and said, "You poor woman…" (What in God's name???) I wonder how he would have treated me if I had said that to him? He would have dressed me down again and laid into me with "Oh you are just trying to control the situation" or something like that! He softly said to her, "Oh Terry you still struggle with trust don't you?" So all impartiality had left the room at that point. Why does she have such hypnotic power over men? She isn't even pretty, in fact she is sort of unattractive (especially with her short ugly hair), she is uneducated and doesn't even look you in the eye–how does she do this to men???

I broke the tender moment they were having and said that we needed to talk about the fact that she was pressing me relentlessly on some deadlines (i.e. she had legal counsel, she was divorcing me, she was going to cash out the pension on the 15th, and she made me sign a form relinquishing my rights to the pension, and that she had diverted her paycheck into her own checking account). She then launched into a teary convoluted story about how she had to pay down the debt. I told Pastor Don she was lying–that she was cashing out the retirement because she wanted to run away. This has nothing to do with the debt. The debt became an issue 10 days ago when she wanted to know how to apply the cashed out retirement funds (which I still disapprove of but I signed away my rights to)–to make a clean financial split so she can run away. This is about Terry shouting at me 3 weeks ago, "I HAVE TO BE RID OF YOU." It is an excuse she is using to set herself up for a quick getaway.

I explained that 2/3 of the debt was my college tuition, the new Honda, the kitchen we had purchased together and the 35 trips we had made to AZ in the last 3 years–(mostly because she insisted that I move my lab to AZ.) Of course she couldn't stand for the truth to be told, so she (and I marveled at this) VERY sweetly said "Geez (aw shucks) I don't understand why you would say I wanted to run away… how could you say such a thing??" She bald face lied to Don and tried to justify paying the Government 40% in penalties and taxes on that retirement money. If she doesn't want to run away WHY CASH it out? Why not roll over a $51,000 gift from her company into our JOINT retirement fund?

I mistakenly said it was about $40K in penalties, so she HAD to correct me right there and say that it was ($51,000 X 40%) $21,000 in penalties. And that makes it all right??? Who gives the government $21,000 right now in this horrible economy when you can just roll it over and not pay a dime? What difference does that make??? If you are committed to staying together, you roll it over into your 401K, you don't cash it out.

She also lied about the form she required me to sign (giving up my rights) and the one simple form that she could have filled out (without my signature at all) to ROLL OVER all $51,000 of the pension money into the 401K, or even my half of the $51,000. I pointed this out and again she just bald face LIED about it. I could not believe this charade of misfits–all of us. I admit I am a misfit–but those two need to also.

Then she said (all sweetly again) that she had sort of *decided a few days ago that she was not going to divorce me*. Wow, thanks for telling me!! I have been in torture for days (years) and she could have told me that??? I went to her 2 times in the last 6 days and openly (and with tears) confessed my sin. She never said a word to me in return, she never confessed ANYTHING to me, but she stayed locked in her room (by the way this is the 16th week of that nonsense). I still don't believe she is not going to divorce me. She then said she still wants a legal separation. Don swallowed her act line and sinker.

Pastor Don then told us that we needed to start coming to his church. I have been going to one of the best churches in Southern California for almost eleven years and now all of a sudden I have to start going to his crappy little church in Upland, California because we are not under enough of his control or something?

Actually what he really said was, "I do individual counseling on weeknights like we are doing now, and then I do group therapy on Sunday mornings at 10:30." Wait a minute–did he just say that preaching the word of God and worshipping with the body on Sunday morning is GROUP THERAPY that HE conducts.??? CAN YOU BELIEVE THAT??? This is when I knew this man is definitely a legalist and a megalomaniac.

I'm sorry folks–I tried. I bought and read the book he asked me to. I confessed my pride issues and listed the top 5 from my own life. I tried to sit under the pounding and abuse for 2 weeks straight. I had to sit there and watch him side with "poor little Terry" who played him like a fiddle. It was too bizarre–I should have acted out like a crazy person or something.…

I quietly told him that it would be hard for me to come to his church on Sundays because I was moving to the coast, 2 hours away. Then I said that I was really having trouble with this being so one sided and that I would have to think about coming back on Wednesday nights. The goodbyes were cordial and nothing further transpired. I did thank him for his valuable time and said goodbye. That was the end of cultic Don.

I did, however, make a copy of the whole section above discussing his cultic counseling and emailed it to him before publishing this book. I knew I would not get anything constructive from him in reply, but I wanted him to know that I was on to his sick game and that I was going to expose him. I heard nothing back–surprise, surprise.

When I got home I parked (her now) Honda in front of the pool but I did not move my van into the garage from its outside parking spot. I will do that tomorrow. I am going to just drive my van from now on. I plan to start packing right away. If Terry will go with me to Pastor Gene for counseling and start coming back to our church and small group, I will commit again to being a humble and loving husband. Otherwise it is time for a separation. We came home separately. She walked into the house (I was in my room with the lights out). She went straight to the garage and opened the door. When she noticed the Honda wasn't there she came into my room (without knocking) and asked, "Is there something wrong with the Honda?" That says it all.…as long as her Honda is OK, who cares if there is something wrong with this marriage?

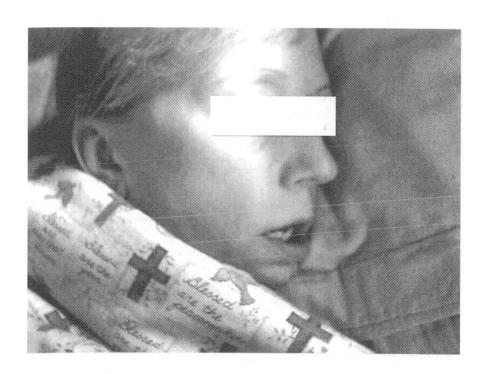

Saturday 11/14/09

Terry informed me a few minutes ago that she had indeed cashed out some of the retirement. She said that she wanted the utilities in her name (gas, electric, water, cable), but that the phones could now be cut off since she already had her new cell phone with a Phoenix number (480 area code). So it is clear that I must find a new place to live and that she is bent on returning to Phoenix.

She also said that she was getting the house appraised as soon as possible for sale-and that my 50% of the profit (which won't be much, if any, since the house has depreciated about $250,000 in the last year) and my share of the pension she would hold for me. I told her I didn't want a red cent from her from anything.

So I guess the counseling we had was great for her – I mean Pastor blaming it all on me and everything. But it was simply no help to me and now she is just acting out the plan that she obviously spent a great deal of time formulating. She lied to his face and was now back on her track – full speed ahead.

The house can be sold at a loss – I don't care. Of course, I have no desire to remain in a home that has had nothing but contention in it for almost nine years. By the way, I told her my Dad died today and she said, "I'm sorry." And walked away.

11/16 – I cut off the cable TV service – Silence from her.
11/18 – I cut off the phone service – Silence from her.
11/19 – I rented a truck and drove away. Silence from her.

Here are more fabulous emails from her between November 2009 and January 2010.

11/21/09 from Terry

Mitch,

This is my new email address: "terryl1991@Gmail.com"; (the letter after the y is an 'L' followed by the 4 digit number 1991). Thank you for leaving your address and phone number. I appreciate your willingness to let me know ahead of time before you will come to the house, thank you. This will be very helpful as I will then move the car from the garage before you come so that you have open access to the garage.

I have no plans to put the house up for sale. I apologize if I was not clear in my explanation when I said I would try to get the house appraised soon; it was not so that the house could be put up for sale, it was so that you could have a figure as to what the house is worth as of the time of your move.

Please let me know where my books are from the 2-shelf bookcase that I mentioned in the note as I do not see them there now.

Thank you very much,

T

11/25/09

M-

Wanted to let you know that I am leaving after work to drive to AZ for Thanksgiving and will be back on Saturday eve or Sunday in case you were planning to do anymore moving this weekend

Thank you,

T

12/05/09

M -

Could you tell me where the toolbox with the green lid and the sectioned brown box that contains all the fasteners are?

I brought those from AZ with me, it took me a long time to collect those items and I would like to use them.

Thank you very much,

T

12/24/09

M -

I have driven to AZ for Christmas and will return late Sunday... in case you wanted to go to the house for anything.

Thanks,

T

Of course I did not answer any of her stupid emails.

1/18/10. Martin Luther King Day – hard rain falling.

I stopped by the house unannounced at 6:45AM. I rang the doorbell just in case she was there, but after no answer I went in through the front door and walked the house. All trace of my former presence in my home had been removed from the walls, and the visible areas of the house, and were stored in several rooms that were closed up. The living room was re arranged and was neat but very stark. All the blinds in the downstairs were closed up tight—it seemed like a cave. She had obviously paid for someone to remove all the leaves and debris from the back porch as it was clean and many bags of leaves were sitting out front for the trash men to pick up. I opened the earthquake container and removed as many cans of food as I could fit into a box I got from the garage. Many of my things that I had left behind had been placed into piles in the garage.

My old bedroom was untouched however, except for some furniture that had been jammed into it. It was quite dirty, and some of my old things were piled into the corners. I did not look in my closet. My old bath was cleaned up and the crystals and geodes that had been on the counter were placed in my old room. All my old things that had been in the medicine cabinet and under the sink had been removed. The master bedroom upstairs had been completely rearranged. The beautiful butterflies in Plexiglas containers that I had hand carried from Old San Juan, Puerto Rico back to the states were removed from the wall and placed into the upstairs room I had used as my lab. In the place where the butterflies had been on the wall was a prominent picture of Jesus. I guess if she stares at Jesus' picture enough she doesn't feel so bad about the pagan way she treated her husband. He must love her so very much. She is so special. I guess I am going to hell.

So there you have it. I have been gone 8 weeks—gone during our 8th Thanksgiving—gone during our 8th Christmas—gone during my 57th birthday—gone during her 56th birthday and my traces are now gone as well.

At 9AM after eating some breakfast, I met with my tax lady and we discussed the particulars needed for me to file separate taxes from her. She will not enjoy the benefits of my company deductions, and I will not report her cashing out the retirement funds on my taxes. She has to drag that one into the IRS all by herself. I hope she gets audited.

4/3/10. Saturday. Still no word from her. Our 8th wedding anniversary is in 3 days.

I envision her as being the happiest psychotic woman in the world. My taxes are done—it cost me $1700 to extricate myself from her financially. Of course, she will need my signature to sell the house and cash out any remaining retirement funds she wants to waste. What's funny is my accountant told me that Terry called her and asked her to do her taxes too. Haha–she is about to have to pay out a bundle for spending all that retirement money. Oh well. Life goes on.

4/23/10 I got this today
   "Mitch,
   I apologize that I haven't been able to get these papers to you until now. I have now saved the funds needed to use Legal Action Workshop (L.A.W.)-[similar to We The People]-as the legal service for assistance in filing the separation papers. Please note that these papers indicate 'divorce' but are the same papers that are used in filing for legal separation.
   The forms require that each of us complete and sign. They are in PDF format because the Word version they tried to send was not Mac-compatible. You can scan & send them back to me or, if you'd prefer to send them direct to L.A.W., let me know and I will send you the email address for the person at their office who is assisting me.
   Thank you very much,
   T"

My Pastor and all my advisors all said, "Get a lawyer". Nope – she can have it all, I really don't care. Here was my response:

"4/28/10
   Terry,
   It was six months ago today that you announced you had legal help and that you planned to get a divorce.
   Today you have almost everything you wanted: me out of your life, your independence from me and from everyone who was involved in your life at church, your precious job, your precious financial independence, your plans to return to Phoenix, your Phoenix phone number, the house, the furniture, all the new appliances, the car, the retirement funds, etc., etc....
   Can I assume that you still do not wish to be reconciled to your husband or to go with me to our pastors at church? I think I must assume that you do not, based upon what you have just sent me. Plus you keep saying, "He knows you too well."
   Since I must assume that you intend to cement this divide, what then is the point of these papers you have sent me to complete? They say 'divorce'

on them—whether or not you intended it this way, divorce still seems to be your hearts desire.

Reconciliation does not seem to be anywhere in your plans.

Jesus said about marriage, "What God has joined together, let man not separate." (Mt 19:6, Mk 10:9). You made it clear that I had to 'separate' from you and so I did. Now you want for the 'separation' to become "legal." Sounds like divorce, ultimately, doesn't it?

Terry, what is the point of disobeying Jesus "just a little"? Jesus sees your heart. How is "just a little" disobedience any better that complete disobedience in His eyes? Divorce is no worse that the 'separation' you seek—it is the same sin in His eyes. You are 'separating' what God has brought together.

You have no Biblical reason for what you have done-and since you have already engineered the 'separation', why stop short now? It did not stop you prior to this moment – it should not stop you in the future if you remain so intent on this.

Just divorce me like you truly desire and be done with it. I will not resist you (Matt 5:39). It is probably for the best anyway because you are only happy when you are completely independent, especially from me.

What does Mitch want? I only want the heart of a Biblical woman-something you do not seem to have. Nothing else on this Earth is important to me. There is nothing else that you now have, or that we "jointly own" that I could write down on these papers that means anything to me at all. I have already forgiven you and released you- take it all with you! Just divorce me and be done with it.

Now, here is a fork in the road, Terry. I have attached a Word file to this email that suggests a Biblical alternative towards this divide. With God's help it might foster the marriage that God designed for us

It is the best I can do right now. It is not ideal but there it is.

You are under no obligation to read it. You are under no obligation to even consider it.

In fact, you can simply delete it without opening it-you won't offend me in the least at this point. My life could go either way, but I would prefer to discharge my duty to God with the vows that I made over 8 years ago. Nevertheless, you may choose to consider it or you may not.

I have complied with all your wishes to date. I will not resist your intentions to be rid of me if you proceed. So just go for the divorce Terry. Forget this nonsense of an unbiblical separation. Move on.

Mitch"

She emailed me back with a new email address: fearnot4me@yahoo.com I think that was some kind of a signal to me that she was all happy with Jesus and all, since I had just finished quoting her the Scriptures that lay her out before God as a complete hypocrite.

She asked me to list all my assets on the pages she had sent me–AS IF I HAVE ANY ASSETS!!!

So I sent this:

"4/29/10

What assets? You have ALL the tangible assets from this supposed "marriage"–the RISP, the Pension, the house, the car, the new furniture, the new big screen TV, the Spa, the newer refrigerator, all the new appliances in the kitchen, the new washer and dryer, your new bed.….

And let's not forget the $7000 trip to Germany, the $2500 week in La Jolla, the $1300 engagement ring, all the Swarovski jewelry–oh yeah and the garnet ring you were so ashamed of you wouldn't even wear it around your family.

What I have are DEBTS-$2500 in gasoline cards and $2,000 on the AMEX card for about 40 trips to AZ in 5 years, $2500 on the Visa for the Spa I bought for you, $2500 on Home Depot for the new appliances that I still pay on.…

So you can write all that out on your pages 5,6,7 and mail them to me and maybe I'll sign them you selfish pagan."

I also did something that I think is really funny.…I Googled her idiot kid and found pictures of him that he had uploaded to his Facebook page. I particularly enjoyed the one headshot of him, where he is looking into the camera with his middle finger extended in the F-you symbol. So I pasted it onto the page and labeled the page "BetterFearGod.doc".

I bet that really made her mad, but she is in such denial over her kid it is not even funny.

She signed divorce papers two days later. I was served the court documents at work on 5/11/10. She even wants her old name restored. Wow I sure had a positive influence on this person, huh?

5/10/10

I drove to the house again early, since I knew she would be at work. It was bizarre. She had a bunch of new Jesus pictures on the walls. I guess it gives Jesus a warm fuzzy to know His picture is everywhere in that peaceful, happy place.

All of the new kitchen cabinet shelves, all of the kitchen drawers were segregated into groupings of utensils, dishes, cups, silverware–everything.... and it was all labeled with post-it-notes that said things like, "This shelf for T," and "This shelf all M". I kid you not!! Here are the pictures to prove it.

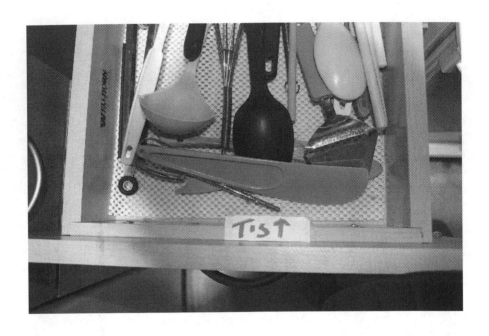

This nut job spent who knows how much time dividing up all the crap in the kitchen with little T's and M's on them—all the stuff I walked away from six months ago. Even the freezer was labeled! I am not kidding. I opened the freezer thinking, "She couldn't have gone this far," but you guessed it—the shelves and even the items on the freezer door were labeled. What is the point of that? I have told her repeatedly that she has nothing I want. I only ever wanted her heart, but she does not have a heart. She is a stone temple pilot. How quickly she offers me the worn Tupperware of a screwed up marriage. What about the real value… the retirement plan we worked on together to grow to $150 K?

You see, I put all my eggs in the "us basket". Everything I had and all my energy and love, I laid at her feet. She stabbed at that basket and stabbed at the eggs. She shattered and cut all the eggs into pieces. For her to label them now "M" with her little post-it-notes and arrows is abhorrent and grotesque to me. That is why I cannot drag any of those shattered eggs into my new life. I want none of it, except the things that remind me of my college sweetheart.

I collected some pillows and other items I wanted and split—leaving little trace that I was there. Good Lord. Thank God this is over. There is, however, one black and white high-resolution CCTV camera that I forgot about and I really do need that, so I will go by again during the day in the next couple of weeks.

5/19/10 I sent this email to her best friends in Phoenix:

Hello Eddie and John. I hope all is well with you.

So Terry served me here at work with court papers last week, so I guess this year of pain and uncertainty is over.

If she had only gone to our Pastors with me things may have turned out differently, but she refused all my requests since June.

I was made to sign away my rights to the pension money, "Or I will make it a death benefit." She can have it all-I only wanted her heart.

She demanded that I leave in November-a long, silent separation and now divorce, "I have to be rid of you!"

Oh well.

So I just wanted you guys to know that I really enjoyed knowing you.

So goodbye then, and God bless,

Mitch

I never got any reply…..surprise, surprise – what wonderful Jesus-loving Christians these people are!!! They make me vomit. They were willing to stand tall with me at my wedding. They got all dressed up and played the "close friend" part as we stood before their Pastor Paul and all his loving disciples and made our solemn vows. Don't they look nice in our wedding pictures? What sweet postures. I should have left their faces unblurred so you can see their sweet Christian expressions. What a lasting friendship we had in Jesus. They came to hear me speak when I appeared at well-promoted Bible/Science meetings in Arizona. They enthusiastically hugged me and told me how awesome my talks were. They came to my home in California, and they welcomed me into their home in Phoenix. Now dead silence. No reply. No, "Mitch–what is going on with you and Terry? Can we pray for you?" DEAD SILENCE.

Where are you now John and Eddie? Where is that awesome Christian fellowship you showed me in the past?

5/26/10

I worked a few hours in Los Angeles and then, knowing she would be at work, decided to swing by the house one last time and to get that camera I need. I rang the doorbell about 6 times and then opened up the front security door and the front door. The living room was even more stark than before. Once again, every shade was drawn and closed tight – I had to turn on lights just to see, and it was 12:30 in the afternoon. I noticed that all of her videos–all the Cary Grant love stories, all the pictures of her brat, etc. had been removed from the living room bookshelf and were nowhere downstairs. One whole bookshelf was completely empty–the other one was overstuffed with all my old videos and stuff. I wondered where she had put all her videos. She must be spending all of her time up in her ghostly bedroom.

The door to the garage was locked from the inside with the deadbolt and when I opened it and looked into the garage I was surprised to see the car gone. I wondered if she was parking it elsewhere-maybe because she feared that I would do something to it. Who drives the car out of the garage, closes the outer garage door and then goes back inside the house to lock the door into the house from the inside? Like I said – none of this ever made sense to me…

As I looked into the kitchen drawers again it hit me that some items from my previous life were in the drawers she had labeled "T". I thought, "How sad this disturbed person is to call my old things hers." A pair of scissors that my ex-wife had bought and used (because she was a seamstress) was one of those items, and I decided, "Heck no!" My college sweetheart had made many articles of clothing with those scissors.

So I took those and then I took paintings off the living room wall that my sweetheart and I had bought together. I also removed my fossils from the mantle over the fireplace and some beautiful shells that I had bought. I went upstairs to find my black and white CCTV camera and noticed she had replaced her bedroom door handle with a knob that required a key. She probably locks herself in there every night thinking she is so safe. I thought Jesus must be so happy and proud to call her one of His own….. doesn't He protect her? Why does she need a locked handle?

I didn't ever have to worry about removing any of her pictures and paintings from the walls because she STILL never hung anything from her past. How bizarre. Maybe she wanted to keep all her pictures in a box because she never planned to be here this long. Eight years is a long time to leave precious family photos in a box.

She had moved one of my small dressers into the other upstairs bedroom that was still open. I went through the drawers a bit just to see what was there and found a card that she had written me years ago. Why had I kept it? The envelope was addressed to " My dear husband Mitch." I wrote on it, "Uh, huh – all lies." And left it on the dresser for her to see.

This time I'm not coming back.

So I expect I will get some sick email or letter from her because I took my paintings and my shells and fossils that adorned her already stark living room. I won't answer. I won't go back. I am happy in my new life now. That old crappy and hot place is now so ugly to me. I am so happy to be living on the coast enjoying the cool weather and away from that disturbed person.

I sort of know in my heart that I want the best for her, but it is so hard to not want vengeance – I am human after all. I promised God I would let it all go, and with His help I am doing so. He will repay her many fold.

6/1/10

Like I said, I expected a sick email from her….here is what I got today:

M-

I was in AZ for my nephew's high school graduation this past week and I notice that there are things gone from the house. Did you come by and pick up some things? If so, that is fine as most of what is here is yours, I understand. If you could please just let me know beforehand that you or others will be coming, I would appreciate it.

Thank you very much,

T

No, "Hello–how are you?" No, "I saw your note about 'all lies' on the card I gave you." Just a clinical, "I notice that there are things gone," and "let me know." I would never go when she was there – I couldn't stand to look at her and hope I never have to again.

Once again, I simply ignored her.

7/8/2010

Well, today she decided to send me a financial settlement agreement. This email came under the subject title, "Important Request"

Mitch,

I have been advised by Legal Action Workshop that the next step in the process is the settlement agreement. Based on what we previously discussed and from information I found online, I put together the following wording describing the items that need to be included in the settlement agreement.

The Workshop has also informed me that a court appearance will not be necessary if agreement is reached.

I am respectfully asking you to review this and to respond back. Please let me know as soon as possible if you agree or of any changes you may have.

Thank you very much,

T

Real Estate Property: xxxx Canyon Dr., Glendora CA 91702, wherein both parties are listed as Joint Tenants in the Deed of Property. Both spouses agree that the property will be sold and proceeds divided equally. Petitioner agrees to continue making the payments on the Wells Fargo mortgage held in her name. Petitioner will be permitted to remain living solely in the house allowing time for her to make the house sale-ready, after which the house will be put up for sale. In the interim, Respondent will be allowed access to the home on pre-agreed upon dates/times in order to obtain any/all of his belongings that are currently in the home.

Spousal Support: Both spouses agree that neither spouse will receive or request spousal support from the other.

Vehicles: Both spouses agree that each will retain the vehicles that are currently in their individual possession and will provide whatever documents may be required to show ownership of such vehicles.

Retirement Accounts: Both spouses agree to waive any/all rights or interest that each may have in the retirement accounts, savings accounts or pensions of the other and all such accounts now individually held and maintained will be and remain separate property of the spouse in whose name the asset is now held.

Business: Micro Specialist: Both spouses agree that the Petitioner waives any/all rights or interest she may have in the business Micro Specialist.

Debts: Both spouses agree that each will be responsible for all debts as previously discussed which are listed as such for Petitioner and Respondent in the Declaration of Disclosure, individually and for any undisclosed debts individually.

Health Insurance: Both spouses agree that Respondent will remain covered under Petitioner's medical/dental/vision/long term care coverage provided through her employment through 12-31-2010, as was previously discussed. If Petitioner's employment should terminate before 12-31-2010, Respondent agrees to secure his own coverage.

Life Insurance: Both spouses agree to keep each other as the primary beneficiary on each other's Term Life Insurance coverage until divorce is final.

What did you notice about her proposed settlement agreement? She wanted to keep her retirement all to herself. What a selfish pig. When we married she had $28,000 in her retirement and it was only collecting annual interest of – what 6%? I convinced her that we needed to go aggressive in the stock market so we grew it to over $100K. Naturally she wanted to keep it all. Sorry Terry–it doesn't work that way.....

Plus my business, Micro Specialist was started almost 20 years before I met her – she actually caused my business to suffer. She has no right to that at all.

Here was my response. I sent it under the subject title, "Important Request – for who?"

"Honestly! Did you think your behavior would result in no pain? I will not relinquish my rights to that portion of the retirement account (RISP and Pension) that is community property. Any increase after April 6, 2001 is community property and the law grants me 50%.

My retirement account has only $3000 in it. Remember who put the down payment into the house and spent all that money on walls and paint? I DID. That was the end of my retirement account, but I was willing to sacrifice it for "us". You now must pay the difference from yours.

Yes, the house must be sold-and soon. All profits must be split. You now sit there and enjoy the benefits of safety, security and continuity in your life-while I suffer the lack of each of those in mine-all at your hands.

As if that is not enough, you propose "settlement" language that denies me my right to community property? You are more selfish than I ever imagined.

Because I never wanted this separation and divorce, because I begged for reconciliation and because you "had to be rid of me" and demanded that I leave-I was out on the street and had nowhere to go. I had (and still have) nowhere to put my share of the community property that we jointly acquired-you have been quite the aggressor here, and I warned you that shipwrecking everything was not in your best interest. It does not make you look so good.

Because I have been denied the security and safety of my part of the community property, the sale of the house could and probably will be seriously delayed until such time as all the household items which are community property are sold off. The delay could last many months. This is the natural result of your rash actions.

Because Micro Specialist was started in 1984, it is not community property and you can lay no claim to it. Besides, it has lost clients steadily since April 6, 2001. I can prove all this in court at no small expense to you. You have been of no benefit to Micro Specialist and it is of no benefit to you. If I can prevail over USC in court, what obstacle will you present?

Also, please carefully note that the community property laws state that for equity-the differences in the values of the vehicles must also be settled. Kelly Blue Book has your vehicle between$16,210 and $17,900. Mine is between $1,860 and 2,410 (not the $5000 you erroneously quoted on your Schedule of Assets and Debts), an obvious inequity.

In addition, as mentioned above, the inequity that exists in all the household furnishings must be rectified. Since you forced me out, and have all that we jointly acquired as a part of the house, that has to be sold and settled. I have nowhere to put the couches, TV, my end tables, or my parents beautiful brass lamps (that you have no claim to). Since you forced your hand, all that as well must be sold or disposed of.

So if you want a court appearance, fine with me. I will bring in my witnesses who will testify on my behalf. You won't look so good after all is said and done.

Furthermore, you lied to the Court when you stated that the date of separation was 5/15/09 on your Petition for Dissolution for Marriage. We separated on November 19, when I moved away, which my many receipts and cancelled checks will show. In addition my Church Small Group threw me a going away party on November 6th before we were separated. This as well will make you look bad to the Court.

However, I will agree to settle and not pursue the above if you do the right thing and simply disperse my half of all retirement gains. You already listed it on the Schedule of Assets and Debts forms that were sent to me from your attorney. Your forms would be the first thing I would file with the court if you choose a court battle. Again, you would not look so good after all this and it could greatly affect any settlement dictated by the Court."

MHA

Oh, by the way, the growing set of tattoos on your son are lovely. I note the new ones added just the other day… Congratulations on that.

Well she must have told him that I had found his pictures, so he made the site private. But not before I downloaded most of them. Like this one:

7/21/10 This email came today:

M,

I have one question that I would like to ask: Could you please clarify for me your statement that you "will agree to settle and not pursue the above if you do the right thing and simply disperse my half of all retirement gains"? I apologize but, I truly do not understand what you feel that is and I am just asking for clarification; please explain.

Thank you.

What is not to understand here? I should get my 50%. I will not drag your butt into court if you just give me my 50% of all retirement funds gains. I sent this to her two days later – and I made sure she got it early Friday morning, hopefully as she was sipping her coffee before leaving at work at 5AM. I sure hope she had a horrible weekend as a result:

Terry,

Yet again, the woman who has 'never had a good relationship with a man' cannot be corrected.

YOU stamped YOUR feet, YOU stabbed YOUR finger in MY face and you screamed at the top of your lungs, "It is between ME and GOD, not YOU," and "I HAVE TO BE RID OF YOU." I witnessed that wonderful display several times.

I begged you to go to counseling with the Godliest pastor I have ever known, from our church of eight years, but you REFUSED because "He knows YOU too well." Don't patients go to doctors who really understand their condition to get well? You have never wanted to get well.

YOU locked YOURSELF in YOUR room for 20 WEEKS, not me-or have you forgotten that little tidbit? (And that wasn't the first time you pulled that little stunt).

Finally after an intervention by my son (and only because Patrick asked) you relented and went to his bizarre pastor in Upland and then you lied to his face. Wow.

Don't let your selective memory and your ice-cold heart forget who forced this situation. I didn't just "move out" as you put it.

And who can forget your angry and loud promise that if I did not sign the pension waiver, you would "make it a death benefit ONLY payable on my DEATH." How lovely was that?

That image of you expressing your inner "Christian" purity and reverence, gentle and quiet spirit will last me for eternity (1 Peter 3:1-4).

How could I live in a house that YOU chose from the ones we looked at, that YOU decreed what the painting scheme should be, that YOU decorated with the wicker we bought and that YOU refused to love me, or honor me, or cherish me in?

How could I live around the things that only served to remind me of how my leadership as a father and head of the home was gutted like a fish?

How could I live around things and memories that only stab my heart again and again, reminding me of the cold and clinical nature of our so-called union. How would that have brought me peace and tranquility?

Dear God Almighty-did you learn ANYTHING about relationships in these 8 years? Anything at all?

"Want" and "deserve" are different things. Just because I do not "want" the soiled trappings of this disaster, does not mean that I do not deserve my share of the proceeds.

I deserve so much more than you are capable of scraping the barrel for. You never deserved anyone like me. Your golden moment in the sun has passed-and your eyes are still squeezed shut. I marvel at your aloofness.

Yes, when we bought the home, your precious retirement was BORROWED against. It was also REPAID with no small effort on my part. My retirement was CASHED OUT, emptied, GUTTED. The $3100 that is in it now if far less than the amount that was in it before I ever met you. I did that for US. I put all I had in the "us basket"-something you could never do. I would still pour out everything I ever had for a life of real love-real connection. You are a missed call in an ocean of static.

The balance due to the kitchen remodeling is your doing, not mine. I didn't stamp my feet and scream "I HAVE TO BE RID OF YOU." I didn't force separation and divorce. I didn't clinically say-"You dear man, can continue to live in this ice prison where I refused to be your partner your lover, your soul mate."

Nevertheless your retirement loan will some day be repaid-maybe even from the proceeds of the sale of 1801. My retirement was sacrificed for the greater good and is GONE.

And don't forget that you barely had $28,000 or something like that in your retirement in 2002. Financially, your retirement is what is it today due to no small effort on my part.

Use this language dear ex-wife and you "will be rid of me" forever:

"Real Estate Property: xxxx Canyon Dr., Glendora CA 91702, wherein both parties are listed as Joint Tenants in the Deed of Property. Both spouses agree that the property will be sold and proceeds divided equally. Petitioner agrees to continue making the payments on the Wells Fargo mortgage held in her name. Petitioner will be permitted to remain living solely in the house allowing time for her to make the house sale-ready, after which the house will be put up for sale. In the interim, Respondent will be allowed access to the home on pre-agreed upon dates/times in order to obtain any/all of his belongings that are currently in the home.

Spousal Support: Both spouses agree that neither spouse will receive or request spousal support from the other.

Vehicles: Both spouses agree that each will retain the vehicles that are currently in their individual possession and will provide whatever documents may be required to show ownership of such vehicles.

Retirement Accounts: Both spouses agree to divide that portion of the retirement accounts and pensions that is subject to community property. The value of Respondent's retirement account to be divided is $0. The value of the Petitioner's retirement account to be divided is $_____.

Debts: Both spouses agree that each will be responsible for all debts as previously discussed which are listed as such for Petitioner and Respondent in the Declaration of Disclosure, individually and for any undisclosed debts individually.

Health Insurance:Both spouses agree that Respondent will remain covered under Petitioner's medical/dental/vision/long term care coverage provided through her employment through 12-31-2010, as was previously discussed. If Petitioner's employment should terminate before 12-31-2010, Respondent agrees to secure his own coverage.

Life Insurance: Both spouses agree to keep each other as the primary beneficiary on each other's Term Life Insurance coverage until divorce is final."

How sick for a "wife" of eight years to want to split every old rusted and crappy kitchen utensil down to the nth degree, and to not want to give me a penny of my share of the retirement money I was responsible for earning. What a fine Christian woman and a wonderful example of Jesus. Well, not the Jesus I know…..but who knows? Maybe I don't know the real Jesus… maybe the real Jesus is on her side! CRAP!

On Friday September 3, 2010 I got this email:
Subject: Information
M,
In case you might be thinking of coming to the house this weekend, I am leaving for a weekend trip to AZ and will be back late Monday.

Except for what is in the kitchen and labeled, all of my things are in the master bedroom. I am using the odd "shell" chair from the living room. The other things that were in the master bedroom have been moved to the boys old room. All of Patrick's stuff is against the west window wall in that room and he knows they are there and will be making arrangements to move them.

It took me a quite a while to review, research and go through the documents that Legal Action workshop compiled which include what you requested. I have signed them and had them notarized per their instructions. You will need to fill in the license plate number for the van on both documents. All of the wording covers everything in the proper legal terms used by the court. The amount of your community interest in my Retirement Plan is determined by the court based on a formula of months of interest (rather than an amount) and is incorporated in the language. I have requested information from my Retirement Plan about the QDRO and will get it to you as soon as I receive it.

These documents also reference the property that each of us "has in our possession". I spoke to the attorney at Legal Action Workshop about the things we have already discussed as yours, which I will not lay claim to, and they are not intended to be inclusive of this reference. The Workshop will be mailing them to you at the Thousand Oaks mailbox, which you will need to have notarized and return to them.

Thank you,

T

Why in God's name would I ever go back to that house? There is NOTHING for me there. Why would I want anything that we acquired together? It is all hot, smelly crap to me. She can drag it behind a freight train for all I care. Why in God's name can she not type out my full name? Is this "T" and "M" thing supposed to be cute, or make me feel all fuzzy and warm? I just want to puke up blood.

Why would I care that it took her a long time "to review, research and go through the documents that Legal Action workshop compiled"? Is that supposed to make me feel grateful or whatever? This is ALL her doing. I will never feel sorry that she had to do this to make the settlement fair. I will never feel sorry that she is going to have to throw away the mountain of stuff that is still there, that she is going to have to get the house "sale ready", that she is going to have to find a realtor, show the house, sell the house and send me the $5.00 that will be earned from flushing our equity down the drain. Get lost woman – drive yourself off a cliff – what do I care? You don't exist.

9/8/2010

The financial settlement documents arrived today. I signed them and left a space between my first name and last name on each instance I had to sign. Then I had it all notarized. I went home and wrote in "God hates divorce" on every instance where I left a space and mailed them off. The judge will probably reject the papers but I don't care. I finally get to express my opinion after 9 years of this nightmare, so I did.

"What I have written I have written." John 19:22. I bet I get some kind of sick email scolding me for that.

To her credit, she did list the retirement accounts, so those will be chopped up and split between us....too bad she already cashed out $50K to pay off the car, the retirement (kitchen) loan and her credit cards. That means her retirement has been earning much less money since she cashed all that out. On top of that – whatever is left now has to be hammered to give me my share, which means she will probably be left with only $25-30,000 in her retirement account and she is already 56 – going on 57 years of age. In order for her to have any money to retire on she will probably have to work until she is 70 or so. Wow...I try to help people and look what happens.

How sad that I signed the documents that she engineered, 9 years to the day that we first met each other face to face. That's right–to the day. September 9, 2001 – 2 days before 9/11, I drove to Phoenix to meet Terry Loretta Shafer for the first time. We had been emailing each other for about 2 months, and I decided that it was time for us to meet. As I approached Phoenix, I called her on the phone and gave her my ETA. She asked me if I would mind meeting her at a neutral place before coming to her home, so I said sure. She directed me to a McDonald's near her home, so I parked my van and waited for her to arrive. About 10 minutes after I parked, she pulled up in her little decrepit Toyota Tercel. I got out of the van and she approached me, she put her hands on either side of my face and said, "You're gorgeous!" We kissed a few times and then we sat in the van and chatted for a few minutes. That night I stayed at a Best Western not far from her home and the next day, I went and picked her up and we drove to northern Arizona – we enjoyed two days of fun at the Berringer Meteor Crater, the Petrified Forest and at other places in and around Flagstaff. I wish someone would have told me that nine years to the day later, I would be signing divorce papers on a failed marriage. I would have walked away from all this before it ever got started.

I wondered however if there was any significance to me signing these papers on the ninth day of the ninth month of the ninth year that I first met Terry face to face. I found this commentary online about the Biblical properties of the number 999:

"The number 999 is the reverse of 666, the number of the Beast of the Revelation (Apocalypse). This arithmetical strangeness demonstrates that the "power" of the Beast, 666, will be "reversed" by 153, the characteristic number of the Christ, to give as result 999, symbol of the application of the divine justice."

Could it be that the divine justice on Terry Loretta Shafer has begun? Interesting.

I also find it interesting that *Tauret* is the name of an ancient Egyptian deity. She was known as the Concubine of Seth (the god of chaos, confusion, darkness, death, destruction, evil, night, retribution and revenge). Huh. Wow. *Tauret* herself was known as a goddess of darkness and revenge, but she was also the protector of pregnant women.

9/21/2010.

I printed off the email she sent me on January 4, 2005 (see above), where she admitted to me that she was not a wife. I wrote on it, "With God, all things are possible." Then I put it into an envelope and mailed it to her as, "T. Shafer" at the Glendora address. A week has gone by and I have heard nothing in return. I don't expect to. Every attempt on my part to reach out to her *from day one* has been met with the cold shoulder. Why should now, the time when our assets are going to be sold off and ripped into two, be any different?

10/4/10 Here is the response I received from her:
"M,
I have just about completed getting the house ready for sale. I have met with a real estate agent and she can meet with you for a presentation or she can email it to you. Please let me know which you would prefer.

Also, please let me know a date and time that you would like to come to pick up anything here at the house that you want. If you do not want to pick up anything else, please let me know if you would like it picked up for donation.
Thank you,
T"

10/5/10

I bought a card to send to Terry. It had two kittens hugging on the front of it. I handwrote the following message on the inside and mailed it to her. "Almost one year since we separated. What has changed? Are you truly at peace over this? We face a steep cliff now. It is still not too late to steer this away from the cliff. I still wish to fulfill the vows I made before God and you. Please agree to go with me to Pastor Gene once or twice a month just to talk. Mitch."

I expect noting but silence but God is my witness – I have tried every conceivable angle here. I cannot be blamed for this.

I hired an attorney in Encinitas to draw up the legal documents to submit to her retirement plan company to slice away my big piece of the pie.…..

I am also going to completely ignore her regarding the sale of the house. I could care less – let her slog through all that crud all by herself. When the sales contract arrives I might sign it – nothing further. She can pay to have it all made ready and sellable. I am too busy now. But, if she does not sign and file the legal paperwork on the retirement split, I won't sign the house sale contract. Pure and simple. I get mine before she gets hers.

I did hear back from her on 10/15/10:

"M -

The value of the ERP was $17,692.19 on 4/5/02; the value of the RISP was $21,069.57 on 4/5/02. Total of both was $38,761.76 on 4/5/02. NOTE: The ERP was rolled into the RISP on 12/16/09.

The value of the RISP (inc. ERP) was $149,180.40 on 5/11/10.

The $12000.00 RISP loan was taken out on 11/17/08 and the balance due is $7497.59

Please advise as soon as possible if you would like to meet with the real estate agent for her presentation or, if she can email it to you.

Also, please let me know the date and time that you would like to come and pick up anything you want here at the house as I need to get the carpets cleaned. If you do not want to pick up anything else, please let me know by 10/22/10 so that I can arrange a donation pick up.

Thank you very much,

- T"

12/15/10

A box arrived today. It had no return address, no note – no explanation. In it were all the bracelets, rings, earrings, pendants and chains I ever bought her – all tucked neatly into a Swarovski box.….. Even the 4-stone, 1-carat diamond engagement ring and soldered wedding band in 14K white diamond that adorned her finger for 8 years. Dear God – what message do I take away from this?

"I just made you up to hurt myself….yeah, and I just made you up to hurt myself….yeah and I just made you up to hurt myself. And it worked. Yes it did. There is no you there is only me. There is no you there is only me. There is no f*&kin' you there is only me. There is no you there is only me. Only. "

Words and music, Trent Reznor, Nine Inch Nails.

AFTERWARD

I judge you not woman. I came not to judge. There is a judge for you – His tardiness is not unplanned. You fake all manner of Christianity – and God hates all of it.

"That is when God will *whistle for the flies* at the headwaters of Egypt's Nile, and *whistle for the bees* in the land of Assyria. They'll come and infest every nook and cranny of this country. There'll be no getting away from them. And that's when the Master will take the razor rented from across the Euphrates and shave the hair off your heads and genitals, leaving you shamed, exposed, and denuded." Isaiah 7:18-20.

Good luck with that Terry, you wanna be Christian woman.

APPENDIX

Please take a moment to email me your replies to these questions. You can answer True or False (or just T/F and the question #). I will also read any comments that you send.

I sincerely thank you in advance for taking the time to do so. My email address is: mitch.armaugh@gmail.com

1. Mitch should never have remarried after his first marriage ended.

2. Mitch should have ended the engagement when he got cold feet.

3. Mitch should have not tried to discipline Ronnie.

4. Mitch should have gone to counseling with Terry even though all she did was cry.

5. Mitch should have accepted Terry's offer to pay for everything and just leave him.

6. Terry is the perfect Christian woman.

7. Terry is the consummate sinner.

8. Mitch is the perfect Christian man.

9. Mitch is the consummate sinner.

10. Mitch should have kept all this to himself.